MEDICINE DOG

The Miraculous Cure That Healed My Best Friend and Saved My Life

JULIA SZABO

LYONS PRESS
Guilford, Connecticut
An imprint of Globe Pequot Press

For everyone who said I couldn't,
and Susan Ainsworth, who said I could,
and
in loving memory of Sam, Sheba,
Eleanor Mondale, and Dr. Katherine Rogers

Project Editor: Lauren Brancato
Layout: Mary Ballachino

Library of Congress Cataloging-in-Publication Data

Szabo, Julia, 1965-

 Medicine dog : the miraculous cure that healed my best friend and
saved my life / Julia Szabo.
     pages cm
 Summary: "Thanks to her dog and his visionary vet, Julia became the
first American to receive stem cells to heal her IBD"— Provided by
publisher.
 ISBN 978-0-7627-9644-1 (hardback)
1. Pets—Health. 2. Pets—Diseases—Alternative treatment. 3. Stem
cells—Transplantation. 4. Veterinary genetics. I. Title.
 SF745.5.S93 2014
 636.089'602774—dc23

                                   2013045435

Printed in the United States of America

10 9 8 7 6 5 4 3 2 1

Contents

I consulted with my two brothers, DR. REASON and DR. EXPE-RIENCE, and took a voyage to visit my mother NATURE, by whose advice, together with the help of DR. DILIGENCE, I at last obtained my desire; and, being warned by MR. HONESTY, a stranger in our days, to publish it to the world, I have done it.
    —NICHOLAS CULPEPER, *THE ENGLISH PHYSICIAN*

PROLOGUE

You will hardly know who I am or what I mean,
But I shall be good health to you nevertheless,
And filter and fibre your blood.

—WALT WHITMAN

On January 9, 2013, my dog and I made medical history. We underwent tandem, cutting-edge stem cell procedures, Desiree in New York City (our hometown) and I in Rancho Mirage, California. At forty-seven, I became the first American to receive adult stem cells, derived from my own belly fat, to repair the chronic gastrointestinal disease I'd struggled with since 1999. At the same time, on the opposite coast, beautiful Desiree—a German shepherd just two years young—became the first New York City dog to have her own stem cells surgically collected, then cryobanked for future use, until the inevitable future date when they are needed to help her heal.

This was the culmination of a strange journey, one that transported me from New York to Spain to California, with several stops in between. It was an extraordinary day of healing that left me feeling brand new. My technical birthday is May 20; I'm a proud Taurus, albeit a cusp baby. But January 9 is my re-birthday, for on that date I felt born again, with a clean slate and a second chance at a healthy, happy life. For Desiree, as for all of her canine kind, every day—even a rainy one—is a clean slate filled with positive potential. I don't know her technical birthday, because I adopted her from an animal shelter, where she was brought in as a stray. So from here on out, January 9 is Desiree's re-birthday, too.

What happened on that day changed both our lives, and I'm convinced that it absolutely saved mine. And to think that I owe it to a motley pack of adopted shelter dogs—fourteen in all over the past twenty years, plus more than a dozen fosters. Those dogs gave me a sense of purpose, bringing order, peace, and a healthy routine to my chaotic, inconsistent existence. They quite literally saved my life. This book tells our story

Desiree and Julia, ten days after treatment, 2013 DANIEL REICHERT

and concludes a fifteen-year odyssey. On my journey, not only was a dog waiting for me when I arrived home (as canine Argos faithfully awaited Odysseus) but also several dogs held my paw every step of the way. This is a canine memoir in which the lead dog doesn't heel, he heals! That's why I call him, and the book he inspired, Medicine Dog.

All dogs qualify as Medicine Dogs, because canine healing power is well documented. Dogs reduce our blood pressure and raise our levels of oxytocin just by letting us pet them. They boost our cardiovascular health by taking us out for regular walks—the heart-healthiest exercise there is, at any age. They lift our mood and lower our stress; they relax muscle tonicity in children with spastic cerebral palsy; they alert to attacks of anaphylaxis and asthma, intervening to save people's lives. The canine's amazing sense of smell can be harnessed to detect cancer or dangerous dips in blood sugar. They're good medicine, Medicine Dogs.

As a journalist, I can vouch that my Medicine Dogs gave me something extra: the motivation to research and report on the most high-tech healing modalities available to dogs. Finding innovative solutions to extend and improve my dogs' lives informed my job as the Pet Reporter and led me to the biggest scoop of my career: the astonishing healing power of adult stem cells for ailing people and pets. I learned about the groundbreaking work of Vet-Stem, pioneer of veterinary regenerative medicine in California, which heals equine and canine patients using the animals' own stem cells. I was so impressed with Vet-Stem and its cell harvesting and culturing technology, I arranged for two of my beloved dogs to undergo the Vet-Stem procedure when arthritis robbed them of their youthful mobility.

My dogs' amazing success with adult stem cells was, for me, a life-changer that motivated me to seek the same level of high-tech healing for myself. This was easier said than achieved, for the treatment my dogs received was not available to human patients in America when I first went about trying to obtain it. I was shocked to learn that dogs could be cured with adult stem cells removed from their own fat, while humans had to settle for antiquated, risky surgical methods. There was something basically wrong with this picture, something I just couldn't stomach.

But I was encouraged to discover that, elsewhere in the world, it was a very different story: People with a variety of life-threatening medical problems were being cured with their own stem cells. Some of the stories told of healing that was nothing short of dramatic. What was going on here? I resolved to be healed the high-tech way, no matter how far I had to travel to achieve my goal. And I dedicated myself to reporting on regenerative medicine for dogs and people, to raise awareness of adult stem cells' healing potential, in the hope that more patients would join me in demanding much-needed change.

The media is rife with stories of human healing modalities being applied to dogs, from high-tech hyperbaric oxygen therapy to homespun homeopathy. But what I was seeking was the opposite: a stem cell procedure that any dog could receive but was as yet not available for humans. Strange as it may sound, getting treated by a doctor precisely the way my vet treated my dogs became my mission. Along the way on this odd and singular quest, I encountered setback after frustrating setback. My dogs' tenacity inspired me to keep on keeping on. My hunt for a good doctor took me across the country and around the world. At a time when I despaired of finding one competent, compassionate physician to help me, dogs—and only dogs—led me to the healer who would finally solve my problem once and for all. Thanks to my tail-wagging Medicine Dogs, I found not one brilliant, caring physician but several—and wouldn't you know, these docs are all dog lovers. Coincidence? I think not.

Stem cells are the future of medicine. But for me, the healing power of Medicine Dogs is equally important and regenerative. So much scientific data exists to prove how good dogs are for human health. Yet despite all that incontrovertible evidence, just how dogs work their medicinal magic remains a mystery. We hardly know who they are or what they mean. But this much is certain: They are healers with an instinctive gift for completing their humans in the healthiest possible way. "Dogs are not our whole lives," said the author Roger Caras, "but they make our lives whole." That they do. "Apply the dog!" is my pet phrase whenever I'm feeling low, physically or psychically. A canine cuddle—or in my case, make that a hound huddle—is all I need to recharge. It works every time. Feeling low? Apply the dog. Need an Rx for longevity? Take two Medicine Dogs, and you won't have to call your doctor in the morning. That's because you'll be at the dog park reaping health benefits—and if he or she is smart, so will your doc.

CHAPTER 1

The Curious Case of K-9 Sam

Everywhere the eye can see, people devise outrageously lame excuses for dumping pets. Got a problem? Here's the "solution": Get rid of the dog! Folks complain about the health-care system, about the high level of stress in their lives, yet they cavalierly toss away the one family member who's scientifically proven to improve their well-being by lowering stress, which we all know to be a killer. In short, they bail on the one family member most likely to keep them healthy and prevent them from having to consult too many doctors. I wish some entity would fund a survey of people who gave up their dogs, asking point-blank just how much their lives were "improved" by this appalling act of betrayal. The results would speak for themselves. In the meantime, I can offer my story as anecdotal proof that it's smart to keep the dog, for Spot can easily save your life.

Right now, millions of Medicine Dogs find themselves homeless at animal shelters. Channeling Iggy Pop, all they are collectively saying is, "I wanna be your dog." I'm thankful for the legions of people around the world who dedicate themselves to homeless dogs' welfare. In the rescue groups I run with, there's a saying that goes: "Saving just one dog won't save the world . . . but surely the world will change for that one dog." In 1996, the world changed for one New York City shelter dog named Sam. He wasn't exactly the canine hero you'd expect to see in a Disney movie: Seventy-five pounds of solid black pit bull, he had hard muscles, soft eyes, bearlike paws, and a head like the "toaster" engine on a vintage BMW motorbike, his magnificent braincase forming a diamond shape. This unlikely dog star walked into my life, stepped into a leading role, then proceeded to rewrite the entire script.

Sam was my second pit bull. The first was a white pit mix named Daisy, adopted from the ASPCA in 1994 shortly after the 9-to-5 world

Sam in his salad days

and I went our separate ways and, with great trepidation, I began a freelance career as a style and culture reporter. Daisy taught me how to be a tenacious news hound by making a couple hours' short work of a formidable chew toy that would have taken most dogs a week to demolish. I thought, if only I could write like that. Following her lead, I wrote like my living depended on it. My favorite subject was Daisy, whose name and likeness would appear in *Allure, Travel + Leisure, Vogue Paris,* and *The New Yorker* (the latter illustrated with drawings by celebrity caricaturist Robert Risko).

Daisy was a brilliant career coach with killer reporting instincts, who taught by example how to be a "dog with a bone." But she wasn't the cuddliest critter in the bestiary, with a cool reserve and imperious air that moved me to nickname her "Miss Dog." Moreover, she was either deaf, or selectively hard of hearing, so she pretty much ignored everything I ever said to her. After a couple of years, I started to think how nice it would be to have a second dog to snuggle with and talk to. And one fateful day in 1996, I happened to read an article in *The Village Voice* about New York City's municipal animal shelter, Animal Care & Control. The author

Elizabeth Hess expertly conjured a scene of horror, where overcrowding and a lack of adopters meant that wonderful family pets were being killed just for lack of space to hold them. Although I knew it would be an emotionally harrowing experience, I had to go there and save a life.

And sure enough, just as the article had described, cages of sweet pit bulls were stacked two high. In one of the upper berths was a large, black stray, age two years, with a white mark on his chest resembling the Batman symbol, and rope burns on his snout and ankles from having been tranquilized and hog-tied just prior to arriving at the shelter. Why anyone would tranq a teddy bear is beyond me, but, sadly, many folks are fearful of big, black dogs, a lingering superstition that results in "black dog syndrome" at animal shelters, where dusky animals (cats included) are the last to be adopted and the first to be killed for lack of space.

Confident in his cuteness, innocent of the fact that he was hours away from being killed, this creature gently reached his paw out to me through the bars of his cage and took my heart with him. He came home that day, September 4, 1996, and would prove to be one of the greatest blessings of my life. Because of the bat mark on his chest, I debated calling him Bruce or Wayne, but Sam was the name that stuck. This extraordinary dog would express joy by flipping over on his back and doing a Snoopy dance wherever he happened to be, whether in the apartment, on the grass, or out on the sidewalk. And when he needed your attention, he'd do that adorable thing with his paw.

He was full of joy, as affectionate as they come, and ridiculously intuitive. One night, while my husband, X, was out working (or whatever he was out doing) late, I turned in but couldn't get to sleep because the heat had cut out and the apartment was quite frosty. So I asked Sam to come to bed and keep me warm. He jumped into bed, spooned me, and nibbled gently at my ear, which instantly warmed me up because the earlobe, I would later learn, is an acupressure point! I don't know how Sam knew, but I do know this: With a dog that sensitive, who needs a husband who stays out late?

Sam endeared himself to all who met him. Well, almost all. About a week after we adopted him, we were out for a nighttime romp in the park when a man emerged from the shadows and unleashed his dog, who

Loyal, dark, handsome: a gal's best friend JONATHON KAMBOURIS

promptly leapt on our Sam, grabbing his head in a jawhold and refusing to let go. This sudden attack was my first exposure to the shadow world of dog fighting, which would later gain national attention thanks to the atrocities committed by Michael Vick. Our boy was losing. I'll never forget how several other dog lovers joined us in trying to liberate Sam from his attacker, but the dog tenaciously hung on to our boy's head. All the while, his owner was pulling him by his taut upper hind legs. This fool move merely turned the attack dog's teeth into meat slicers, cutting even bigger slashes in Sam's flesh; we all yelled at the man to quit.

Nobody on the scene was carrying a breaking stick—the tool used to un-wrench a dog's jaw in just such a situation—and in the heat of the crisis, I didn't think to hunt for a twig that might have served that purpose. Attempts to scream and kick at the attacking dog were utterly useless; he was RoboPit. My stomach churning and my blood aboil, I reached my hand into the melee—but that dang dog turned just long enough to bite me, then sank his teeth back into our Sam. Somehow, my quick-thinking husband managed to put an end to the hostilities with one brilliant maneuver: He grabbed the conjoined dogs and flipped them over. That did the trick. In an instant, the dogs were separated and X had a firm hold on Sam, embracing him protectively like a bodyguard.

We examined the damage done to our poor beaten baby. Sam's ear was almost severed and his poor head hung low, wet with blood pouring from deep puncture wounds. The owner of the canine attacker, his unscathed dog now properly leashed, saw fit to calmly look me in the eye and say, "I guess that'll teach you never to let your dog off leash!" At that instant, I would have gladly relieved this man of his paltry endowment with my own teeth, and suffered the legal consequences, but there was no time to waste—Sam had to be rushed to the emergency hospital ASAP.

He spent a week in the Animal Medical Center's ICU; that hospital stay was followed by intensive home care. Vet techs marveled at how stoically Sam endured hydrotherapy and other painful convalescent maneuvers. At home, where we did low-tech hydrotherapy with our humble hand-shower attachment—which had to sting something fierce—sweetheart Sam would lick us, as if thanking us for helping him heal. He came through just fine, with some scars to remind us of what he'd survived.

Daisy went through her long life with no health issues to speak of and only one skirmish that required stitches. Sam, on the other hand, confronted numerous health calamities and introduced me to many excellent doctors. You might say Sam became a one-dog physician-referral service.

Survival was Sam's greatest skill. He triumphed over a bout of hypothermia, crumpling at my feet after X took him for a long, brisk tour of the New York City Reservoir on a subarctic winter day . . . then anterior cruciate ligament (ACL) rupture . . . followed by partial tail amputation, after his poor tail was accidentally struck by a car door . . . then root canal. Sam emerged from that excruciating dental procedure with a flashy gold crown on his eye tooth that made him look like an extra in an old-school James Bond flick. I nonchalantly missed routine doctor and dentist appointments for myself, but if Sam needed medical attention, it was always a matter of deciding which state-of-the-art animal hospital would best serve his needs. With stainless steel in his leg, gold on his tooth, and an iron will to live, my multi-metallic mutt was, in my eyes, the worthy, latter-day counterpart of a canine I'd admired in childhood: "Maximillion," the Bionic Dog of TV fame and constant companion of my idol, Lindsay Wagner, star of *The Bionic Woman.*

One of the good doctors I met thanks to Sam is Dr. David Jay Friedman, whose reputation as one of New York's best plastic surgeons precedes him. One day, Sam was so happy to see me when I returned home that he jumped on the bed, the better to give me a properly welcoming hug. He was grinning wide, and one of his fangs got caught on the corner of my mouth, resulting in a gash and a bloody mess. Poor Sam was mortified. "OMG, I'M SO SORRY," read the thought bubble over my dog's worried, wrinkly-browed forehead. I assured Sam I wasn't angry with him, then high-tailed it to the ER of the nearest hospital, conveniently located a few blocks from our apartment. I was lucky that it was Dr. Friedman's day on duty; he boldly boasted that he could stitch up my lip so that, once it healed, I wouldn't remember which side had been cut. If you can do it, it ain't bragging—that's exactly what Dr. Friedman did. To this day, I still don't recall which side of my mouth was stitched!

Because Sam was so special—and so black, which made photographs and painted likenesses a challenge—I commissioned an out-of-the-ordinary

Bronze bust of Sam by sculptor Jennifer Weinik   MARIE FETZER

portrait to remember him by: a life-size bronze bust by the Philadelphia sculptor Jennifer Weinik. Sam sat patiently for Jennifer (actually, as frequently happens in these situations, artist and model had quite the love affair). With her signature attention to detail, Jennifer replicated Sam's happy grin down to the serrated edges along his lower lips and saw to it that the bust, too, would sport a gold crown, giving the left eye tooth a high polish to contrast with the rest of her sculpture's dark patina. The result of her artistry is a monument that—like the dog it's modeled on—was built to last.

Sam vaulted over his health hurdles with ease and grace. But in 2008, it looked as if he'd finally met his match. As a youngster, he would urinate by lifting his hind leg with a balletic extension to rival the young Baryshnikov. But by the time he hit thirteen, the most he could do was answer nature's call with all four feet on the ground, looking dejected and sad. Sam was succumbing to the crippling effects of advanced osteoarthritis—what one of my neighbors quaintly called "a visit from Mr. Arthur." Except Mr. Arthur's visits were becoming more and more like assaults with a blunt object. With Sam in his crosshairs, Mr. Arthur was like the crazed, cane-wielding, little old ladies of Monty Python fame—on a mission and out for blood. I'd been giving Sam joint-support supplements for years, including omega-3 fish oil, glucosamine, plus naturally anti-inflammatory curcumin and cinnamon, but drew the line at NSAIDs because of their documented impact on the liver and kidneys. But what he really needed—what no pill or oil could assist—was for the cartilage surrounding his now–un-cushioned joints to regrow, permitting normal leg movement.

One afternoon in mid-April—a day that drove home for me why T. S. Eliot designated that month the cruelest—Sam's hind legs collapsed under him and he wiped out on the sidewalk, around the corner from our apartment. Seeing me struggle with two dogs, one collapsed and one mobile (Pepper, Sam's girlfriend), a neighbor kindly stopped to offer help. She's a makeup artist with psychic abilities—hey, this is New York, where folks have talents in many directions. Taking Pepper's leash while I maneuvered Sam, she told me Sam wanted me to know that he was still a warrior and would still bravely give his life for me, that what pained him most was not arthritis, but feeling diminished in my eyes. I was touched by these psychic sentiments but could focus only on getting Sam safely home. I managed this by supporting his rear end from underneath with his leash, like a sling, while my psychic friend walked slightly ahead to offer Sam encouragement. Knowing there was no way my back could survive being the hind-leg support for a seventy-pound dog, I jumped on the Internet and began Googling for a solution to help Sam walk on his own again, even if only for a short time, as he neared the end of his life. That solution turned out to be stem cell regeneration therapy. It costs anywhere between two thousand and thirty-five hundred dollars—it's covered by several pet insurance carriers (although coverage varies, and most policies have an exclusion for pre-existing conditions and congenital defects)—but dog lovers will tell you it is worth every penny, and then some, to see a formerly crippled dog walk with confidence again. Motivated on my dog's behalf as never before, I arranged for Sam to be treated with his own stem cells as soon as humanly possible. His poor bones were grinding against each other without a cushion; I winced to see him suffer with each halting step, keenly feeling his discomfort. Sam needed cartilage regeneration, stat, and that's precisely what stem cell therapy achieves.

Incidentally, going the distance for ailing loved ones runs in my family, and we've always been on the cutting edge. In 1961, my mother was inspired by reports of the photojournalist Margaret Bourke-White's battle with Parkinson's disease. Bourke-White, one of *Life* magazine's four original photographers, had undergone a daring brain surgery, chronicled in the magazine, in which a hole was drilled in the patient's skull; my mother coordinated with her sister to have the same operation performed on my grandmother, whose name was Julia, in London that same year. (By the way, Bourke-White, or "Maggie the Indestructible" as her colleagues called her, had two Medicine Dogs, a pair of Afghan hounds, and would take them for outings while supporting herself with a walking stick.)

Back in New York in 2008—a couple of weeks, dozens of phone calls, and three vet visits after I resolved to put my crumbling dog back together—on a day I'll never forget (April 30), Sam came through a stem cell treatment for osteoarthritis with such flying colors that his many admirers in our neighborhood, jaded New Yorkers all, dropped their jaws to see my old dog walking tall, noticeably stronger than he'd been in years.

Stem cells get their name from their appearance; under a microscope, they resemble stems, as in mushroom stems. That first Google search on the topic revealed that the mainstream media offered no shortage of stories about embryonic stem cells, the controversial organisms that the Christian right faithfully fights against. The media's insistent focus on embryonic cells—each story never failing to extol their "pluripotent" property, meaning they can differentiate into all cell types—made it easy for the casual reader to assume that the only type of stem cells of interest to scientists were harvested from aborted fetuses. No less an authority than Dr. Sanjay Gupta, CNN's chief medical correspondent, summarily stated, in 2001, that "the most useful cells come only from embryos."

But that was not the case. The real, underreported story—the one that held healing promise for Sam and, later, me—took some digging to uncover: how adult or autologous mesenchymal stem cells, also known as ASC, derived from a patient's own tissue, could be re-injected into the patient's body to repair certain body parts, with the goal of putting them back in working order. And no embryos are harmed. (*Autologous* means the cells' donor and recipient are one and the same, and *mesenchymal* describes cells that form connective tissue and blood vessels.) I've always been a sucker for the underdog—and the underreported story. Now, here was a scoop that combined the two. But reporting it would first mean undoing years of negative press.

In 2008 we were nearing the end of the George W. Bush administration, which actively opposed embryonic stem cell research. The year before, during a 2007 concert in Las Vegas, legendary folk singer Mary Travers alluded to W's anti–stem cell stance by describing ASC as "not the kind of stem cells the president doesn't like—these cells know exactly who they're going to be when they grow up." Travers underwent a stem cell bone marrow transplant doctors hoped would cure the leukemia that would ultimately take her life in 2009. She was deftly using humor to cut through the media-made confusion that hounded this very serious subject: In some circles, the mere mention of the term "stem cell" was—and still is—enough to close a book, end a discussion, empty a restaurant, shut down a party. That's because many people still automatically presume all stem cells are embryonic cells.

For obvious reasons, anyone who is anti-abortion or pro-life will automatically side against the medical use of stem cells if it means destroying embryos. Yet this was only half the story. Most people simply didn't know about the amazing regenerative power of the autologous cells we all carry around in our bodies—or how easily they may be surgically harvested from one part of the body (or, in the case of umbilical cord blood, cryobanked after giving birth), then re-injected in the same body to help it heal. ASCs aren't pluripotent, but they're plenty potent nevertheless.

Injected into the bloodstream, they go to work like the honey-I-shrunk-the-submarine in that Raquel Welch sci-fi classic *The Fantastic Voyage*, traveling until they locate the body part that needs a healing assist. That's pretty amazing, if you ask me—and well worth its fifteen minutes of media fame. Yet people didn't know about this aspect of ASCs because they didn't hear about it in the news. Sam's experience, and my dogged reporting about ASCs and their implications for human health, enabled a lot of people—myself included—to understand something vitally important about the stem cell debate: that this "controversial" treatment doesn't have to be controversial at all.

Stem cells are the body's master cells, an army of microscopic mechanics that can travel anywhere in the body to repair and regenerate damaged tissue. This special healing force—picture the cellular equivalent of the Green Berets, Shayetet 13, or Spetsnaz—lies dormant in our bodies, waiting to be surgically extracted, then introduced to the part(s) of the body that could use backup. When a patient receives an injection of his or her own stem cells, it's as if a crack reconnaissance team is deployed—only instead of search-and-destroy, these cells are on a mission to search-and-repair. Do I sound like I'm giving you a hard, ahem, cell? Adult stem cells really are all that. And here's the best part: There's no risk of rejection. Your body basically puts out a welcome mat for its own cells, recognizing them not as foreign invaders but some of its own, allies sent to regenerate diseased, injured, or worn-away tissue.

Each of us—human, canine, feline, equine—has a reserve of these cells in our bodies, stored in our adipose (fat) tissue (there are also reserves elsewhere, notably in our bone marrow and, if humans have a baby, our umbilical cord blood). The fat is easily extracted via liposuction—yes, a "tummy tuck," in cosmetic-surgery parlance, only this one isn't done for looks. I don't know anyone who loves her own belly or thighs; but think of these "imperfect" parts as a kind of custom medicine chest, harboring adult stem cells stored in that extra fat we're all trying to work off, and one's view of bellies and thighs swiftly changes for the better. Meanwhile, in an exciting new development announced in March 2013, ASC derived from small samples of menstrual blood (termed endometrial regenerative cells, or ERC) are being applied to treat heart disease. This technology promises to deliver cell therapy to large numbers of cardiac patients, permitting a whole new point of view on periods that takes the "s" out of "the curse" and turns it into the cure for heart failure, the number-one killer of women. It would appear that the human physiology has a built-in sense of poetic justice.

The problem with pluripotent embryonic cells is that they don't play well with adult tissue. The age difference is hard to overcome. Explains Dr. Fabio Solano, MD, general and colorectal surgeon at Costa Rica's Cima Hospital, "Adult stem cells play a natural role in repair of damaged tissue in the adult; in contrast, fetal stem cells do not properly 'know' how to communicate with adult tissue." There's a generation gap—actually, more of a canyon—between them, as embryonic cells want to grow into a fetus. Introducing hyper-young cells to staid, grown-up tissue is a recipe for abnormally rapid growth in one place, mimicking another, tragically epidemic example of too-rapid cell growth: cancer.

Religion and science—it's hard to imagine stranger bedfellows. But today, for the first time in history, religion and science are now on the same page. ASC, the stem cells that do no harm to fetuses, actually work; embryonic cells do not. This is why the Catholic Church supports ASC research, morally and financially, even going so far as to fund regenerative clinical trials. And it explains why the most exciting breakthroughs in cell medicine have been made in the most righteously Catholic of countries: Spain, birthplace of the Inquisition.

Galileo Galilei defied the Vatican by insisting, rightly, on the heliocentric model of the cosmos when the pope and cardinals preferred a cosmology in which the sun spun around the Earth, i.e., them. What would Galileo say now that the Vatican is talking scientific sense, and the Diocese agrees with the diagnosticians? This extraordinary development is not a story the mainstream media feels comfortable reporting. The notion that a Vatican-approved medical protocol might actually work makes reporters queasy; most have been reluctant to cross that church-state line by promoting a medical therapy endorsed by religious entities and individuals. And so, article after biased article paints ASC therapy as a "dangerous" modality, describing treatments as quackery and equating them with snake oil. Happily, there's one niche in the mainstream media where ASC is described accurately, without bias: human interest stories about pets. Everyone can agree that it's inspiring to read articles about arthritic dogs given a new leash on life with their own stem cells; it's impressive to see video footage of four-footed patients, post–stem cell treatment, walking with their old casual confidence and to hear testimonials from these animals' overjoyed owners.

The pioneer of cell medicine for animals is a visionary veterinarian named Dr. Robert J. Harman, who invented technology to harness the healing power of ASC on behalf of dogs, cats, and horses, and called it Vet-Stem. Headquartered in San Diego, California, Vet-Stem's state-of-the-art facility—with its space-age apparatus designed to extract cells from fat samples, and its fancy freezers for cryopreserving cells—is as high-tech as anything one might see in a sci-fi flick. The super-sanitary atmosphere at this place puts some human hospitals I've seen to shame. Moreover, Dr. Harman (or as I call him, Dr. Bob) has coauthored research papers together with medical doctors on the human side—that's how well he knows his stuff. And yet, Vet-Stem's procedure of harvesting cells from fatty tissue is straightforward and simple. It does not require a fancy specialty hospital staffed by board-certified surgeons with extra degrees and letters after their names. Any veterinary surgeon—from rural country doc to urban clinician—can perform it after completing Vet-Stem's three-hour-long online course. I'd like to think that, were he alive today, the Scots country vet Alf Wight—better known to legions of animal lovers the world over by his pen name, James Herriot—would get Vet-Stem certification in a New York minute.

For years, the Humane Society of New York has been my go-to place for hound healing, but it is not a fancy specialty hospital by any stretch. It's the no-frills clinic of a nonprofit animal shelter founded in 1904, in a narrow, five-story building where space is always at a premium. And yet, the Society offers some impressive services, including care for exotic animals (birds and reptiles); excellent dental cleaning; sophisticated diagnostic tools; and behavioral consultations with Broadway's go-to animal trainer, Bill Berloni, winner of a Tony Award for Excellence in Theater. The Humane Society's best-kept secret weapons are its rock-star vets, notably the superbly skilled surgeon Dr. Elizabeth Higgins. It was at the

Humane Society clinic that Sam had undergone many of the procedures he'd required during his lifetime, from tooth cleaning to tumor removal. He adored Dr. Higgins, so I asked if she would please obtain Vet-Stem certification to perform the high-tech tummy tuck on my brave old dog. We're very grateful she said yes.

And so, per Vet-Stem's protocol, a sample of Sam's fatty tissue was surgically harvested from his groin under anesthesia, then FedExed in a dry-ice-insulated collection kit to San Diego. There, the tissue sample was placed in a centrifuge and harvested for stem cells, then vials of cells were repacked in dry ice and overnighted back to New York. In the intervening day and a half, I was instructed to alternately cold-pack and hot-pack the surgical site. In lieu of taking a hot pack to the groin, Sam preferred sunbathing on the stoop of our building; happily, the weather complied.

Meanwhile, in San Diego, the Vet-Stem team of doctors was doubtful about the quantity and viability of Sam's cells, given his advanced age. For Operation Stem Cell to have a shot, we needed three vials, one for the stifle of each hind leg, plus another vial for an intravenous injection. Sam's liposuction yielded more than we needed, much more—fourteen vials, to be precise, each one containing some three million healing stem cells. That's one vial for each year of Sam's remarkable life to date, and every single vial was viable! Three of those precious tubes were overnighted back to the Humane Society clinic. The contents of two were injected directly into my dog's afflicted joints, where they would enable Sam's connective tissue to repair itself; the goal was for the cells to regenerate his cartilage, so his poor old leg bones would stop grinding against each other with no cushion. The stem cells in the third vial, injected intravenously, would search Sam's body like microscopic hunting hounds hot on the scent, seeking other damaged parts that needed a cellular assist. (The remaining eleven of Sam's surprisingly viable vials were stored on ice in San Diego for his future use; he'd eventually receive three more "booster" injections.)

My expectations were realistic. I never thought Sam would emerge from this procedure a magically changed dog; as a journalist I'm duty-bound to remain skeptical, even when I've jacked up my hopes. So I told myself I'd be thrilled if Sam could walk like his old self again, the way he was the day before he collapsed on the street and could barely hobble home.

During recovery, Sam preferred sun baths to hot packs.

I just wanted him to stand strong. The morning that FedEx guaranteed Sam's cells would arrive from San Diego, X and I chauffeured him to the Humane Society clinic. Sam attempted to jump out of our Volvo wagon—and promptly wiped out on the sidewalk, his ego seriously bruised.

That afternoon, Doc Higgins called to say that all had gone well and Sam could come home. In fact, the Humane Society minivan was making rounds to run errands, so she offered to drop off Sam. Waiting at the corner of First Avenue and 90th Street, I was ready to help my dog dismount from the van, which was much higher off the ground than our Volvo. But Sam had other plans, and he was in a hurry. "I've got this," Sam seemed to say as he brusquely pushed past me and leapt out of the van, making a perfect landing on all fours. As if to announce his next trick, he turned around with a look that clearly said, "Wait—there's more." Sam took a few steps, slowly but much more surely than he had that morning. And then, after giving me a knowing glance (just to be sure I was watching his every move), Sam turned his back to me with theatrical flair, and . . . lifted his leg to pee. Hello again, Baryshnikov. He'd only emerged from sedation three hours earlier. Had Broadway Bill Berloni coached Sam in milking the spotlight-stealing dramatic gesture? I would have rubbed my eyes in disbelief but was too delirious with joy. I didn't own an iPhone at that time, but even if I'd had one, these events were happening so fast I probably wouldn't have successfully captured them on video anyway.

I got Sam upstairs more quickly than I had in months—he didn't need my help climbing the steps of our front stoop, thank you very much!—then grabbed my clunky Sanyo cell phone to call Vet-Stem. Describing the last half hour with breathless excitement, I asked, "Did I just see what I just saw?" They'd heard stories like this before: "We tell people to expect results anywhere from three days to three weeks to three months," said Dr. Harman. "But it's not unheard-of to see results in three hours. And," Dr. Bob added with characteristic compassion, "for a male dog to be able to lift his leg again makes such a difference in his quality of life—it's a guy thing." I remembered my psychic neighbor's words about Sam still seeing himself as a warrior.

After a week of alternating hot and cold compresses, and sitting on our stoop to soak up more joint-warming rays, Sam began regressing in age before my eyes. In chronological terms he was still ninety-eight in dog years, but Vet-Stem gave him license not to act his age. No longer fourteen years old, he was a canine Benjamin Button: fourteen years young, and getting younger. Pretty soon, his behavior was that of an eight- or nine-year-old dog. He resumed doing those cute things I hadn't seen in years, starting with the Snoopy dance on his back. He trotted confidently down the sidewalk . . . navigated steps with poise . . . flirted aerobically with female dogs many years his junior . . . dug in his heels with bionic stubbornness when he didn't want to move in the direction I was heading. X always used to joke that Sam had a terminal case of the blues; it was now clear that Sam's new theme song was "I Feel Good," and there was nothing terminal about him.

People in my neighborhood who remembered seeing Sam struggle, stiff-legged, on walks noticed the difference right away. Many dropped their jaws to see my old dog walking tall, his clock visibly reversing itself. They didn't bother asking how or where their dogs could get the same procedure. Immediately, they fast-forwarded to the $64,000 question: How and where could they—or their mothers or brothers or sisters-in-law—get this procedure for themselves? Mind you, these people were part of the toughest possible demographic—jaded New Yorkers—and they were impressed.

Wow—can they do this for people, too?

I was the Pet Reporter for the *New York Post* with a weekly column in the Sunday paper, and success stories of cutting-edge veterinary procedures were my stock in trade. I'd broken news about medical breakthroughs, ranging from botanical chemotherapy to bionic animal limbs, and was proud of the positive feedback I received from readers and media colleagues. But I'd never seen a response like the unanimous one I received after Sam's stem cell success: appreciation of an animal's recovery that prompted enthusiastic inquiries about similar human treatment options.

Wow—can they do this for people, too?

That's the question my dog and I kept hearing over and over on our walks together, until we heard it so often that it began to sound like a mantra.

So . . . can they?

The answer was yes, and no. Obviously, the technology existed and it worked, but it was not FDA-approved for use on people. Vet-Stem's many success stories were offering compelling proof of ASC's efficacy in the form of canine, feline, and equine case studies. Throughout medical history, the biggest breakthroughs in human medicine were tested out on animals first. Now, dogs' joints could be regenerated with their own cells, while the state of the art for humans was . . . getting the joints of cadavers implanted in their limbs. It seemed veterinary medicine had officially outstripped human medicine. "Stem Cell Therapy for Pets" read a headline in the July 14, 2008, issue of *Time* magazine. "Sorry, people: A new treatment for ailing joints is only for pooches (and cats and horses)."

There was hope, however: By this time, America had a new president, the candidate I'd proudly cast my vote for. Barack Obama promised to open the door for stem cell research—embryonic stem cell research. Unfortunately, the media continued reporting on stem cells the same way it had during the previous administration, by emphasizing embryos. Like everyone else, the president received his news from the mainstream media, and adult cells were still not yet ready for prime time. But overseas, it was a very different story. Americans who had run out of treatment options on US soil were finding unheard-of relief from a variety of "incurable" ailments—including arthritis, multiple sclerosis, Duchenne muscular dystrophy, and paraplegia—at Central American and South American clinics offering treatment with adult stem cells. These people were, and still are, routinely disparaged as "medical tourists," and their doctors as unethical "quacks."

One month and a few days after my dog underwent his stem cell procedure, surgeons at the Hospital Clinic in Barcelona, led by Professor Paolo Macchiarini, carried out the world's first tissue-engineered whole organ transplant, using a trachea (windpipe) custom-made with the recipient's own adult stem cells. The patient, a thirty-year-old Colombian mom of two named Claudia Castillo, needed the transplant to save a lung after tuberculosis had damaged the left bronchus (branch) of her trachea. To fabricate the new airway, doctors took a donor trachea from a recently deceased patient and applied chemicals and enzymes to wash it clean of the donor's cells—all that remained was a collagen scaffold, which was then seeded with Claudia's cells, a mixture of ASC from her own bone marrow plus cells lining her own trachea. After four days in the lab, in a rotating bioreactor, that cellular cocktail morphed into the cells that normally surround the windpipe—and the transformed trachea was ready to be transplanted into Claudia's body. One month later, a biopsy of the site proved that the transplant had developed its own blood supply; four months later, the patient still showed no signs of rejection. "We are terribly excited by these results," Prof. Macchiarini said. "She is enjoying a normal life, which for us clinicians is the most beautiful gift."

Since 2008, dogs like my Sam have benefited from high-tech healing, while human patients who could be enjoying a vastly improved quality of life have been instead made to feel helpless—as helpless as my dog must have felt when his hind legs collapsed beneath him. I could relate to that terrible feeling of helplessness. Nine years earlier, prepped to undergo middle-of-the-night surgery in a hospital ER, I'd experienced it myself.

CHAPTER 2

Sick as a Dog

As a journalist, I've written and spoken openly about many events in my life, yet I've never written before about surviving septicemia, also known as sepsis or blood poisoning, and I do so now as a way of (1) being thankful, and (2) raising awareness that this too-often-fatal condition could befall any one of us, human or canine, at any age. I was thirty-four when a bacterial infection hijacked my bloodstream, dangerously raising my body temperature, dramatically lowering my blood pressure, and threatening to shut down my vital organs. The year was 1999, and I was at the top of my game as a fashion journalist in New York City, with a biweekly column in the *New York Post* called "Fashion City" and a coveted front-row seat at runway shows many of my colleagues would have killed to eject me from. My eye was trained to observe and report on the tempest-in-a-thimble stirred up twice annually at New York Fashion Week—hem and hair lengths, fashionable fabrics, heel heights, and other earth-shatteringly newsworthy topics—and my job was to keep the conversation going, in between those milestone events, with celebrity-driven stories. All the while, I was obliged to maintain the appearance of a fashion plate on an unfashionably tight budget, so imagine my delight when celebrity photographer Roxanne Lowit told me that Isaac Mizrahi had remarked to her how well I wore a silk blouse of his; later, legendary lensman Bill Cunningham of the *New York Times* snapped me wearing a Prada skirt-suit. My biggest scoop for the *Post* was a column about a new cable TV series starring Sarah Jessica Parker, whose pilot portended to be deeply driven by designer clothes. I predicted that *Sex and the City* would be a fashion show, and my column—in which SJP dished, deliciously, about her personal favorite shopping resources and her desire to make the show's characters accurate portrayals of the uniquely, inherently stylish

New York Woman—started the media-wide trend of covering HBO's long-running mega-hit series from a fashion angle. The rest was pop-culture history. And then everything fell into proper perspective when I almost became history.

I was very lucky to survive; many sepsis patients didn't, including Gustav Mahler, Mary Wollstonecraft, Alexander Scriabin, Yuriko Miya-moto, William Henry Harrison, James Garfield, and Calvin Coolidge Jr.; the thirtieth president's sons were out playing a game of tennis when the younger of the two, sixteen-year-old Cal Jr.—wearing tennis shoes without socks—developed a blister on his right foot, which progressed into the blood poisoning that killed him on July 7, 1924. It's sobering how the most sophisticated, state-of-the-art, contemporary emergency room is sometimes no match for a fast-moving blood infection, especially if it's resistant to antibiotics. Once a patient goes into septic shock, it's too late. Even a very closely monitored patient can succumb; I didn't realize until recently that sepsis is what killed both Christopher Reeve and Pope John Paul II, and who was more closely watched than everyone's favorite Man of Steel and man of the cloth? Superman and the Pontiff were, of course, also major figures on opposite sides of the international stem cell debate. Becoming an advocate for the disabled after the 1996 equestrian accident that severed his skull from his spine and left him paralyzed, Reeve was an outspoken supporter of embryonic stem cell research.

I lived to write about my sepsis and to take a stand on the stem cell controversy—fated to cross paths, stem cells and I had a date with destiny, although I had no way of knowing it back then. I have no doubt my dog over dosage, if you will, is the reason why. The average animal lover has one or at most two dogs; I have "only" four today, but in 1999, X and I had many more than that. One Medicine Dog is a potent healing force, but he can only do so much. The extreme stress of my unhappy marriage put me in such bad shape that I needed the continuous attentions of a seven-pack of Medicine Dogs. Looking back, it's not hard to see how the steady buildup of toxicity from my unhappy marriage, my low levels of oxytocin, and my adrenal glands' relentless release of the stress hormone cortisol would culminate in a spectacular illness requiring emergency surgery. My spousal situation was diseased, with frequent bouts of acute suspicion,

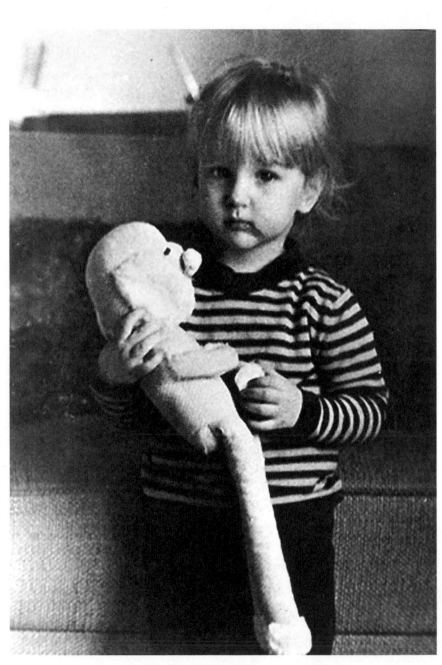

Me and my real, imaginary friend, circa 1968

worry, and outright fear. Had it not been for my dogs' therapeutic presence, the surfeit of stress-induced hormones in my system would doubtless have finished me.

The calmness of canines is one of my earliest memories; I don't know what it's like not to be surrounded and soothed by dogs. I was a confirmed dog person even before I ever had an actual puppy. As a child, I was a collector of plush poodle toys known as Hugniks, re-dubbed the *pudli*, which is the plural of poodle in Hungarian, the language of my ancestors. They fell apart at the seams from my constant pawing at them—I distinctly recall falling asleep every night while stroking the nearest one's long, floppy ear—so my mother stitched them back together like the most competent vet. These real, imaginary dogs were my constant companions, even after I got a real puppy of my own, Bodri the puli (Hungarian sheepdog), sweet black-and-white runt of her litter. Real and imaginary dogs were especially important to me during the extreme fear-of-death phase of my childhood, when I would lie awake at night and freak myself out about not being alive. It nearly sent me into a panic. So I suspect I've been loath to face the fact that septicemia was my bona fide brush with death—and the death I feared most wasn't my own, but the demise of my marriage, then just seven years young. Septicemia almost killed me, but before it did, I thought I'd already cleared the toughest hurdle of my life: the first trial separation from my husband.

I adored that man. The day after we met, he wrote me this note: "Dearest Julia, I did not know this was possible, now I know anything is. Love, X." Our wedding day, September 10, 1993, was a day I'll never forget; we were married in the chambers of the Honorable Bruce McMarion Wright, justice of the New York State Supreme Court, whom we both deeply admired for his radical activism, elegance, and wit. A poet as well as a jurist, he surprised us by reading e.e. cummings' beautiful poem "Since feeling is first." Then we rode away on a vintage BMW motorcycle for an overnight stay at the Royalton Hotel. The one-night honeymoon was a gift from my then-boss, the late Liz Tilberis, editor in chief of *Harper's Bazaar*. To impress Liz, also known as La Blanche (as art director Fabien Baron called her, a nod to her stunning white hair), I wore a black minidress by Moschino, styled X in a vintage Emilio Pucci necktie, and arranged for my bouquet of roses—by Liz's favorite floral designer Miho Kosuda—to match the tie's fuchsia, white, and baby-pink palette. I was thrilled when La Blanche smiled her approval of the decidedly not *Town & Country* wedding-day photos.

When we first met, X was the "perfect friend"—in author J. R. Ackerley's phrase—whom I'd dreamed of my whole life: so brilliantly witty, handsome, charming, and earthy, with such blue eyes! With his broad shoulders and karate-sculpted physique, he looked as breathtaking in a business suit as in a motorcycle jacket (my preferred getup for him). All that, plus he was wonderfully caring. Ever since my college days, I would experience extremely painful menstrual periods, stricken as if by a club with excruciating back pain and cramps; I'll never forget the first time this happened while in X's presence, and how swiftly he morphed into EMT, doctor, and nurse all at once, spiriting me home in a cab, carrying me upstairs, and out-mothering my own mommy with tender ministrations. I didn't keep track of Aunt Flo's ETA—major denial MO much?— but X did. As time passed, X seemed to relish picking fights, out of the blue and over nothing, at precisely that time of the month, then point to the calendar and announce, as if making some *aha!* medical discovery: "So *that's* why you're such a bitch." I was shocked, but I firmly believed X's previous PMS-care persona was the real one, whereas this cold, calculating humiliator was just an act, so I waited for the warm, nurturing lover I knew to show his sweet face again. I would wait—steadfastly, stubbornly, stupidly—for seventeen years. Things didn't get better; they got worse. And the flaws in my "perfect friend" were thrown in relief by my real perfect friends, the four-footed ones.

Rescued dogs offered generous helpings of the warm, nurturing presence I missed in my marriage, and I began collecting them like the stuffed *pudli* of my childhood. My dogs—*pitbulis* as my mother wittily dubbed them—filled a widening emotional void in my life caused by my beloved husband's increasing coldness. After Sam came home, I was so grateful to the shelter where I'd found him that I began volunteering to walk dogs and assist with pit bull adoptions. What I saw there sharpened my skills as a reporter and observer. If X was a vicious entity lurking behind a super-cute mask, pit bulls were quite the opposite. They were nothing like the reputation the media had manufactured and whipped into a foamy frenzy. Pits were, in fact, adorably affectionate dogs, unfairly saddled with a "vicious" mystique. The very first specimen I ever met was a brindle male who belonged to a neighbor at the apartment building where X and I first resided together in 1993. I'll never forget the day that dog sweetly stood up in the elevator to give me a hug. I'd heard and read only horror stories in the media about dogs who looked like this and was pleasantly shocked to see that the reality was infinitely more cuddly. This dog was downright adorable, doing the two things I would come to love most about his kind: wiggling (i.e., wagging his tail aerobically) and piggling (snorting and snuffling with porcine pleasure). I resolved to do whatever I could to help out this maligned breed's reputation, and to use my work as a journalist to right the wrongs the media was relentlessly feeding the public about pits. What a difference the passing of two decades makes. Today, the nicest people own pit bulls and express a desire to adopt them, and there are many rescue groups dedicated to pulling pits off death row at animal shelters. But in the late '90s, pit rescue and rehab was something very few people did, and many people I encountered had no hesitation to opine aloud, "Shouldn't you be rescuing people *from* pit bulls?"

When X and I realized our dream of having a small country place, we arrived in the Catskill mountains with our terrific trio—Daisy, Sam, and Pepper—but the canine count quickly escalated. We visited the local animal shelter upstate and came home with two gorgeous furry creatures: Sheba, a red border collie, and Tiki, a chow-rottweiler. Not long after, at the same animal shelter, I found the most extraordinary creature: a little brindle pit named Brittany, a name I could not abide because of the then-enormous popularity of a teen sensation named Spears. This dog was breathtakingly beautiful, with amber eyes to match her coppery, tiger-striped coat, My Little Pony eyelashes, perfectly cropped ears, and the cutest undershot jaw. One had to think seriously about upsetting the balance by adding another dog to the pack, but I couldn't stand to leave this captivating creature behind without at least some warm bedding, so I gave her one of the thick acrylic horse blankets we kept in the car for the canines' comfort. The following weekend, we returned to the shelter; the staff had cleverly arranged to have Britannia, as I'd renamed her, spayed.

"Look, your mommy's here!" the kennel worker announced as we walked over to my new best friend. Upon seeing me, Britannia did a three-foot vertical leap in the air. She came home that day.

I distinctly recall being impressed by the expert way Britannia's abdomen had been stitched; clearly, the precise needle artistry, resembling as it did a museum-quality patchwork quilt, was the calling card of a perfectionist lady surgeon. "Was the vet who did this spay a woman?" I inquired of the shelter staff; she certainly was. Dr. Jo Olver of Jockeyport Livery Stable and Veterinary Services became one of my go-to vets, despite her practice being one long hour's drive away from our country seat. Thanks to continuously running ozone machines, the hospital was as pristine-clean in smell as it was in appearance. But Dr. Jo's needlework was her practice's best advertisement; several thousands of dollars were spent at Jockeyport in the ensuing years. It was the first time I actively sought out a doctor, regardless of location or how far I had to travel to get there,

The Brindlesteins: Britannia (right) and Haus

rather than just patronize the nearest one—and it wouldn't be the last. My dogs, I decided, were well worth going the extra mile, or 54.4 to be exact.

Britannia got herself a husband when an ASPCA humane law enforcement officer called to let me know that she'd rescued a brindle male pit who'd suffered terrible abuse at the hands of a convicted rapist. Without hesitation, I took the dog, whose name was House (re-spelled H-A-U-S). The two brindles, as if recognizing each other as the same striped subset of the same species, instantly bonded as a couple. I dubbed them the Brindlesteins.

My aerobic accumulation of animals was out of the ordinary, to be sure. I would have been ripe for an episode of *Hoarders,* had the show existed at the time. Dogs provided the unconditional love my husband could not. The ones I found homes for renewed my faith in love and second chances; the ones who stayed with me inspired everything I did. Some dog lovers worry that they won't live long enough to have all the different types of dog they'd dreamed of having; I'm not one of those dog lovers. Rescuing and fostering enabled me to enjoy the company of a few really wonderful breeds before they went away to their forever homes, including a Norwegian elkhound, a keeshond, and a treeing walker coonhound. Thanks to the mixed-breeds, I had a chow *and* a rottweiler, a Lab *and* a shepherd.

In keeping me happy and distracted, the permanent and temporary dogs had their work cut out for them. X became more and more hostile, issuing insults that were almost too shocking to be taken seriously. During one argument, he told me, "You deserve to be euthanized." This stranger was a far cry from the young man in the leather jacket who'd reeled me in by describing a magical motorcycle ride in Westchester county, along a road lined with flowering trees; at precisely the right moment in spring, vrooming on that fabled path would cause the petals to cascade down on the rider. X promised many times to take me for that ride, but something always took precedence and it didn't happen. One day, standing in line at the supermarket, I was overcome with sadness about my miserably flailing marriage. I decided to separate from X and began searching for an apartment of my own. When I found one, X was very upset and burst into tears. He undertook a charm offensive, bombarding me with roses and pleading mash notes. But I explained that if our marriage had a chance of working, putting space between us was the only way to find out. Besides, I'd be just ten short blocks away. I took two dogs—Britannia and Haus, who were actively inspiring me by enjoying the kind of nice relationship X and I couldn't manage—and moved to my new place, a small one-bedroom on the third floor of a brownstone walk-up in Spanish Harlem.

My mind wandered back to the time shortly before I met X. What, and whom, had I missed in those intervening seven years? I'd once briefly dated an up-and-coming young psychiatrist but ended the relationship because I thought he was kind of arrogant—in a word, doctorlike. Once settled in to my new place, I summoned the courage to contact Doc. We went out on a few dates, even a double date; try relaxing during a sushi dinner with not one but three psychiatrists! Doc had said he was a dog lover, but when my friendly brindles eagerly swarmed him, with wide smiles and wagging tails, he couldn't have looked less comfortable. I'd given Doc the benefit of the doubt, figuring surely he'd be intelligent enough to look past the media's relentless depiction of pit bulls as demons. But like so many people, he couldn't see my dogs as dogs; they were just four-footed newspaper headlines waiting to happen. When a colleague mentioned a media power couple in the market for a rescued golden retriever or yellow Lab, I tried preaching the pro-pit gospel, but they had their hearts set on a Ralph Lauren dog. Never turning down a chance to save a life, I found a sweet, pre-owned dog named Fred at an animal shelter upstate that was a mix of both breeds; I scooped him up and promptly adopted him to the couple, who were thrilled. That led to another double date; meeting Fred, Doc turned into a playful little boy. "Now, THAT'S a DOG!" he said, approvingly. At that moment, I knew our relationship wasn't going to work out. Dogs, and the often complex issues they raise, were important to me in my work and my life, and Doc wasn't getting it. My first assessment of him had been correct, it seemed.

But there was no time for a serious discussion with Doc because, in short order, about two weeks after moving, I was overcome by debilitating pain in my stomach and lower back—much worse than the kind that used to presage my period. Figuring I may have pulled something during the move, I took two Tylenols. The pain only grew worse. I woke up in the middle of the night, sweaty and chilled, with abdominal cramps and overwhelming fecal urgency—except once squarely seated on the john, nothing came out despite my best efforts. Standing up, I saw stars. I thought I was going to black out. I sat back down and tried not to panic. Finally, I dragged myself back to bed; Britannia and Haus were on silent high alert the entire time.

The next morning, I staggered through the dog-walk. Afterward, I called Doc, who gamely offered to give me a prescription for Valium. He'd often joke that, being a shrink, he wasn't a "real" doctor—but he did have a handy script pad. "I used to get that lower back pain all the time, from playing tennis," he said cheerfully, dropping the script off at my apartment after work. Like most doctors, he was confident that a pill existed to cure whatever might ail you—even mental illness, which has its own well-stocked psycho-pharmacopeia. I had no reason to doubt him. But what neither of us knew was that my problem was already way past a pill's power to fix. The pain was escalating. Hauling myself up the two carpeted flights of steps to my new apartment was a serious effort. I put Haus in boarding, figuring I could cut my dog work in half by taking care of just one. But even Britannia was too much—especially with her notorious pulling power, which the noted animal behaviorist Dr. Peter Borchelt had once estimated to be about one thousand pounds—and I didn't want to risk, say, passing out on the street and having Britannia run into traffic. Putting her in X's custody until I felt better was the best thing for Britannia's safety. I called X and asked if he could please take Britannia for a few days. He came over, scowling, to collect her. "I hate people who say 'I can't,'" X said.

"But I really can't walk her—my back is killing me," I whined. Turning to walk Britannia down the stairs, he replied, "You'd be surprised at what you can do."

I was now dogless—not a comfortable condition for me!—and feeling too sick to stay alone, so I called my parents, who told me to come on over. I set up camp on their living-room sofa and settled in for a nap with their two cats. My dad was nice enough to bring the Valium script to the pharmacy and have it filled; I took two. But two hours later, I felt too feverish to sleep. I called Doc to report this new development. Concerned, he offered to make a house call. It was certainly an odd circumstance in which to meet the parents of someone you'd recently started dating, and I give Doc a lot of credit for overcoming the awkwardness of it to try to help me. I began to rethink my gloomy diagnosis of our relationship. Doc came over, greeted my folks in a businesslike fashion, and told me it didn't sound like I had a back problem. He asked me to lower my pajama trousers. Then he quietly announced, "We're going to the emergency room." I was dumbfounded. What had he seen down there? My parents automatically started pulling on their coats, but Doc gently told them there was no reason for us all to sit around and wait—he'd take me and call them with developments. Now my hard-to-impress parents were impressed.

We took a cab to the nearest hospital. It turns out I was spectacularly sick. The nurse in admissions took my temperature; I had a high fever, 105. No wonder I'd been seeing stars: I had a systemic infection, septicemia. My blood was poisoned. What Doc had seen was an angry red boil on my right butt-cheek, the result of an abscess; pus had been collecting down there for days, displacing the tissue to create a container for itself, and my body was reacting violently to the presence of that pus, marshaling its forces to fight the infection. The official diagnosis? Perirectal fistula (PF) and abscess. The pus-filled abscess was the result of leakage from an abnormal opening, or a "fistula," in my gut. There was no time to waste: I had to undergo emergency surgery for an incision and drainage—I&D for short—to remove the toxic pus that was trying to kill me. Incidentally, I would later learn, dogs typically develop symptoms of sepsis in the gastrointestinal tract first. Dogs are my sentinels, as this book will demonstrate, so it's somehow appropriate that the GI tract was my medical ground zero, too.

Lying awake in the ICU the night before undergoing a risky operation to reattach his skull to his spine, Christopher Reeve recalled in his memoir, *Still Me*, how "the door flew open and in hurried a squat fellow with a blue scrub hat and a yellow surgical gown and glasses, speaking in a Russian accent." He announced that he was a proctologist, come to perform a rectal exam—but he was actually Robin Williams, come to cheer up his old friend. It worked: "For the first time since the accident, I laughed," Reeve remembered. Anyone would be delighted by a bedside visit from "Doctor" Robin Williams; alas, that's not what I got. Given barium to drink,

I managed to force it down in three wincing gulps, only to be told they wouldn't "take the picture" after all. To compensate, as this was a teaching hospital, a team of some six interns arrived, and each one examined my rectum. The doctors-in-training were proportioned like football players, with beefy fingers and hands. About an hour later, another intern entered the room. My eyes immediately went to his hands, which were small and slender. "Where were you when it was rectal exam time?" I joked. Happily, that wasn't his mission, so I was spared yet another excruciating probe.

The chief of surgery was called in; he arrived between 2:00 and 3:00 a.m., by which time I had already been wheeled into the OR, and a male nurse—there wasn't a female anywhere in sight—was helping me remove my contact lenses, improvising a lens case with two small saline-filled plastic cups. The surgery chief, Dr. Schmerz (not his real name), introduced himself. The next thing I remember is waking up in the ICU. I was on my back, the weight of my body pressing down on my freshly-carved right buttock, causing me to instinctively start squirming in search of a less searing position. A lady nurse appeared, and I was relieved to finally see a woman—until she sharply told me to stop moving. To my left, my un-lensed eyes made out a familiar figure: Doc, looking bleary from staying up all night with hard contacts slowly affixing themselves to his eyeballs. Standing there clutching my clothes and coat, he looked adorable, like a faithful dog—like Fred! My heart swelled and I reached for his hand, so grateful and proud to know him. He'd saved my life: Without immediate medical attention, I would have died.

"Thanks for staying," I said, squeezing his hand.

I was rigged with a morphine drip for the pain, which was nothing to sneeze at: With all sorts of nerve endings, the crack is an extremely sensitive body part. And that's where Dr. Schmerz had been obliged to make an incision five millimeters wide by five millimeters deep, draining thirty cubic centimeters of "foul smelling pus" from my abscess. The wound could not be stitched shut; it had to heal on its own. Gauze packing had been placed in the incision to prevent the edges of the doctor-made wound from closing too fast and creating yet another infected abscess. Making matters even more uncomfortable, Dr. Schmerz had seen fit to make the incision surprisingly close to my labia.

The next morning, two residents, a woman and a Sikh man wearing a turban, approached my bed. Observing that the Sikh had the most beautiful face, not unlike Naveen Andrews in *The English Patient*, I thought, *What a nice hospital, where the doctors look just like movie stars* (such euphoric observations are not uncommon while high on morphine, even if one's doctor is not a turbaned Sikh). My reverie was rudely interrupted. The residents were there to change the gauze packing keeping my wound open. Without telling me what to expect, with a swift yank the doctors did what they came to do. I understood how Christopher Marlowe's King Edward II must have felt when assassins applied the hot poker to his asshole. Apparently, I was later told, my scream filled the ward, the butt of jokes at follow-up rechecks with Dr. Schmerz. Recovering from that shock, I appreciated that this is how animals experience critical care in vet hospitals. Sadly, we can't explain to ailing pets the pain we're about to inflict in an attempt to make them well. We can just give them painkillers. Unless they are sedated, pain must come to them as an excruciating shock. But I daresay the two doctors treating me that morning could have given me fair warning—or some kind of bullet to bite. Why hadn't they?

The following day, I repaired to my parents' apartment to convalesce. Home nurses arrived daily to clean and repack my wound. Fashion Week was about to start in a few days, and there I was, unfashionably flat on my back. I received a call from my editor at the *Post*. She had good news and bad. Someone had already stepped into my position as fashion critic; my colleague wasn't just subbing for me at the shows, she was taking my job. I was still recovering from that blow when my editor quickly unfurled the silver lining. The paper had liked my occasional articles on dogs—notably the one about designer dog accessories—and wanted to try out a weekly pets column. Would I be interested? Would I ever! Was she kidding? Report and write all day about dogs and cats and other species of companion animal, my favorite subjects? Leave "Fashion City" for an exciting new urban frontier, the petropolis? Have a platform from which to advocate on behalf of animals, especially my beloved pit bulls? Yes, please! When do I start? There were only so many things left to write about fashion; pets, and the serious issues they often raise, from politics to health, offered an opportunity to really hone my journalistic chops. At that time, serious reporting on pets was nonexistent; if a dog was mentioned in a news story—say, as the one who alerted a family to a fire in their home—there was rarely any description of the animal. That had always bugged me; now, here was my chance to do the kind of responsible, accurate reporting I myself wanted to read. And it went without saying that now I'd be able to make a difference on behalf of pit bulls, the dog so routinely demonized by the mainstream media. I jumped at this once-in-a-lifetime opportunity. It wasn't good news, it was *great* news. I was game to embark on my new career, to put my nose to the ground, and to get on with the new life I was looking forward to when my surgery derailed me.

At one follow-up exam, Dr. Schmerz explained how bacteria from liquid stool could contaminate my bloodstream, by leaking through the fistula in my gut—basically, the less solid my excrement, the greater my chance of reinfection and a relapse of septicemia. "So don't get diarrhea," the doctor concluded. How would I manage that?

"I don't know," he replied. "Just don't."

Basically, I had to get my shit together, and I was on my own to figure out how.

Doc was still in the picture. For the first time since before my hospitalization, we spent the night at his place. Feeling much better than I had in weeks, I ventured to hope that we might do The Deed—and figured I couldn't be in better hands than here with Doc. I had every confidence the sweetheart who'd spent the night at the hospital with me would do everything right. Instead, he withdrew and settled in to sleep.

"I don't do pus," he cracked. Lo and behold, Prince Charming turned into a turd.

"The pus was removed in surgery, remember?" I explained. "There is no more pus."

Doc was silent. Lying beside him in the dark, feeling very alone, I thought about the two doctors in my life. The one at the hospital was cavalierly telling me not to get diarrhea without providing a clue as to how, while the one in bed with me just saddled me with a heavy hang-up about my apparently pus-filled privates. Whom did I have to sleep with to find a physician with better bedside manners? As if the unchecked emission from his mouth wasn't noxious enough, Doc farted in his sleep all that night, our last together; it was his turn to end the relationship, and he did. Thereafter, I sensed that two topics with which I was now very intimate—anorectal pus (actual or perceived) and the pit bull polemic— would likely be roadblocks to any new relationship I might try to start. Everything happens for a reason, as the saying goes. I'd been wrong about pus being a thing of the past. In the coming years, as the surgical inci- sion turned into a chronic, nonhealing wound, there would be more pus and lots of it. So Doc really wasn't the one for me. Dogs, those blessed creatures, are unfazed by humans' gross emissions, but people are often too squeamish to deal with unpleasant bodily eruptions, even when such things ooze from their own bodies. On a subsequent visit to the hospital for a recheck, I'd expressed concern to a kind, young female resident that my condition had put an end to my dating prospects, repeating Doc's pus comment as proof. Surprised, she asked, "And he's a doctor?"

"Yep, a psychiatrist."

"Oh, a shrink," she replied with a dismissive hand wave. "That doesn't count. You need to find a *real* doctor."

Amen! But, as I would learn, that's much easier said than done. For all his shortcomings, at least X loved pits. With gratitude and hope for a new start, I took my husband up on his numerous offers to start over again with him, negotiated with my landlady about terminating my lease, and returned to live with X.

CHAPTER 3

Deep Doo-Doo

This is a medical memoir and a tribute to the healing power of companion animals and stem cells. But in the simplest terms, it's about how a pack of adopted shelter dogs helped me get my shit together—at a time when there was shit in my blood, my doctor didn't give a shit, and my spouse couldn't stop being a shit. Now, a brief aside about that word: When we can't use the S-word innocently and cleanly, to refer to the natural function it so succinctly describes, the result is a hang-up—and hang-ups aren't healthy. Fecal matter is an excellent barometer of wellness, so it's high time to approach this "taboo" topic with the same healthy innocence displayed by our canine cohorts. Dogs live in a parallel universe where there's no shame in shit. In fact, it's often cause for celebration. When we humans can talk about it, calling it by its proper name, then we'll be able to communicate more openly with our doctors, and the result will be a better understanding of health overall.

Dr. Jane Wilson-Howarth, fellow of the Royal Society of Tropical Medicine and Hygiene, authored an excellent book with a wonderfully stiff-upper-lip title: *How to Shit Around the World: The Art of Staying Clean and Healthy While Traveling.* Yet six years after that book's publication, an esteemed GI specialist would tell me how it surprised him when, describing their defecations for diagnostic purposes, many patients still cover their mouths, mortified. Dogs have no such issues. Ever notice how Spot will express the relief of a good bowel movement by kicking gleefully with hind legs at the earth underfoot? In the years following my emergency surgery, I envied dogs that sweet relief—pooping became that unpleasant an ordeal. How many horrific ways can one suffer on a toilet? Innumerably many, as I would learn. If the opposite of sublime relief is demonic possession, picture being at once exorcist and exorcee—that's

For dogs, there's no shame in shit. DANA ROSE LEE

how it felt to be coaxing out crap as if evicting Satan from a particularly comfy place. There were times when, lightheaded and practically passing out from straining to poop, I sat on the toilet and saw stars, just as I had two nights before my trip to the emergency hospital, times when the agony of diarrhea caused me to call out to my mommy even when she was miles away. The invention of the smartphone was a godsend during those awful instances when fecal urgency would strike during, say, a conference call; thanks to the mute function, my business colleagues didn't know that my attentive participation was affirmed between bouts of toilet trauma.

Surviving sepsis wasn't the end of my medical problems. It was only the beginning. The pathogenesis—or disease-causing mechanism—of my septicemia was a perirectal fistula, the Latin term for which is *fistula-in-ano*. *Fistula* is Latin for "pipe," so picture an abnormal passageway, or tunnel, connecting the inside of the anal canal to the skin around the anus or buttock. Fistulas can arise between any two parts of the body that don't normally connect, but they are most common in the digestive tract. Those most prone to developing fistulas are people who have Crohn's and ulcerative colitis—the inflammatory bowel diseases collectively termed IBD, which affect some 1.4 million Americans, including Pearl Jam's lead guitarist, Mike McCready, an inspirationally outspoken IBD advocate. Dr. Schmerz didn't seem to think I had Crohn's or colitis, yet my PF symptoms were practically the same. If not closed by some means, my fistula would continue to threaten my life by continuously leaking fecal matter into my bloodstream, where it definitely does not belong.

Fistulas have challenged history's most skilled physicians, starting with Hippocrates. According to the *International Journal of Colorectal Disease*, "Fistula-in-ano has been well known for millennia because of its profound negative impact on the patient's quality of life." If you're a fistula patient, you're in "deep doo-doo," to quote President George H. W. Bush, and so is your surgeon. It's impossible to keep the surgical site completely clean. As Haig Dudukgian and Herand Abcarian wrote in the *World Journal of Gastroenterology*, "A common theme in this disease process in all its forms is the presence of stool within the wound, both before and after treatment strategies. Surgeons abhor the thought of stool in surgical wounds, yet in fistula-in-ano we have to accept the fact that a fresh surgical wound will be bathed in feces on a daily basis." As patients of anorectal surgery, we must accept that same fact, and—as I can personally attest—it's pretty dreadful.

I experienced relapse after relapse of reinfection and the early stages of septicemia, constantly dreading extreme exhaustion, fever, wrenching abdominal cramps that left me wincing and ashen, and demonic bowel movements that made me pant as if I'd just run a race on a full stomach. As the years wore on, to my utter mortification, I also experienced surprise flatulence while out in public (sometimes in mid-sentence). Working in my favor was the fact that the surgical incision that saved my life never completely healed; it would provide an exit pathway for pus to drain away from my body. Every few months, septicemia would start—then stop when drainage began. Living with such a chronic condition left me vulnerable to other problems, actual and potential. Of the latter, the one I feared most was colon cancer. Yet Dr. Schmerz could offer no practical advice. Only other fistula sufferers can do that; most doctors just can't imagine what it's like to live with something like this, and even the ones who treat fistula patients are more concerned with their own pressing issues, such as keeping the surgical site clean post-operatively; they have no time to spend on patients' everyday hygiene and toilet troubles. Remember what one of the priests says to Linda Blair's movie mom, Ellen Burstyn, in *The Exorcist:* "There are no experts. You probably know as much about possession as most priests!" Substitute fistula for possession and doctors for priests, and you have an accurate summary of what it's like to live with this condition. To cope, you will have to become so resourceful that, by the end, you'll be as expert on the topic as a physician, if not more so.

In the West, more men than women develop anorectal fistulas; but in sub-Saharan Africa and Asia, it's women who suffer most, as obstetric fistula continues to plague those of childbearing age, although it was largely eliminated elsewhere in the world by the early twentieth century. Thankfully, the Worldwide Fistula Fund is dedicated to helping the world's poorest women and eradicating fistula worldwide. Now imagine being a monarch in the seventeenth century, with no dog to comfort you and a royal pain in the ass to distract you from affairs of state. Louis XIV of France, the Sun King, didn't have to imagine such a scenario; he lived it. From his birth, history's most famous fistula patient had every detail of his physical condition recorded daily by the royal physician. French for doo-doo is *caca,* and the infant heir apparent to the throne of France was dubbed *le dauphin* (a smiling dolphin even appears on his coat of arms). As was the case for all *dauphins* before and after him, the little prince's excrement—*caca dauphin*—was closely monitored for color and consistency, as telling signs of health. If, as the grown-up Louis famously proclaimed, "*L'état, c'est moi*" ("The state, it's me"), then millions are in deep doo-doo if the crowned head is anorectally aggravated. The active king had logged many years of riding horseback, often in heavy armor, so his condition was attributed to that. Infamously careless about matters of personal hygiene, Louis XIV gave fair warning to courtiers to open a window in advance of his entering their air space, so it's reasonable to suspect that an unclean crack, not excessive equitation, conspired to bedevil his bottom. On January 15, 1685, the royal physician noted a swelling in the king's anal area. By February 18, an abscess had formed, followed by a fistula on May 2. Enemas and poultices didn't work, so a surgeon was summoned. Back then, surgeons were esteemed on the level of butchers and barbers (no offense to either profession), but physicians were prohibited, by order of the Catholic Church, to cut into the human body—alive or dead. The king was ailing; cutting him was now the only option.

It's stressful just trying to fathom the stress endured by the man charged with cutting the king of France: surgeon Charles-François Félix, who respectfully requested six months to prepare for this historic procedure. He used that time to—ouch—conduct experimental operations on peasants who didn't need surgery; several died, and God only knows how many suffered painful post-surgical complications. For his famous patient, Félix invented tools that are now displayed at the museum at Versailles: a precise, finely curved scalpel and a heavy-duty wrought-iron retractor. Finally, Félix was ready; the operation was performed, without anesthesia, on November 18, 1686, at 7:00 a.m. In the crowded OR were Madame de Maintenon, the king's mistress; his son the dauphin; his confessor; his physicians; and the minister of state. The operation was a success, and the royal patient—exhibiting admirable calmness while his surgeon sweated bullets—was back in the saddle in three months' time.

The status of surgery was exalted overnight; public lectures on the topic were delivered in the king's garden, and many courtiers, in the first instance I've heard of a medically inspired fashion statement, took to wearing chic "bandages" (white sashes) tied below the waist to honor the king's bravery in surgery. The surgeon who made it all possible, Monsieur Félix, was rewarded with money, a title, and an estate. But Félix retired from practice, and subsequent centuries would see many of his colleagues vexed by *fistula-in-ano,* performing surgeries that too often left the patient incontinent. Who knows how differently anorectal surgical technology might have evolved had Félix continued wielding the implements he custom-crafted or taught his procedure to other surgeons. But Louis XIV famously, and rather obnoxiously, said, *"Après moi, le deluge"* ("After me, the flood"); after he overcame PF, some two centuries of his fellow fistula sufferers were left in a drowning pool.

Another breakthrough was sorely needed. Historical documents suggest that a century prior to Félix's great achievement, fistulas were already taxing medical resources. The reputation of this unfortunate condition was well enough known that fistula became shorthand for precisely what Bush 41 meant by deep doo-doo: an icky, sticky political problem. In 1581, M. Walter Haddon wrote a religio-political tract titled "Against Jerome Osorius, Bishop of Silvane in Portugal and Against His Slanderous Invectives," which describes the doo-doo du jour as "the fretting fistula within the bowels of the Christian commonwealth." Twenty-two years later, in 1603, the first performance of *All's Well That Ends Well* at the Globe Theater would once again draw on what seemed to be common knowledge: that a fistula is a shitty condition to have, whether the sufferer is an individual body or the body politic. In Act 1, Scene 1, Shakespeare dramatizes the concept by naming the problem plaguing the king, crowned head of the body politic:

BERTRAM
What is it, my good lord, the king languishes of?
LAFEU
A fistula, my lord.
BERTRAM
I heard not of it before.
LAFEU
I would it were not notorious.

Like Bertram, I'd never heard of fistulas before I got one myself. But as I learned more about my condition, I came to realize that in the United States, today, the fistula in the commonwealth is the stem cell debate, which has caused confusion to the point of shackling medical progress while patients are literally dying for cell therapy. Christopher Reeve was renowned for his talent for embodying a range of personae on stage; little did he know that he would come to experience, in real life, the Shakespearean king's medical dilemma in *All's Well That Ends Well*:

He hath abandoned his physicians, madam; under whose practices
he hath persecuted time with hope, and finds no other
advantage in the process but only the losing of hope by time.

People wonder why Reeve didn't seek treatment overseas when obviously money was no object. I see it as a matter of medical diplomacy: His fame having elevated him to a status that demanded noblesse oblige, he could no more travel outside the United States for treatment than Louis XIV could have sought treatment in, say, Spain. Superman steadfastly awaited the day when "the American Way" of medicine would cure him right here at home. Sadly, he learned, the hard way, what it meant to "persecute time with hope." And with Reeve's passing, we lost a dedicated cultural leader and patient advocate.

Any pathogenesis can be acute, recurrent, or chronic; in the case of my PF, it would turn out to be all three: acute at first (when it almost killed me), then recurrent, and finally—after several years of nonhealing—chronic. At one of my follow-up appointments at the hospital, my reporter's nature attempted to understand what was happening to me. The chief of surgery had surprisingly few answers. This much was certain: The hospital ordeal I'd just endured, at great expense of money and pain, was just a temporary fix. The surgery had merely prevented death this time. Nothing had been done to correct the condition that necessitated the surgery. What, I wanted to know, could be done to heal my intestine and stop this cycle of disease? Only two things: a stent (i.e., plug), which could easily migrate, or a seton, a silk cord tied tightly around the intestine immediately above the perforation. With the seton approach, the damaged part of the intestine atrophies away, leaving the patient incontinent for several weeks, a condition that sadly remains permanent in many cases. This was, in my view, a totally unacceptable risk, so I chose to live with PF rather than chance incontinence. Although I was now the Pet Reporter, I still had a soft spot for style; my line had been, until recently, all about silky threads, but this application was definitely not fashionably correct! What would Isaac Mizrahi say? Here's what I said: "I'd rather be dead than incontinent." Except this was no joking matter: If I became septic again, I could very well end up dead.

I found it hard to believe that in 1999, just months shy of the turn of a new millennium, there didn't exist a more state-of-the-art, twenty-first-century PF remedy than stents, setons, or diarrhea avoidance. Yet it didn't seem to me as if Dr. Schmerz was trying very hard to find a creative solution. Part of the problem was the sad fact that anorectal diseases, to borrow the comedic catchphrase of the late Rodney Dangerfield, "don't get no respect." Dealing as they do with butts and assholes, they're an easy target for tasteless humor, even among physicians who ought to know better (paging Doc). So I shouldn't have been surprised when the doctor entrusted to treat my problem made it the butt of an unfortunate joke. Sadly, despite our time together in the emergency OR, and the year during which I had to keep coming back to him for rechecks in an attempt to figure out why my wound was refusing to heal, Dr. Schmerz never warmed up to me; we were just two ships passing one night, and he preferred to keep it that way. His one attempt at humor wound up being as cutting as his scalpel. To wit: At a post-operative checkup, I described some trouble I was having as a result of the proximity of the incision to my other plumbing. One problem was really weird: Every month, I would notice blood emanating from the surgical wound; then a day or so later, I'd get my menstrual period. I connected the dots: I was getting my period first through the incision, and then the usual way. That kind of freaked me out. So I asked Dr. Schmerz why hadn't he made the incision a bit farther out on the butt-cheek?

"Because we saved your butt!" he said with a smile.

That was so funny I forgot to laugh. I pictured this pre-performed one-liner getting a hearty laugh from the all-male team in the operating theater, my exposed posterior rising from a sea of sterile blue OR toweling, and felt a hot rush of humiliation. (I believe it's safe to assume the Sun King's surgeon never cracked a joke about treating his patient "where the sun don't shine," at least not in Louis's presence.) There were so many things Dr. Schmerz could have said during that year, anything to make those hospital visits more informative and less depressing—notably the excruciating one during which I underwent an exam by proctoscope, which, despite the exploratory discomfort, yielded no new information whatsoever. But he didn't give a—well, you know. It's cause for celebration when a medical professional displays a healthy sense of humor, not laughing at his patients, but with them. I wish more doctors would be open to questions, and more willing to seek answers and solutions, instead of just shrugging and saying "I don't know." Is that too much to ask?

It didn't used to be. In my teens, my mom—the mother of all Medicine Dogs—took me to an orthodontist to correct my seriously crooked teeth, which she blamed on my aversion to drinking milk. Micromanaging my mouth, she refused to allow any of my teeth to be extracted—and today I'm very grateful that she did, although it meant having to wear braces longer than I would have had she let him pull a tooth or two. Happily our orthodontist, Dr. George Silling, was up to the task and diligently complied with Mommy's request. Although it would have been easier for him to just show us the door—that's how most doctors today handle overly interactive patients—he rose to the challenge of straightening my pearly whites without pulling. He'd even spend time patiently explaining the straightening process to me, how it would take a bit longer, and my teeth would be quite tightly packed together. "But your mother doesn't want me to pull any of your teeth, so that's why we're doing it this way," the good doctor would say.

No wonder he had quite the loyal following, including one very famous patient. One day, as my mom and I were heading in, a drop-dead-gorgeous girl and her mom were on their way out. The girl looked familiar to me—she was my contemporary, but whereas I was a classic ugly duckling with Coke-bottle glasses and railroad-track braces, she was a certifiable swan with no apparent flaws and no visible metal on her teeth. Ushering them out, Dr. Silling introduced us: "Do you know Brooke Shields, the actress?" Everyone knew beautiful Brooke at that moment—she'd recently been profiled in *New York* magazine, my favorite publication since childhood, on the occasion of her star turn in the movie *Pretty Baby*. Once seated in Dr. Silling's chair, I made a smart-alecky comment: "So, you're the orthodontist to the stars, huh?" He nearly fell over laughing, and every time I saw him thereafter, he'd always quote that remark with a chuckle, proudly copping to his celebrity-doc status. An inquisitive reporter even back then, I asked him why the lovely Ms. Shields didn't have braces on *her* teeth? Dr. Silling cordially explained that she did; he'd rigged special invisible orthodontics for her, affixed to the back of her teeth, so they wouldn't upstage her work as an actress and model. Nice doc!

Today, I see just how spoiled I was to have such an accommodating doctor who cared. That set the standard for me. Fortunately, my good luck with dentists continued. I'm lucky to have my teeth tended by Dr. Jennifer Jablow, herself a dentist-to-the-stars (and dedicated dog rescuer). But I was to wait a long time before finding a non-dental doctor with a bedside manner as nice as Dr. Silling's. It was also hard to find one with his high level of competence. In my experience, doctors simply weren't nearly as thorough or intuitive as the vets who treated my dogs, who thought around problems with impressive attention to detail, truly cared about their patients' comfort, and treated them with basic respect. It would take me several years to find a doctor as compassionate, competent, and respectful as the vets who treated my dogs—or one with a bedside manner as appealing as that of the dogs themselves. Whenever I'm feeling poorly and must repair to bed, some of my sweet Medicine Dogs come over to the bedside to offer snout nuzzles, while others leap gingerly onto the mattress to stand over me with worried looks, as if asking what they might bring or do. These behaviors are unspeakably adorable and amazingly therapeutic.

To fully appreciate the Sun King's bravery in biting the bullet and undergoing anorectal surgery while fully conscious, it helps to know that, almost 200 years later, the first New Yorker to undergo ether anesthesia was an anorectal patient whose name is not known; nineteenth-century doctors understood that heroism of the sort Louis XIV displayed could not reasonably be expected. In November 1846, Dr. John Rodgers used ether anesthesia during the treatment of a perirectal abscess at the New York Hospital in New York City; it was one month after dentist W. T. G. Morton first demonstrated the use of ether anesthesia at Massachusetts General Hospital in Boston. But while anesthesia methods made significant strides, anorectal surgical solutions took baby steps—until the second year of the twenty-first century, when a Spanish surgeon proposed to treat fistula patients by using their own adult stem cells to regenerate tissue at the site of the fistulous tract, effectively closing it. The first to offer a truly innovative solution to this age-old medical problem, Dr. Damián García-Olmo, practitioner and professor of colorectal surgery at La Paz University Hospital in Madrid, completed the first phase 1 clinical trial in 2004 and is a pioneer of cell therapy (*terapia celular* in Spanish). As the first to make a connection between fistulas and stem cells, he secured his place in medical history. But I had no way of knowing any of this in 1999, nor the fact that Dr. García-Olmo would eventually become an important person in my life.

Problems of the posterior lagged way behind in commanding some doctors' respect, as Schmerz's callous crack about saving my butt indicated. But at some hospitals, anorectal disease is taken quite seriously—and nowhere more so than at St. Marks Hospital in London. The only medical institution in the world to specialize in intestinal and colorectal medicine, it began in 1835 as a seven-bed clinic called The Infirmary for the Relief of the Poor afflicted with Fistula and other Diseases of the Rectum (The Fistula Infirmary, for short). It was the brainchild of surgeon Frederick Salmon, who performed some 3,500 operations, and whose satisfied patients included novelist Charles Dickens and the Lord Mayor, William Taylor Copeland. Providing specialist treatment free of charge to London's poor, the infirmary moved successively to ever-larger premises. Among its celebrity benefactors were Dickens and Lillie Langtry, the beautiful actress who was the mistress of the Prince of Wales; to raise funds for the hospital, she organized a charity matinee at her theater in Drury Lane.

With the diagnosis of PF comes a sincere appreciation of a reliable bowel movement, which is such an elusive goal for millions of constipated Americans that we spend some $700 million on over-the-counter laxatives. Meanwhile, at the other end of the consistency spectrum, some 15 million Americans with irritable bowels drive the market for anti-diarrhea drugs. Lacking compassion or constructive guidance from my doctor, I gave up on conventional physicians and became my own de facto doc, trying to figure out how not to get diarrhea and keep myself healthy overall. I was off to a great start, for I had the best live-in wellness coaches: my dogs. I'd long ago realized that what came out of them depended on what I put in them; slowly, it dawned on me that I could control the consistency of my own stool with what I ate, too, so that it stayed in the desirable zone between rock-hard and soft-serve. Basically, I trained myself to take health cues from my dogs. Following their lead in medical matters may sound frightfully primitive, but it's worked wonders for me. My dogs offered moral support while I suffered for years on the toilet seat. They knew exactly what I was doing (or trying to do) there and felt sorry for me. How do I know? One very busy day, Pepper experienced fecal urgency and kept trying to get my attention every which way she knew how. When I still failed to understand her very clear message, she "told" me she had to "go" by sitting down next to the toilet and staring intently at me, as if to say, "That thing you do here? I need to do that now, outside." I took her out immediately, and she went right away. Complying with New York City's Canine Waste Law, I did "doo" diligence by picking up what she produced. The so-called "pooper scooper law" was enacted in 1978, yet there are still many people who flout it shamelessly. But I'm grateful for this law, because it forced me to take responsibility for my dogs' shit—and, in so doing, enabled me to cope with my own. Too many of us can't handle shit, and, as a result, many serious health issues go undiscussed and undiagnosed, when they could instead be treated with openness and the best that modern medicine has to offer. Thanks to my dogs, I handle shit every day. I've learned to make peace with it and accept it unconditionally: To scoop it and eliminate all trace of it—eradicating its lingering, molecular scent—from surfaces both hard and soft, and, yes, to talk about it candidly as the normal, natural bodily function it is.

John Updike has my eternal respect for gracefully deploying the word *diarrhea* at the coda of his moving elegiac poem "Dog's Death." Like the poor puppy Updike describes, I hated it when a liquid, projectile bowel movement, or a battery of them, rendered me helpless; unlike a dog, I had the power to prevent it from happening, in myself as well as in my dogs. So, when Dr. Schmerz gave me the strange marching order "Don't get diarrhea," I was determined to follow his non-advice. Dogs, who instinctively self-heal, teach by example how to get one's shit together. They do a few things as part of their regular routine that we would all do well to imitate:

They start their day by making number two.

They hydrate without hesitation (which is why it's important to keep a dog's water bowl filled).

They eat grass when they sense tummy upset, knowing instinctively that it will induce vomiting and/or pooping, quelling gastric upset and promoting digestion.

They squat to poop.

The first directive is ideal, but it isn't always easy to incorporate into one's schedule, especially if one is pressed for time. It would take a long time—years, in fact—before I would achieve early-morning relief. As for the second point, I've always had what I call a drinking problem—but instead of alcohol addiction, mine was about not getting enough water. But ensuring that my dogs always have fresh, clean water motivated me to keep myself hydrated by drinking half my weight in ounces of water each day. It took me many years to adopt the third page from my dogs' digestive playbook, ingesting grass. The first time I tried a wheatgrass shot, I gagged. But since learning that wheatgrass's active ingredient— chlorophyll—is a potent digestive aid, I'll force myself to swig a shot of green once a week. As for squatting, the fact that dogs don't use a toilet automatically makes their defecation process far more efficient than that of the average first-world human. Health-conscious people are starting to realize that the toilet—whose design hasn't changed since the eminent Victorian Thomas Crapper invented it—is a culprit of hemorrhoids, constipation, ulcerative colitis, irritable bowel syndrome, colon cancer, appendicitis, and heart attacks. Humans, like dogs, instinctively squat to poop, because the position naturally promotes defecation; toilet-sitting, on the other hand, results in straining, which causes a temporary disruption in cardiac flow. Happily, now there are platforms available that adapt traditional toilets to permit squatting rather than sitting.

Incidentally, squatting is how we Westerners made number two until the mid-nineteenth century; chairlike toilets, or stools, were the realm of royalty, and there was no higher honor than to be appointed Groom of the Stool, or the courtier trusted to attend to the monarch's privy chamber. Dogs rule in my heart and home, so I'm proud to serve them. As both scooper and scholar of poop, I know what to look for before, during, and after a dog dump, from the expansion of the sphincter that signals defecation is imminent, to the drop of liquid at the tail end of a bowel movement, which indicates that the anal sacs have successfully expressed themselves and are in good working order (if not, they need to be expressed by a vet). It's the least I can do to reward my Medicine Dogs' excellent bedside manners. Of course, bedside manners are as important in a lover as in a healer, and, sadly, my husband's left much to be desired. I didn't learn until later that mine was a textbook example of a verbally and emotionally abusive marriage. By then, it was too late—I was already addicted to him as to sister morphine. I honestly believed I'd never meet anyone as intelligent and fascinating as X. I was chronically infatuated with him. Every time I tried to leave him, he cried and begged me to come back, and back I always went, whereupon he'd quickly morph from sweet Dr. Jekyll into snarling Mr. Hyde. Not long after I returned to live with him, X's hostility became unbearable. His cruelty found an easy target in my bottom and its attendant problems.

"I think you got this because you let somebody fuck you in the ass," he announced.

Putting aside the rudeness and vulgarity of this idiotic statement, let's look at the logic, or lack thereof: Even if I had done that, which—newsflash!—I hadn't, there's no way such activity could have resulted in my condition. Remember, it had started with an abnormal opening in my rectum. Some*thing* had fucked with my gut. It would take years before I'd meet the doctor who'd explain what that was. For now, I knew this much: It wasn't what X was saying it was, and his accusation hurt, a lot. In moments of extreme nastiness—of which there were many, increasing in frequency all the time—X made reference to "your third asshole."

The first time he did this, I naively responded, "You mean my second?"

"No," he clarified. "The third one's your mouth."

What a cheap shot! In 1644, John Bulwer—physician, philosopher, and advocate for the deaf—wrote, much more elegantly, "The mouth is but a running sore and hollow fistula of the minde." The heavy disgust on the part of both parties in my crumbling marriage was not exactly conducive to the trusting relaxation required to become intimate. At a time in our young lives when my handsome husband and I should have been enjoying each other at least once a day, months went by without any action at all. Our sexual estrangement stretched into a year, then another, not unlike the ever-lengthening "healing" time of the chronic nonhealing wound on my butt. I requested a divorce for the umpteenth time. To my surprise, after repeatedly refusing to comply or promising that he would make that process drag out for thirty years—did I mention he's an attorney, and a litigator to boot?—X surprised me with a complicated document he'd custom-drafted. Our divorce was finalized in May 2001. And then the shit hit the fan.

CHAPTER 4

Wellness Watchdogs

In the spring of 2001, my now ex-husband decamped to our country place without me. He'd finally agreed to make the dissolution of our marriage final and legal by offering to draft our divorce agreement himself. He cried broke—he'd been unemployed for months—so I gave him one last payment of money. Immediately before putting the Volvo wagon in drive and heading north for the highway, he left me with these parting words: "I'm the only one who will ever love you." What should have been cause for celebration—the butthead was finally out of my life, and together, my third asshole and I could start fresh—swiftly turned into the first day of a period of high mourning. I'd wanted X gone, but no sooner was he out of there than I wanted him back; funny how that works sometimes. The root cause of the trouble was that X had taken the dogs with him. We'd agreed that life would be more pleasant for them in the country. So it wasn't X I really missed; it was our dogs. The gaping hole in my existence was caused by the absence of those healing hounds. My bed was utterly devoid of the comforting, cuddlesome, canine presence I'd grown accustomed to; there were no sweet snoring sounds to help me drift off, no soothing snouts to nudge me awake. Worst of all, there was no Britannia to spoon with! No longer a venue for sweet dreams, that bed was just a mattress covered with sheets depressingly devoid of dog hair. As I kicked myself for allowing X to take the dogs, the thundering silence of a home—if a dogless apartment could even be called that—without a single canine companion quickly became overwhelming and unbearable. It was the most brutal kind of withdrawal to be separated from my Medicine Dogs.

The excellent *Elle* columnist E. Jean Carroll, in her typical no-nonsense style, advised me to just go out and adopt five more dogs. Heeding her wise counsel, I set out looking for just one. At the Bergen County Animal

Shelter in Teterboro, New Jersey, one of the residents, an adorable white pit bull named Snowball, resembled the love child of Daisy and Sam, and—miracle of miracles—was good with other dogs and mellow around cats. There'd be no need for a church-and-state separation of my feline and canine population. I adored Snowball, but his cute antics only reminded me of Daisy, Sam, and B even more. I wrote X a heartfelt, tearful letter begging him to come back, and Express Mailed it to the house upstate. Shortly after that, I encountered one of the many characters who made my Upper East Side neighborhood so . . . endlessly entertaining. Perhaps you know the type: dog walker and busybody, eternally minding everyone's business but her own. She stopped me on the street to let me know that she suspected X was involved with "that friend of yours who rescues dogs." When I asked her how she'd come to that conclusion, she responded that it was "just a feeling." It was a feeling I'd had before many times, too, but X had assured me so often and so vehemently that he "never had anything to do with her" (his standard boilerplate) that I believed him.

We'd met L together, in 1997, at an event in the Bronx's Van Cortlandt Park. At that time, pit bulls were the object of such widespread fear and loathing that when you crossed paths with a fellow pit lover, it was like meeting a long-lost sibling and cause for celebration. X and I had only had two pits at that juncture; L had four and ran a rescue group dedicated to saving pit bulls. Like me, she had a hard time leaving a shelter without taking a dog out. I immediately began thinking of ways to help her rescue effort, because it was also my rescue effort—anything to reduce the number of pits being put down every day. I pitched a story to my editor at the paper, got the green light, and in classic *Post* fashion the grabby headline read, "Killing Dogs: It's the Pits." It was a kind of performance art to place a pro-pit story in a tabloid known for its splashy, exploitative coverage of these "dangerous, vicious, child-killer" dogs. I've always loved performance art, so I was especially proud to scoop this cuddly controversial story. Such is the *Post*'s following among competing newspaper editors and television producers that, in short order, L was profiled by other newspapers and then made appearances on local TV.

L invited X and me to sit on the board of her nonprofit, which we did gladly. Bonding over our mutual passion for dog rescue, she and I brainstormed strategies for raising the public's awareness about pits' positive potential. "Remember the dog in *Flashdance?*" she'd say. "He's a pit, and a sweetheart! We need to get those images circulating." I was impressed by her enthusiasm and creativity, admired her tenacious determination on behalf of our mutual favorite dog breed, and considered her a close girlfriend; as friends often do, we commiserated about this and that, and men. But what I didn't know was that L and X were much closer friends. I began to suspect something was up when, one weekend, L came in to Manhattan from the Bronx—a schlep—and surprised us by showing up outside our apartment building. She said she happened to be in the neighborhood and would love to help walk our dogs. I wondered about why she would leave her own dogs unattended to spend time with ours. As we all walked the dogs together, the air was charged with conspiratorial looks and smiles darting between her and my husband. I started to feel first like a third wheel, then sick to my stomach. I looked pleadingly at X and tried to convey—silently, then with subtle hints—that we had other things to do that day, things that didn't involve L. My attempt at communication with my spouse had no effect; that only works between committed couples. He continued chatting—you might say openly flirting—with L, so she continued to overstay her welcome.

In the months that followed, I told myself it couldn't be possible that L was actively pursuing X with intent to seduce. I mean, he was my husband, she was my friend, we all worked together saving dogs, and surely women didn't do that to each other? Especially women who team up to rescue pit bulls, the most loyal species of dog there is? When L announced that she'd like to visit us in the country and bring her dogs, ostensibly to scope out property for a sanctuary, I was queasy but still welcomed her. Our little upstate cottage was starting to become a graveyard for the many fix-it projects that X promised to complete but never got around to starting. But that morning, anticipating L's arrival, X leapt up bright and early to assemble a spacious outdoor enclosure for her dogs, to keep them separate from ours and prevent a fight. I'd never seen him work at any home improvement project so diligently and efficiently before. L arrived, and we showed her around our property and the nearby towns. A few hours later, when the visit was over, there was a very awkward moment, while we all said goodbye, as X and L kissed full on the mouth. I was speechless: Those two were on a collision course, and they didn't care if I would get mowed down. Not long after that, I looked at X and made this rather dramatic declaration: "Please, let's resign from L's board now and have nothing more to do with her. She will destroy us. We'll find other ways to help pit bulls." We resigned, and I figured that was the end of that.

Some weeks after I mailed my former spouse that pathetic honey-come-home letter, he called to say he'd be in the city attending to some errands; could he stop by for a visit? X came over and told me that he'd received my letter and left it, unopened, on a shelf in the intervening weeks. Quietly, cuttingly, he proceeded to lay a spectacular guilt trip on me, reminding me that he wasn't the one who'd pushed for the divorce. He was never at fault; I was. Then he dropped a bomb. He and the dogs weren't alone at the house; L was living there too, with her pack (which was now up to ten). That explained the phrase he'd judiciously inserted in our divorce agreement, stating that he "may live there with whomever he chooses." L had worked long and hard to seduce X away from me, despite (or perhaps because of) my confiding in her numerous gruesome details of our unhappy marriage. It took her four years, but she finally achieved her goal. So, here was—in the words of Woody Allen's *Crimes and Mis-demeanors* character—"my worst nightmare realized." L had succeeded in taking everything I had: dogs, husband, house. I nearly collapsed. Actually, I did fall on the floor. Seriously, now, of all the women X could have moved into our house, he had to pick that one?

"L was never your friend," X clarified. "She hates you. She was always *my* friend."

He rose to leave, and I broke down. Calling my childhood friend M to wail about what had just transpired, I raised her concern enough that she begged me to take that day's appointment with her shrink. I'm glad I did. The late Dr. Conalee Levine-Shneidman was the first person in my life who neither told me what I wanted to hear, nor gratuitously insulted me. An Upper West Side Jungian psychiatric practitioner of the old school, she was precisely the healing force I needed at this critical time, and the few hours I spent with her bought me clarity, resolve, and peace of mind, to the tune of $190 for a forty-five-minute session. I'd idiotically filled up the first session by talking a blue streak; thereafter, I timed myself, taking up no more than seven minutes before turning the floor back to the doctor.

One day I answered my phone and L was on the other line. We'd had several unpleasant phone exchanges since X's disclosure of her presence in the house, and I wasn't relishing the prospect of another telephonic showdown. "Is he standing right there?" I inquired.

"No, he forgot to take the phone with him," she whispered in a voice completely absent of malice. This was one of the many pleasant aspects of life with X, who took the handset of the cordless phone with him while running errands, so you couldn't make a call that he couldn't overhear.

L began speaking urgently, as if making a call to 911. "Julia, listen, I want to tell you how sorry I am that I didn't believe you. Everything you told me he was doing to you, he's now doing to me!"

I was speechless. But there was no time to formulate a response.

"Gotta go—he's back!" With that, she hung up.

By August, X was making more frequent trips to the city and stopping by to visit me. The smart thing to do would have been to let him stay with L, but I believed I could make this work, and my goal was a happy reunion with my dogs. He had some choice words to say about my seeing a therapist: "Haven't diminishing returns started to set in?" Despite his initial hostility, sitting together on the floor of that apartment, we came close to communicating in a constructive way about our relationship, and how it had unraveled. At my next psychiatric appointment, I described some of our exchanges. "He needs therapy," Dr. Levine-Shneidman said. X had always steadfastly refused therapy, couples as well as solo. "I'm not crazy," he'd tell me. "*You* are." In that case, the good doctor—rightly deducing that I was hell-bent on making the terrible mistake of re-partnering with X—assured me, "If you insist on staying with him, I can help you." Unfortunately, lacking health insurance, I couldn't afford what threatened to become a substantial psychiatric tab. It pained me to end my therapy sessions, but end them I did. I would have to navigate the choppy waters of my diseased partnership all by myself, with no psychiatric guidance. I renewed my dedication to learning to drive—something I'd put off doing for years—and mastering the steering wheel became something of a psychiatric substitute, a less expensive way to empower myself.

Meanwhile, out in the world, the stem cell debate continued apace. However, having no personal stake in it myself at that point, and no reason to write about it (yet), I didn't engage. On August 9, 2001, seventeen days after Pope John Paul II had sternly addressed him at Castel Gandolfo urging the United States to stop embryonic stem cell research, the deeply religious George W. Bush overcame the ethical dilemma he'd been grappling with to announce that federal funds may be awarded for research using human embryonic stem cells if the following criteria were met:

The derivation process (which begins with the destruction of the embryo) was initiated prior to 9:00 p.m. EDT on August 9, 2001;

The stem cells must have been derived from an embryo that was created for reproductive purposes and was no longer needed;

Informed consent must have been obtained for the donation of the embryo and that donation must not have involved financial inducements.

The National Institutes of Health, the Federal government's leading biomedical research organization, implemented President Bush's policy, funding research scientists to conduct research on existing human embryonic stem cells and, in the NIH's words, "to explore the enormous promise of these unique cells, including their potential to produce breakthrough therapies and cures." Knowing what we do today, in hindsight Bush 43's criteria for federally funded human embryonic stem cell research were not nearly as reactionary or obstructionist as many recall them to be. But mention stem cells to the average liberal and, in short order, you'll hear a passionate denouncement of Bush 43, when in fact the president's restrictions reveal a surprisingly open mind, considering the unshakeable nature of his faith.

One month and two days after the announcement of Bush 43's stem cell policy, on the morning of Monday, September 11, the airborne terrorist attacks on the World Trade Center and the Pentagon, and the thwarted flight aimed at either the White House or the US Capitol, left little room in the headlines for consideration of scientific research—or, in fact, anything else. Terrorist cells, not stem cells, were now the focus of media attention. That very morning, X had an appointment at the World Trade Center, to interview for a job. However, he'd overslept, awaking to hear that he'd been spared and, later, gloating that an attorney he'd hated was among the nearly three thousand people killed. I'm sad and embarrassed to report that I agreed to reboot the troubled relationship that made a seven-pack of Medicine Dogs, plus a few psychiatric sessions, so very necessary to my survival. (Incidentally, X and I were not alone in our ill-advised re-marital mission; on and after 9/11, many couples who'd resolved to divorce withdrew their petitions voluntarily, giving commitment another shot as a leap of faith in the face of terrible tragedy.) X promised to end it with L once and for all this time. It would take a few months to help her get relocated, but he was on his way back to me. He had one key condition: I

Britannia, country couch potato and Afghan hound impersonator

was never to talk to L or meet with her, ever. At the first opportunity, I met with L. No longer able to afford my therapist, I craved a chance to analyze X with the help of the only other person I knew who'd been as close to him as I had. The trauma of my marriage didn't just happen to me; it happened to her, too. Over lunch, we agreed that there was something wrong with X, and L confided that her mechanism for coping with his Jekyll-Hyde transformation was telling herself, "The man I loved doesn't exist." I'd accepted that long ago, but I was very glad to be getting my dogs back—something L could certainly appreciate—and glad she and I could salvage some kind of cordial rapport, if not a friendship in the conventional sense. I was grateful that the "father" of my dogs was coming home because instantly my furry family would be restored to me.

For me, that September was memorable for another personal milestone that was also professional: Bulfinch Press published my first book, *Animal House Style: Designing a Home to Share with Your Pets.* It was terrible timing to have a book, especially one's first, published days after a national tragedy that shook us all to our core. Added to that was the very sad fact that one of the people who appears on several of the book's pages was firefighter Timmy Haskell; he and his brother and father, also firefighters, were all killed that day trying to do their job. But my goal for that book was to help the dogs and cats who were routinely surrendered at animal shelters "because they destroyed the furniture." So I did what I could to promote it, in honor of the many dogs and dog lovers who perished on 9/11, the heroic search-and-rescue and therapy canines who bravely answered the call of duty on that day and in the terrible weeks that followed—and the many animals who wound up homeless at animal shelters. With photographs I hoped would offer incontrovertible proof that a house isn't a home without at least one animal in residence, I aimed to encourage folks to hightail it to their nearest animal shelter and adopt without delay.

By Thanksgiving, L had relocated and I was reunited with my dogs and X. We resolved to clean up our country house and make it a nice place to live, for the dogs and us. I was contacted by a magazine editor with great news; she wanted to feature my book. We met for lunch and bonded instantly. I told her about my other big project of the past two

Reunited, and it feels so good. DANIELA STALLINGER

months, getting back together with X. She immediately hit on a new feature story concept: "Decorating to Save a Marriage." She wasn't just saying that—she really meant it. The magazine, she promised, would commission designers at no cost to us and secure donations of key home-improvement elements. My task was to engage and pay a local contractor, then, when all was decorated and done, I'd be paid to write the story. Talk about a plum assignment! Having written about so many beautiful homes belonging to other people, it was exciting to have the opportunity to write about my own soon-to-be beautiful home. We began discussing when she'd drive up to take the scouting shots. I'd written many features about couples collaborating on home design, and even coauthored a book on this topic titled *Living Together*. Here, my beloved and I would be putting the transformative power of design to the test. Could it really save us? Completing my first book had been an epic struggle, with X thwarting the best efforts of movers, upholsterers, painters, and, finally, photographers. "There will be no shoot today!" King X would decree with imperious "off-with-their-heads" finality, and it would take much begging to get him to cease and desist obstructing the business at hand. But in this instance, I managed to win over his practical side when I told him the magazine would be arranging for free paint and French doors in the living room. Sold: He'd always wanted French doors in there.

We began renovating our house, a process that can strain the strongest relationships. Fully believing that design would save us, I forged ahead like some kind of aesthetic zealot. My editor's vision of marital bliss through masonry and bricks became the bed-warmer that defrosted my coldest winter mornings. Focusing on the positive, I repeated to myself that X and I had much to be thankful for: We lived in our very own super-dog-friendly house, where, pretty soon, the home fires would be burning bright. The magazine did more than just provide paint; they flew in a decorative painter from Sweden, Robert Persson, whose work appears in the home of the king and queen of Norway. Robert happens to be violently allergic to animals, so we were obliged to evacuate all of our animals from the premises, schlepping them back to our Manhattan apartment, while he applied his trompe l'oeil magic to the walls of our little cottage. Before leaving, we put our dogs in their high-fenced outdoor runs and

collaborated on staining the floors ourselves. "Here was the hard work of relationships made tangible, with results you could see as well as feel," I wrote.

I'd poured my soul into that renovation, and the text was written from my heart. But things were not as picturesque as those beautiful magazine storyboards suggested. Circumstances had been going steadily south throughout the weeks of renovation, with X becoming increasingly abusive, and me doing my utmost to conceal our sad reality from the magazine team. Finally, it came time to photograph the finished interiors. On the first of a two-day photo shoot, the stress of having to cater to five very demanding people—the editor, the super-queeny decorators, the photographer, and his assistant—all issuing orders in his house, where he fancied he was the one in charge, began to push X to the breaking point. His for-publication persona was cheerfully brewing espresso, griddling pancakes, popping popcorn, and serving these refreshments to our guests; when the visitors weren't looking, he seethed. At one point, my editor called to me from the living room; X and I were standing in the kitchen. Rushing toward her with X at my back, I tripped over a telephone wire in the pantry. I was cruising for a spectacular wipeout when X caught my left arm with one hand. Turning to thank him for the neat save, I noticed his other hand was drawn back into a tight fist.

"I'm sick of your fucking clumsiness," he hissed almost inaudibly.

Time stopped, as if I'd stumbled on a Lifetime movie at the laundromat and couldn't change the channel.

"Julia, are you all right?" My editor called out from the living room. X snapped out of his bullying fugue state, narrowly avoiding what would have been a very public display of domestic violence, and we proceeded to the living room to join the others as if nothing had happened. I never mentioned the incident to X, or tried to make sense of it, because I honestly think he wouldn't have remembered, or would have denied it, and that would have merely started another fight. After the shoot, the chandeliers and furnishings that the magazine had trucked in from New York City were carefully packed up and removed, and we were left to reinvent our interiors within the freshly painted walls. Hey, at least they couldn't pack those up and take them, too! Which is how X hit on a new emotional-blackmail MO—threatening to throw black paint over Robert's painstaking artistry became his new menacing refrain. (Of course, X rarely displayed his dark side out in public, so friends and acquaintances—especially the female ones—were convinced that I had to be exaggerating the details of my private domestic hell, never failing to remark on how handsome and chivalrous X was. He did have a talent for playing a perfect Prince Charming, bowing and kissing ladies' hands.) Naturally, I'd become quite attached to our new wall decorations that so sweetly brought the outdoors in, down to the foliage and the likeness of one of the squirrels often spotted scampering across the lawn. In an odd coincidence, Robert had signed the top of one wall with his name followed by his hometown, *Falun i Sverige* (Falun in Sweden)—a city put on the map by various post-9/11 profiles of Osama bin Laden in the media. Newspaper and magazine articles reprinted a group snapshot taken in 1971, the year that twenty-three members of the bin Laden family visited Falun while one of Osama's elder brothers conducted business with Swedish automotive giant Volvo; that picture made it hard to fathom how a smiling sixteen-year-old boy in a green button-down shirt and blue bell-bottoms could have morphed into the murderous Al Qaeda leader who, then still at large, had succeeded in terrorizing the entire world.

Later, close friends and casual acquaintances told me I looked terrorized in the magazine photograph with X, who encircled me with his arms and scowled at the camera. The only one who couldn't see it was me. So much effort, on the part of so many people, had been spent on feathering our "love" nest; I was determined to tough it out, "for better and for worse." Call me Pollyanna, pit bull warrior: Things would get better, they just had to! Besides, this little house was my darling dogs' home, and they made everything worthwhile. And so, life settled into a routine, with me doing my work from our country home and honing my cooking chops (it was either that or put pizza and Chinese food on heavy rotation). The pups made the work of food prep fun, eagerly accepting offers of carrot peels and other dog-safe detritus. Making meals with the dogs was always more enjoyable than sharing them with X; we'd sit in deafening silence as he read the newspaper at the table. The one time I protested, he slammed his fist next to a plate with such force, it jumped and clattered.

If he did speak, his conversation left much to be desired. Many times X would remark upon how my butt had fallen and I was rapidly losing my figure. One day, I happened upon a stash of lingerie I'd purchased at a sample sale. Closing myself in the bathroom, I tried on stretchy-lace bikini bottoms and wasn't entirely horrified at the state of affairs back there—the scar was concealed, and the actual silhouette of my butt wasn't so drastically changed. But after an attempt at seducing X while wearing the scanties was rebuffed, I was crushed.

One day, I checked the call-answering system on our apartment's land line and retrieved this message: "Just so you know," said a deep, husky female voice I did not recognize, "I've been fucking your husband, and he's really good." I put the phone on speaker and replayed the message so X could hear it too, horrified upon hearing it again that something so hideous could violate the atmosphere in our newly beautified living space.

"Whoever it is," X said, "she sounds like a lot of fun!"

After such a remark, I just couldn't bring myself to be physically intimate with him again. It was the last time I would ever turn to him for anything resembling solace. My dogs were now officially the only reliable guardians of my emotional and spiritual well-being. They were my wellness watchdogs, and I counted on them for the warmth I wasn't getting from my cold human partner. At least I could cuddle with them and confide in them, even if they couldn't talk back! They offered consistency in the face of X's increasingly abusive behavior; they were my calm, warm port in the stormy weather caused by my increasing estrangement from my former spouse. Looking back to those dark, dogless, post-divorce days just prior to my reconciliation with X, I knew that life without the Medicine Dogs was no life for me. OK, so this wasn't much of a life, but I had no intention of going through the wrenching heartbreak of losing even one of these dogs ever again. That resolve was about to be put to the test.

CHAPTER 5

Back to the ICU

We'd been spending most of our time in the country; X was still unemployed, so I supported our enterprise with my freelance writing. I loved being in our newly redecorated house; despite the vanishing act of the fabulous furnishings featured in the magazine shoot, despite having to share the place with my psycho ex, this was home, and I cherished it. The smallest domestic chore became an exciting event, from trying a new recipe, to building a fire in the new Jotul wood stove, to hanging laundry out to dry and disinfect in the sun, to, yes, scooping poop out of the yard and dog runs. The dogs loved spending quality time with each other in the great outdoors, exercising in the two runs we'd built and landscaped for their romping pleasure. My favorite magazine at the time was *Country Living*; I felt fortunate to be living the country life in my very own home—or, to use a quaint British term, rusticating. It would provide me with excellent material when, the following year, I became *Country Living*'s "You & Your Pet" columnist. But, whether I was playing country mouse or city squirrel (the animal X always said I most closely resembled), my most inspired writing sprang from caring for my dogs. Little did I imagine that events surrounding one of those beloved dogs would conspire to give me some of my best material—and biggest heartache. For some of us who live to write, great material comes at a price.

As I received recognition for my pet reporting, I began making appearances on television, which necessitated making occasional trips back to the city (The Matrix, as X and I jokingly called it). I was invited to be part of a TV special about pets; they were filming in Manhattan and didn't have the budget to travel upstate. So X and I accommodated by packing up the bestiary and decamping to our apartment. A camera crew arrived to capture footage of me with my dogs. From the start of the

Mittens Mindlestein and me

several-hour-long shoot, Britannia, my brindle beauty, seemed not herself. She wore a pained expression, and her cropped bat-ears, normally erect, were lying flat on top of her head, as if pasted to the spot. Things went downhill from there. She turned down her food, so I made her scrambled eggs, one of her favorite treats, which normally would motivate her to do her signature three-foot vertical leap in anticipation of egg inhalation. She tried to eat the eggs, but choked, unable to swallow them.

"Your dog looks like she's sick," one camera operator remarked.

"I know," I said. "I'm waiting for you guys to finish so we can take her to the vet."

Finally, the crew left, and off to the vet we went. Britannia stood still on the street, refusing to walk. X picked her up and we speed-walked six blocks to the nearest hospital, run by my friend and former schoolmate, Dr. Jennifer Chaitman. I noticed Britannia's hind legs were thrust out stiffly behind her, as if paralyzed. What was happening to my baby? We left her with Dr. Chaitman, who conferred with her colleagues and called me to say, "I know this sounds strange, but we all think it's tetanus." That explained the stiffening of Britannia's limbs and her inability to eat—tetanus is also known as lockjaw. The pained expression on her poor face and the half-mast position of her ears were classic symptoms of facial paralysis. Although common in people and horses—among its notable victims was Traveller, the gorgeous, sixteen-hand American Saddlebred who was General Robert E. Lee's favorite horse—tetanus is very rare in dogs. So, who should beat the odds by contracting tetanus? Who else but my dog! I prayed that strange ailments wouldn't start plaguing my animals just to make my columns more interesting.

Tetanus, a combination of the Greek *tetanos* (taut) and *teinein* (to stretch), is an infection of the nervous system with the bacterium *Clostridium tetani,* with the distinction of being the only vaccine-preventable disease that is infectious but not contagious. Its terrifying symptom of rapid, body-wide muscle stiffening resembles strychnine poisoning, making a tetanized body appear demonically possessed as the neurotoxin tetanospasmin runs riot through the system. Although stepping on a nail is a very common way to contract tetanus—that's precisely how poor Traveller got it—the deadly infection can take hold in other ways. The initial exam showed no evidence of a puncture wound anywhere on B's body; how had tetanus made its way in? There was no time to try solving that mystery now. The immediate challenge was to get the antitoxin into Britannia as quickly as possible—but all the animal hospitals in New York City and its environs were clean out of tetanus antitoxin. For forty-five nail-biting minutes, Dr. Chaitman stayed on the phone with the Department of Health, which had supplies of antitoxin, explaining why she desperately needed just one vial of the serum to save her patient's life. As my dog's extremities continued to stiffen, the vet calmly, patiently read tetanus chapter and verse to the DOH operator from a veterinary textbook. She described the rarity of the case, the lack of antitoxin at area vet hospitals, and the critical urgency of obtaining a vial of it ASAP, or the patient would soon die.

After saying he'd think about it, the DOH operator came back with this verdict: He couldn't give us the antitoxin for "just a dog." I called this heartless functionary in a frantic, futile effort to persuade him to change his mind. He stood firm. Begging and pleading, I offered to make him a hero in the *New York Post*. Maybe he was a *Daily News* loyalist, because he was utterly unmoved. I hung up and screamed at the phone, "You better pray this dog doesn't die, because if she does, I will find you." At that moment, I became a patient advocate—for my dog. She was hardly "just a dog" to me. I vowed to do whatever it took to save her life. Marshaling the tenacity that was Daisy's gift to me, I called dozens of animal hospitals outside of New York with the determination of the proverbial dog with a bone. Here I was reporting the life-or-death story of my own dog's illness in real time. Call after call ended with the same answer—tetanus was so rare that hospitals just didn't need to keep the antitoxin. Sorry.

Wait a minute—horse vets needed to keep the antitoxin! I almost broke down in tears when the first equine hospital I called agreed to give me a vial of the precious antitoxin Britannia needed. This was an upside-down version of the famous story of Balto—instead of a team of sled dogs, racing to beat the clock to bring the diphtheria antitoxin to Alaska's sick children, we were humans making a mad dash across the snow to save our dog. While I stayed home to care for the rest of our pack, X saddled up to undertake the heroic round-trip drive on icy winter roads, returning at 6:00 a.m. with the precious vial of serum. The dose was enough for a horse—literally—so Dr. Chaitman injected just a portion of it into Britannia, refrigerating the rest. I went to visit the pretty patient that afternoon; she looked bright-eyed and relaxed. I felt confident she'd make a quick recovery in Dr. Chaitman's hospital, where a tech was on duty 24/7.

That night, at 2:00 a.m., I received the call nobody wants to get. Dr. Chaitman told me Britannia had collapsed and was having trouble breathing, but her hospital wasn't equipped with a ventilator. We had to rush Britannia to the emergency hospital right away—it was our only chance to save her. X drove our Volvo, also known as Pitmobile, like Batman on speed to Dr. Chaitman's, where we picked up vet and patient and spirited both to the same hospital that had saved Sam seven years earlier. Dr. Chaitman took the passenger seat and I dove to the back, sitting cross-legged on the folded-down bench seat, holding my panting dog in my lap. The car flew down Second Avenue. For the first and only time, I invoked my dog's ancestry as a fighting canine to prime her for the battle of her life: *"Fight! Fight!! Fight!!!"* I whispered in her ear, visualizing tetanus as a bloodthirsty opponent she could easily defeat by sinking her pretty undershot jaw into its neck and refusing to let go. Upon arrival, Britannia was raced through admissions, with Dr. Chaitman—who had done her residency here a few years earlier—quickly, expertly explaining the case to the vets on duty, and handing over the vial containing the remaining antitoxin. The emergency vets promised to do what they could.

This waking nightmare was uncannily similar to what had befallen me just four years earlier; this time, a potentially fatal infection had hijacked my dog's entire system, rapidly shutting it down. Whereas I'd been sick as a dog, Britannia was sick as . . . a horse. Together, my dog and I had stumbled on a mother-daughterlode of writing material I never wanted to have to drill. But I had a job to do, so I wrote about Britannia and her struggle, to help educate my fellow pet lovers about this dire danger in case they should ever find themselves among the unlucky minority of canine tetanus cases. And one of the things I urgently wanted to convey to readers was the importance of getting dogs' teeth regularly examined by a vet. That's because, just like my systemic infection, B's also began with an abscess: Tetanus had found a portal into Britannia via an oral abscess. Unbeknownst to me, a rotted tooth was lurking in that pretty mouth of hers. A routine dental exam would have revealed this ultimately life-threatening problem, and it could easily have been fixed. Britannia must have eaten something out there in our yard in the country (she was not above this, alas) and that something was contaminated by tetanus spores. This explained why the first manifestation of infection was her facial paralysis—the spasms struck the muscles closest to her mouth. Now, the abscess was discovered and being addressed, and the mystery of how Britannia had contracted tetanus was solved, but it might be too late to save her.

Later that morning, I went to check in on Britannia. She was splayed out like a zebra rug, entubed, her mouth stuffed with what looked like the hose of a vacuum cleaner. A drug called "The Paralyzer" was coursing into her veins to keep her from moving. Thankfully, the ventilator was doing the hard work of breathing for my dog, but actually seeing her hooked up to this machine was difficult to bear. I could sense how trapped and terrified she felt, and that made me feel trapped, too. "How long will you keep her this way?" I asked the critical-care specialist.

"Three days," the vet said. "Because of her breed, she can handle it."

The pit bull has a strong constitution, it's true, and I will always go to the mat for my disease-fighting dogs, but three days seemed like an eternity of torment for this little creature. "Two days," I said firmly, as if negotiating a hostage's release. If Britannia wasn't breathing on her own after that, I informed the vet, I was prepared to return and euthanize her. Well, my girl must have heard me, because she started breathing on her own after a day and a half! She was far from out of the woods, however. She took up residence in the ICU, where the cocktail of antibiotics, sedatives, and anti-spasmodics she was given created complications, including seizures. Because her jaw was still locked and she couldn't swallow, food was being pumped into her via a stomach tube. I was permitted to visit Britannia every day; upon seeing me, my poor angel would try to scrape herself together and rise to greet me. One time, I noticed she was asleep, so I tiptoed over to her crate. "Stein," I whispered—it was one of dozens of her nicknames, short for Mittens Mindlestein, which rhymes with Brittens Brindlestein, because I am apparently insane. I was overjoyed to see her eyeballs roll open. She recognized her silly nickname! I wasn't the only one under this dog's spell; she had the rapt attention of the entire hospital staff. Like the human hospital where I was treated four years earlier, this one is a teaching hospital for vets, so all the doctors took turns treating Britannia, for the rare opportunity to gain experience working on a tetanus case. B's charisma and beauty kept the docs coming back even when they didn't have to. When I took her in for rechecks, vets I'd never seen before dropped to their knees upon seeing Britannia, showering her with hugs and kisses. She basked in all that attention. I tried telling her how lucky she was not to receive serial rectal exams.

After two weeks, Britannia was finally cleared to come home. The bedroom became her private recovery area, and I kept the sanctum dark and quiet so as to speed recovery. Not wanting her to feel left out if she smelled food, I wolfed my meals outside the apartment, in the hallway or on the street. My mom was nice enough to make soup for me and bring it over. At night, monitoring my dog for tetanic seizures, I had to be ready to jump up and (1) awaken her from vivid dreaming, and (2) administer an injection of Valium into her butt—her butt!—to stop the convulsion. Happily for us both, we never had to do a nocturnal injection, but there were plenty of active dreams—including one in which Britannia, taking a huge bite out of some imaginary thing, unintentionally sank her teeth into my back (happily, despite impressive indentations, the skin wasn't broken). The sleep we lost messed with my ability to function. An Internet search led me to the work of Susan Raimond. The California harpist's specialty is playing music that is scientifically arranged, to be "heard" by the body's cells and promote relaxation, per the principles of cytocymatics (how sound affects cellular material). I left Susan a message, she called me back, and we began a friendship that has survived a decade. I would learn that she's achieved astonishing results calming anxious animals at shelters, hospitals, and zoos; from dogs and cats to gorillas and giraffes, all have succumbed to slumber within minutes of hearing the harp healer's music. And while most animal lovers can't bear the thought of medical testing on animals in laboratories, Susan bravely got permission to go into some of the most harrowing environments, playing her harp to offer monkeys and other stressed-out test subjects some much-needed enrichment and relief.

That same year, 2003, was a milestone on the adult stem cell timeline, as veterinarians began using adipose-derived regenerative cells, harvested with Vet-Stem's patented technology, to treat equine orthopedic injuries. One of the very first patients to undergo the procedure was a Dark Bay horse named Jantastic; foaled in March 2000, she was bound for racing glory. But September 7, 2003, was a dark day on this brown beauty's timeline; during the training leading up to her first race, the filly injured her right front superficial digital flexor tendon. Ten days later, on September 17, the tendon underwent Vet-Stem treatment. After stem cell therapy, Jantastic resumed workouts and ran her first race at Golden Gate Fields in May 2005, coming in third; in subsequent races, she came in second, then first. Stem cells enabled this elegant equine to fulfill her destiny as a racehorse. She's now a brood mare and dam of champions. So much money rides on sport horses; it's no surprise, then, that the development of this exciting technology was spurred on by these magnificent creatures and their medical needs. But it's not just about money; horses, like dogs, inspire deep love—and when you love someone, you want to protect that person (or animal) from injury, or arrange to make everything better when something breaks down.

Loving a racehorse can be a painfully high-stakes proposition. During a typical Triple Crown, the odds are ten to one that at least one horse will sustain a career-ending injury. Too often, historically, serious injury didn't just finish a horse's career; it ended his or her life. "Horses are very fragile, weighing over a thousand pounds and walking on toothpick legs," says Dr. Bob, "so orthopedically, they are disasters waiting to happen— and they won't tolerate casts or slings very well." A native of La Jolla, California, and a self-described "very passionate equestrian," he began riding at age twelve; by fourteen, he was working as "kennel help" in a small animal clinic, where he "fell in love with veterinary medicine." His lifelong dedication to healing animals has had a tremendous therapeutic side benefit for humans. As more and more people saw the dramatic effects stem cell therapy was having on horses, many made the connection to their own health needs, wondering "Can they do this for people too?"—the very same question Sam and I heard in the days and weeks following his successful Vet-Stem procedure. Horses with joint trouble have Dr. Bob to thank for pioneering the technology that spares them an untimely retirement or death; dogs like my Sam, meanwhile, can thank the vet's wife, Sue Harman, a trainer and holistic healer: "Sue inspired me to consider moving into treatment of dogs and cats," he says.

Despite succumbing to an ailment that usually befalls horses, my Britannia mercifully never experienced an equine-style orthopedic injury or arthritis, in part due to her petite size (not a lot of weight taxed her joints) and to the fact that, unlike poor Sam and his ACL rupture, she'd never damaged any of her limbs; such damage causes premature joint degeneration. So Britannia never needed stem cell regeneration therapy. Nonetheless, in caring for her, I experienced some life-changing epiphanies. The first had to do with food. Although the scandalous pet food recall of 2007 that claimed so many innocent lives with melamine-tainted "food" was as yet four years off, I'd been aware of other dangerous additives in pet food for some time, and diligently avoided brands whose ingredients included the pesticide ethoxyquin, a known carcinogen. The hospital, however, had sent Britannia home with a supply of prescription dog food in cans, which I was instructed to pump into her via the feeding tube the hospital had installed in her gut. I read the ingredients and balked when I noticed that ethoxyquin was high on the list. It seemed to me as if inserting this food directly into her stomach was a recipe for cancer down the road; if she were ingesting it the usual way—taking it in her mouth and swallowing it—at least her saliva would dilute it, and the ingredients might not be quite as potently toxic by the time they reached her gut. I substituted the toxic prescription food with a pesticide-free brand of over-the-counter canned dog food, and I vowed to override any such poisonous prescription in future. To ensure that the nontoxic grub would travel through the tube, I pureed it in a blender with filtered water, approximating the liquid consistency of the prescription diet. I nearly lost it when a single green pea survived the blender's blades and got stuck in the tube on its way to B's stomach, but luckily managed to flush it through with filtered water.

For creatures that cannot speak, animals are much more communicative than, say, certain spouses. They do whatever it takes to let us know when they are ailing—and when they're on the mend. They also manage to "tell" us about a situation that needs tending, even if it means risking that we'll make fun of them for acting weird. Around this time, I started a stint as the "Pet Penthouse" correspondent—and token straight person—on Sirius OutQ's very gay *Frank DeCaro Show*. When one caller described how his dog was suddenly displaying odd behavior by obsessively licking at the same spot on his, the caller's, foot, I counseled the man (1) not to laugh at his dog, and (2) to seek medical attention ASAP, because Spot may have smelled something off and had no other way to get his attention. Dogs, after all, can detect cancer with those exquisitely sensitive sniffers. The following week, the caller called back to say that there had been a calcium deposit on his foot, and his Medicine Dog was rewarded with a steak dinner. As Britannia started to feel stronger, she conveyed her improvement to me with not-so-subtle gestures. First, she leapt from her cozy nest on the floor up to the bed, the better to spoon with me, as had always been our nocturnal custom. For her next trick, she "told" me that she was sick and tired of eating food without tasting it. How'd she do that? By removing the plastic cap on her stomach tube with her front teeth and spitting the thing out at my feet, making defiant eye contact with me as she did so! I always knew Britannia was one brilliant bitch, but this profoundly impressed me. I called the emergency hospital immediately to let them know what had happened, asking if I could please bring B in right away to remove this thing. They said I had to schedule an appointment, and the earliest one wasn't for several days. I knew that Ms. Rule Britannia, now clearly back to her old self, wasn't willing to wait that long—spitting out the feeding-tube cap had been fair warning—and I didn't want to wake up to discover that my precious patient had injured herself by gnawing that device right out of her belly. So I took her back to Dr. Chaitman, who expertly yanked the tube. Immediately afterward, Britannia trotted around as if she'd jettisoned a ten-pound shackle.

When Britannia first came home, I devoted a column to her, worrying aloud about the tab we were running at the emergency hospital. After the story was published, a benefactor contacted the hospital directly to pay the balance of our bill. Her name? Mary Tyler Moore. America's eternally beautiful sweetheart is an honest-to-goodness, real-life saint and a genuine lover of animals. I took Britannia over to meet her guardian angel in person. By way of offering thanks, B stretched out on her back to request a celebrity belly rub—and got just what she asked for!

I learned a few more valuable lessons from Britannia's illness, which would help keep my own health intact. What I didn't realize then was that my girl's cells had been through hell and needed protection and rehabilitation. Instinctively, however, I sensed that the pharmaceutical assault she'd just come through was enough for two dog lifetimes. I wanted to purify her atmosphere, inside and out, and in doing so I collaterally purified my own. Wanting Britannia to have no contact whatsoever with sulfates, phthalates, and the other toxic ingredients so frequently found in home cleaning and personal grooming products, I became vigilant about selecting chemical-free dog shampoo, plus human hair-care products, cream, soap, dishwashing liquid, and laundry detergent.

For myself, to prevent overtaxing my liver, I stopped taking aspirin or Tylenol for pain, either toughing it out or, in the event of bruising or trauma, using the homeopathic remedy *Arnica montana* (in the case of nerve injury, such as the time I slammed a door on my finger, I also used *Hypericum perforatum*, St. John's wort, which succeeded in saving the nail on that digit). Soon after discovering arnica, I learned that I could safely and simply administer it, in a lower dose of three pellets rather than five, to dogs who'd sustained bruising or trauma. (Simply tuck the pellets into the pocket on the dog's inside lower gum, and gently hold the snout shut as long as Spot will tolerate this, to give the medicine a chance to dissolve.) As for antibiotics, I began to appreciate that, as important as this class of medication is in a medical emergency, it must not be overused; diligently avoiding antibiotics wherever possible, I substituted olive-leaf extract, nature's antibiotic and a potent antiviral. Most important, I wanted to discontinue use of toxic flea-tick medications for Britannia and her pack mates, and I began to research natural alternatives. With amazing timing, at the health food store I was handed a flyer describing a product I'd never heard of before: neem oil, product of a tree that grows all over India and is known as "the village pharmacy" because extracts of its seed, leaf, and bark can cure so many ills. Besides being unusually emollient and beneficial for the skin and hair of any species of creature, neem is also a biopesticide. Mosquitoes and fleas give it a wide berth. Ever since, my dogs and I have all relied on neem soap, shampoo, and oil. For ticks, we use food-grade diatomaceous earth, which desiccates the varmints to death without harming their animal or human hosts.

Thanks to many gifted healers, my beloved dog was wrestled from the jaw of death. Britannia's medical experiences moved me to focus my reporting on companion animal health; thereafter, I became obsessed with learning the newest and latest in veterinary technology, and what was available to extend pets' lives to the fullest, whether they faced life-or-death illness or more common, run-of-the-mill ailments. Long after Britannia survived tetanus, I was still hot on the scent for things to keep her well, always curious to know what new technology had to offer in the event that, heaven forbid, any dogs I loved should ever receive a devastating diagnosis. My dog became my bona fide muse, inspiring me to take pet reporting in new directions of scientific inquiry, and to use the media's reach and influence to challenge vets into trying out new treatment modalities. I couldn't have asked for a cuter muse than my B-witching, brindle bullydog, who became the star of my column, as captivating to me as Traveller the horse was to his rider. Incidentally, General Lee's beloved steed was also much written about, and inspired several lyrical descriptions, including poetry by Stephen Vincent Benét and prose by Richard Adams.

The Civil War horse survived many battles but lost his life to tetanus in 1871, the year he stepped on a nail and was euthanized with a bullet. My brave Britannia was lucky to trounce tetanus and lived to inspire a painted portrait by my talented artist mom. Years later, I find myself still reporting that little dog's story, always eager to learn about new healing modalities that might have made our battle against tetanus easier to win. If I had to do it over again today, I'd arrange to have Britannia placed in a veterinary hyperbaric chamber. Tetanus is an anaerobic bacterium that thrives in environments that lack oxygen, making it highly susceptible to destruction by oxygen at a level higher than atmospheric pressure. Tetanus remains a rare affliction in canines, but it's nice to know that hyperbaric oxygen therapy (HBOT) could help the next odd dog out make an excellent, speedy recovery.

Writing or speaking about my beautiful brindle's ordeal never fails to make me cry, yet I push through the tears to share that extraordinary dog's teaching lesson: Take care of your dog and she will take care of you, in ways you might never imagine. The time, effort, and, yes, money spent on Britannia was perhaps the most important investment I ever made in my own health, with returns that continue to this day. Experiencing illness and recovery with my dog restored my faith in many things, but most of all unconditional love. So what if X was still making nasty comments about my appearance and anatomy—Britannia and I loved each other, in sickness and, yes, health. Although I imagined it must be nice having a person to go to the mat for, I didn't dare hope that I would ever find this kind of nonjudgmental, accepting rapport with a fellow human. I was about to be very pleasantly surprised.

CHAPTER 6

Playing Doctor

Sex is vital for your cellular health—just ask Brian R. Clement and Maria Clement, cofounders of the Hippocrates Health Institute and coauthors of *The 7 Keys to Lifelong Sexual Vitality*. This lucky couple, both PhDs, get to "play doctor" and write from experience about why doing so is good for us all, and what we can eat to keep us in our best, sexiest health. I asked the Clements how long is too long to go without. Here's their response: "The minimum for the majority is twice a week. After an absence of seven days, the production of sperm and eggs reduce. It is the old adage 'use it or lose it.' Many may say it is too long to go without for more than one day." But you needn't ask a doc—just observe your dog. Even long after they were neutered and spayed, my dogs—notably Sam and Pepper—enjoyed celebrating their couplehood by, well, coupling up as often as the spirit moved them. In the case of Britannia and Haus, my girl was definitely the "top"; I never saw Haus mount her, but I did catch her dominating him many times! Sadly, even as I observed all this happy, healthy action in my own house, it didn't sink in for a long time that I was seriously deprived. At age thirty-eight—the prime of my life—I wasn't getting any at all and figured I had no chance of getting any ever again, thanks to the surgical disfigurement of my butt, the devastating remarks of X, and my continuous relapses, complete with oozing pus. How attractive is that?

Try wearing a surgical scar like mine with your bikini, or your bikini wax. Try explaining that scary-looking scar on your butt, where the skin folds inward creating a kind of sinus, to your waxing technician. The one I'd gone to for years, at Elizabeth Arden, preferred to avoid it entirely, leaving the area hairy—an unfortunate contrast to the bare skin on the opposite buttock. The high price of waxing was just not worthwhile without a neat result, so I gave it up. I was a proper hairy monster, not quite as

Britannia was brilliant in bed. JANISE BOGARD

fuzzy as Sheba with her plush, double coat, but just about. When I had to represent in a fashionable fashion—to make TV appearances promoting shelter animals and pet products—I wore a short, black skirt with high heels and dark knit tights that effectively cloaked my hairy legs. The rest of the time, it was trousers and heels all the way. In the absence of a sex life, my choice of heels had a helpful side benefit; walking in them, as urologist Dr. Maria Angela Cerruto of Verona, Italy, would later assert, helps to keep a woman's pelvic floor toned and improve pelvic organ health. And I needed all the help I could get.

My relationship with X had again deteriorated to the point where I was crying every day and felt compelled to escape by moving out. I found a two-bedroom apartment on an as-yet-un-gentrified, tree-lined block of Manhattan—an amazing find—and moved there. I was writing three books at the same time—one about mutts, and the other two about recipes that were safe to share with pets—so I threw myself into my work and continued to allow my sex drive to atrophy until it was very close to death. I didn't know it at the time, but part of my ability to ignore this most natural of urges was attributable to the daily soy-milk shakes I was having for breakfast, flavored with bananas and frozen blueberries. Unfermented soy has a dampening effect on the libido; making matters even worse, it just wasn't agreeing with my digestive system, and I would often wind up doubled over with stomach cramps after drinking my first meal of the day. In the peace and quiet of the "room of one's own" that Virginia Woolf was so right to say every writer needs, I got a lot done. And then, this native New Yorker experienced something very un–New York–like right in the middle of her fabled hometown. In the city where it's perfectly normal never to get to know your neighbors even after decades of living side-by-side, I became fast friends with two gay men in the apartment two doors down the hall from mine. How on earth did that happen? How else: Their dog broke the ice. Leo and Corbett were brothers, both brilliant, creative, and accomplished. You know how anyone with a matchmaking mind might muse, upon learning of an ineligible catch of a man, "Maybe he has a brother?" Well, these guys had not one but two—both straight. The elder, a worldly PhD, had an exciting job that took him all over the world. Here was a bona fide international man of mystery. I'd heard so much about this charismatic brother, descriptions of whom made him sound like a dashing figure lifted from the pages of a spy novel, that I figured he couldn't be all that and real, too. Then I finally met Austin and he was all that, plus gorgeous and funny and very real. He was also an animal lover; the dog was his pet, whom he'd left in his brothers' care.

There was palpable chemistry between Austin and me. This became apparent the night he came to town and his brothers invited me to dine out with them. We had a lovely time, with Leo and Corbett repairing to the *ristorante*'s garden for a strategic smoke-and-joke, leaving their brother Austin and me alone for several lovely minutes of bonding. After dinner, we returned to the brothers' beautifully decorated apartment. On our walk home, a homeless man greeted Leo warmly and pressed upon him a framed painting of a still life with wine bottle—a gift Corbett urged him to refuse because of the surfeit of framed artwork already decorating every inch of their apartment's wall space. It was getting late; Austin rose, picked up the actively resented artwork, and announced that he was walking me home. Ha! It wouldn't be a long trip. We strolled the few yards to my apartment, then sat down for a long chat. He told me about his divorce, his travels, his son; I told him about my divorce, my dogs, my surgery. I spared no unpleasant detail about said operation, but he was unfazed by my unvarnished account, merely shrugging at the grossest parts and offering his sympathy. From that night forward, every time intimacy ever looked imminent, I would perform this easy, um, stick test to find out what a guy was really made of. I knew I never wanted to become attached to someone queasy (like Doc) who would get all weirded-out about pus, so full disclosure became my personal "mensch-ometer," enabling me to learn quickly who was or was not a good guy. Well, here was a very good guy, perhaps one of the last few left on Earth. One thing led to another, and we repaired to my bedroom, where Austin requested a fashion show of high-heeled shoes. I had plenty of those. "Kiss me," he said somewhere between the Manolo Blahniks and the vintage Viviers. I gladly complied. Then I warned him, again, about my scar; he matter-of-factly assured me—again—that it didn't bother him. Mind you, my legs were extra-hairy at this point, hobbitlike in fact; full disclosure about that didn't faze him either. Nothing I could say put him off—not that putting him off was my goal. Suddenly realizing that my life's timeline was about to get a monumental milestone added to it, I excused myself to do some speed primping in the bathroom.

What ensued made that night one of the most memorable of my life. Finally, I got to understand why positions of great power are risked, even lost, for one amazing night of lovemaking. Austin was at once hot and sweet, compassionate and commanding—a real man, a mensch. I don't want to kill anyone with terminal TMI, so I'll just say that Austin put his money where his mouth was to show me that my scar really didn't bother him. Whoa! Dogs do many things to heal themselves and each other, including something we've all seen: licking their own and their pack mates' wounds. This divinely doglike man did the same for my injuries, the physical as well as the psychic ones. Austin fell asleep but soon opened one eye to find me staring at him, wide-eyed with disbelief, the way you do when suddenly your bed isn't a piece of furniture or a place of rest, but an admission-free amusement park—when suddenly you appreciate Milton's phrase "what hath night to do with sleep?" Austin didn't mind my staring; he just smiled, closed his eyes, and snuggled deeper into the pillow—exactly like one of my dogs.

The next morning, I awoke to find that the hunk I'd had the vivid dream about was lying right there beside me. So the previous night had not been a mirage conjured by my overlong sexual drought. He turned to face me, and the X-rated dream sequence began all over again. When he left, I was completely in the moment and surprisingly realistic. With a level of confidence I didn't think I could muster, I didn't fret about whether I'd ever see him again; I felt grateful we'd had this time together. There are people and animals with deep scars who live their entire lives without being made to feel whole; I'd almost been one of them but was spared. I wasn't going to be greedy now. Besides, Austin had to get back to work—and his office was clear across the world. He'd performed his healing mission, playing doctor, and even making a house call. I had to let him go.

That day, I tapped into something I've since come to call The Zen of Carol Burnett. The marvelous Ms. Burnett used to end every episode of her variety show with a ditty that begins, "I'm so glad we had this time together . . ." This time might be half a life or half a day—so cherish it now, before it's too late. Dogs' lives are never long enough, despite our best attempts at extending them, and that's the main reason I've taken great comfort from the Zen of Carol Burnett, and hope you will, too. Whether you're sending a beloved dog to the bridge or bidding a lover adieu, remember that love doesn't die. It's never goodbye—it's just so long, until we meet again. I did meet Austin again, three months later; it was a brief encounter, but magical nonetheless, and it left me so satisfied that I didn't even think about sex (except the sex I'd had with him) for the ensuing—are you ready?—four years. The previous period of abstinence had been a time of frustration and stress—celibacy caused by the low body image that was one of my surgery's side effects, compounded by X's lack of compassion. This four-year period, on the other hand, didn't feel anything like a drought; it wasn't sad or pitiful in the slightest. The years flew by. I was thirty-eight and feeling like a teenager again. And for every uncomfortable or difficult situation I encountered, I had a different, wonderful Medicine Dog standing ready with a healing lesson to teach. I became super-productive at work, cohosting a television pilot for Fine Living Network called *Sit, Stay, Style* while completing my three pet-lifestyle books. Looking at photographs of myself that year, I see a confidence I never had before. The self-esteem I'd left behind in the operating room back in '99, which had been thoroughly drained from me, returned in full blossom. In an odd move, I gave up my apartment in Austin's brothers' building and moved back in with X. He forced my hand; he was paying me visits every day, threatening to make public scenes in my lobby until I returned to live with him. So I reluctantly agreed to give our cohabitation yet another college try. Although there were plenty of Medicine Dogs already on duty in the animal house ward, another was acquired in short order: a gorgeous pit bull named Angus, one of the great loves of my life. Angus, lucky devil, had an open arrangement with two lovely bitches, Lupa and Dora, and neither girl dog seemed to mind sharing her boy with her "sister wife."

Four years is a very long time to deprive oneself of the rejuvenating release of lovemaking. But for a good, long while, my newfound self-confidence enabled me to rise above X's daily verbal assaults. I rededicated myself to my mission: promoting animal welfare in the media. To compensate for the profound personal lows, fortune smiled and allowed me to experience tremendous professional highs. I scored an on-camera audition to be a pet expert for a brand-new talk show hosted by Rachael Ray; although I didn't get the gig, it was truly an honor to be interviewed. I worked on the startup of the dog-product web retailer Fetchdog, where the actress Glenn Close—my boss's wife—honored me by narrating a video I scripted. Hearing this great artist interpret my words, using her signature combo of classical grandeur and jazzy improv, was a career Everest all by itself. I directed a short film about my friend the fashion designer John Bartlett and his three-legged dog Tiny Tim; it won Best Documentary at the 2007 North Shore Animal League DogCatemy Awards Gala, which Sheba attended as my date. I was interviewed for "Why We Love Cats

Sheba with Howard Stern and Richard Belzer, 2007 DogCatemy Awards Gala

and Dogs," part of the prestigious PBS *Nature* documentary series. Then I authored a fourth book, *Pretty Pet-Friendly*, a sequel to *Animal House Style*. In retrospect, I'm amazed at how much I accomplished during that time of enormous physical and emotional upheaval. Those Medicine Dogs were really doing their jobs.

In return, I relentlessly doctored them, serving as a kind of medical impresario to ensure that they always received the integrative procedures and meds I'd researched for my column. When I discovered that Lupa suffered terrifying seizures—on a routine walk, she began shrieking and slamming her body against a doorway—I arranged for a vet to put her on a plant-based anticonvulsant called Lepsilyte; composed of the botanical ingredients valerian and skullcap, it's a dogsend for pets with seizures. With her daily dose, Lupa remained completely seizure-free and safe from the liver-eating side effects caused by the conventional remedies, phenobarbital and potassium bromide. My own muscles stiff from days spent at the computer, I underwent regular treatments with Dr. Joyce Nawy, a chiropractor whose gift for healing helped keep me in one piece, always ready for a dog-walk. After that, I wanted my senior canines to experience the amazing, bodywide relief of a chiropractic adjustment, so I investigated veterinary chiropractic and took the dogs for regular treatments with Dr. Jill Elliot.

By the end of 2007, however, Sam—the chief Medicine Dog—had begun to deteriorate. Health nuts talk all the time about antioxidants and supplements that boost cellular health, and I was dutifully pumping Sam full of those, notably omega-3 in the form of Nordic Naturals oils for pets plus milk thistle to protect his liver and kidneys and prevent his eyes from becoming cloudy. He was also taking FlexPet, the dog version of the human joint supplement Flexcin, as well as a then–brand new product called Vigorate, the vet-developed canine version of the human supplement Juvenon, designed to boost the mitochondria, which supply the body's cells with energy in the form of ATP (adenosine triphosphate). His food was liberally seasoned with turmeric and cinnamon, plus probiotics and coconut oil. Thanks to the *cordon sanitaire* that protected Britannia and all the other members of our woof pack, harmful chemical preservatives didn't have a chance to come anywhere near Sam if I could help it. Still, despite all that plus regular veterinary chiropractic sessions with the excellent Dr. Elliot, Sam was oxidizing before my eyes, his face frosted all over with white hairs, his gait slowing down to a crawl. He was no longer doing the cute, happy-puppy things he used to do throughout his adulthood—flipping over on his back to do the Snoopy dance was now a thing of the distant past. Humping his girlfriend Pepper? Forget about it. He didn't even have the strength to hold his leg up to urinate, so he relieved himself with all four feet on the ground, looking miserably emasculated as he did so. The joy of life was visibly draining out of him. Some might say fourteen is a grand old age for a big pit bull, and it's time to just let go and let nature take its course. That's not my style. I expected Sam to make it to sixteen at least! Yet it didn't occur to me to be proactive by researching innovative options for Sam's arthritis until that day he collapsed on the sidewalk. Had I given myself a head start, the dogged reporter in me would have discovered sooner that Vet-Stem, having succeeded in getting almost two thousand injured horses back up and running, had just begun applying its groundbreaking technology to dogs earlier that year, in May 2007. I suppose after years of working for newspapers, I needed the hardest possible drop-deadline to get any job done. Within a few months, the assignment arrived, and the deadline was yesterday. My crash course in high-tech healing was about to begin.

CHAPTER 7

Evicting the Heartworm

It was May 2008, a few weeks after Sam's surgery, and I was busy chronicling the saga of Sam and his stem cells for the *New York Post*. Because my column was by this time quite short on space, I was obliged to channel my fellow fistula patient, Mr. Dickens, by serializing Sam's story, delivering the stem cell news in installments complete with cliffhanger endings like "To be continued" and "Stay tuned." Part one in the series was about Sam's collapse, discovering Vet-Stem's existence, and looking forward to Sam's being the second New York City dog to undergo this exciting procedure. The very first Vet-Stem patient in our hometown was Stevie, beloved pittie mix of animal activist Simone Reyes, who was on the verge of rising to fame as Uncle Rush's "Boss" on reality TV's *Running Russell Simmons*. Stem cell pioneers are not only the doctors making regenerative medicine possible for patients on two and four legs but also the people who undergo stem cell surgery, or arrange procedures for their pets, because they help to advance science for all of us. Simone certainly qualifies as a stem cell pioneer; I have to hand it to her for finding out about Vet-Stem and bringing it to the attention of her dog's doctor. Here, Simone recalls how Stevie responded to treatment with her own stem cells:

> *I would say that it absolutely improved her quality of life and gave her more mobility as she grew older in years. After the stem cell procedure my ex would often remind me that Stevie was trotting along with us and her brother Cassidy, going much further distances than she was able to go before. I wish that I had known about stem cell therapy when Stevie's sister Pikachu was alive; perhaps it could have helped her as well. Dogs' mobility is one of the most important things*

A rejuvenated Sam enjoys aerobic flirtation with a much younger bulldog named Bella.

they have—a dog's life is about exploring and taking in new smells and being able to walk side-by-side with their guardians. It was a joy to be able to see Stevie have another chance to do things younger dogs and their guardians take for granted. I had to say goodbye to Stevie in 2011. There isn't a day that goes by that I don't send prayers up to heaven to her and gaze lovingly at her photographs that are framed all over my house. Over the years, making the decision of when to let go has always been one of the greatest challenges of my life. Ultimately I found trying to remember that letting them go a day too early rather than a minute too late is the most loving thing a parent can do.

With dogs, sadness lurks even in the happiest moments, because their too-short life spans mean every victory is only temporary. That's why I was grateful for the chance to share Sam's Vet-Stem experience with interested readers of the *Post*. Describing my rejuvenated dog's every move, I wasn't alone in thinking those moves were really something to see. "What a legacy," one reader wrote. Others let me know that they were planning to get Vet-Stem for their dogs, which made me happy. What there was no room to write at the time was that the human medical realm's big news for American orthopedic patients was . . . hip arthroscopy and resurfacing. Each year, some eighty thousand Americans tear a cruciate ligament—the exact same injury sustained years earlier by Simone's Stevie and my Sam, which brought early arthritis to their afflicted joints—and fifty million Americans cope with the challenges of arthritis. Just a few months before Sam was treated with his own stem cells, Vet-Stem was featured on ABC's *Nightline*. Overjoyed owners of four-footed—now sure-footed—patients were calling Vet-Stem to ask where they, too, could be treated with their own stem cells. Looking at Sam post-surgery, it wasn't hard to see why: Dr. Bob and his Vet-Stem team had Benjamin Buttoned my beloved dog. I'd adopted Sam as a fully-grown adult, so I never got to see how he looked as a pup. But after what I'd seen thus far—a formerly hobbled dog taking steps at a fast clip and jumping up to the bed with ease—I fully expected to wake up one morning and find that Sam's improbably youthful stem cells had dialed his biological clock all the way back to the beginning! Sam was no longer one of the estimated twenty million American dogs who suffer from debilitating arthritis. He had it, but it no longer had him.

In the midst of all this hound healing was a lot of human hurting, as the two people in the animal house tried in vain to achieve something resembling marital harmony but only succeeded in becoming more and more estranged. There was no stem cell cure for this, in any country in the world, and the redecoration of our country house, like a botched facelift, had failed to rejuvenate our wedded bliss. The Medicine Dogs felt the stress, faithfully responding by generously dispensing their powerful affections right and left like so many frantic doctors trying to battle a plague; with both X and me for patients, the poor creatures had their work cut out for them. Earlier that year, just a few months before his sidewalk collapse led to his successful stem cell procedure, Sam was feeling—understandably—poorly. One of his pack mates, sensing weakness caused by what must have been a feeling of terror that his legs might not support him when he stood on them, impulsively decided to put Sam out of his misery with her bare teeth. I'm mortified to say that dog was my beloved Britannia. Please don't hate her; she wasn't being vindictive or mean. Those are human attributes, and we must be careful not to over-anthropomorphize our adorable pets. Britannia was merely acting on instinct. Real life with dogs is quite different from a G-rated Disney movie. Dogs are descended from wolves, and when one member of a pack is ailing, the others have been known to dispatch him, to prevent the weakened wolf from slowing down the others and making the pack as a whole vulnerable to predators. To my horror, I got to witness nature's not-so-nice, R-rated side right in my own bedroom.

I was lying in bed surrounded by canines, with Britannia at my side and Sam on the floor to my left, when suddenly Britannia pounced on Sam and went for his throat. Swinging my legs to the floor to separate the dogs, I didn't look out for my left ankle, which collided with B's teeth. Within seconds, X came dashing in from the kitchen, lifting Britannia away from Sam and holding her aloft. I examined Sam, and thankfully he'd escaped with no puncture wounds and only a few scratches. But I was shocked to see, upon looking up, that X, whom Britannia worshipped, had her collar in a death grip; he was twisting and tightening it, and she was visibly struggling for air. I told X to stop; he coldly said he'd have no problem killing her if she attacked Sam again. At that point, I stood up and informed X, in no uncertain terms, that if he killed her, I would kill him.

"Oh yeah?" he sneered, his grip on her collar tightening.

"Let her go!" I screamed.

He didn't, and I couldn't use force on X because the other dogs, feeling confused and compelled to do something to stop the madness, might turn on each other and start an epic dog fight, which could result in a lot of injury. Between the feuding humans and the stressed-out canines, there was already way too much adrenaline pumping in that small space. Finally, X saw fit to carry Britannia out to the kitchen and set her on the floor; she was coughing and gasping for air. I calmed her and made sure she was OK, popped pellets of arnica into Sam's mouth to prevent bruising, then repaired to the bathroom to flush my ankle with povidone-iodine. The battle lines were now drawn and our dogs were not strong enough to keep X and me together. No longer uniting us as a couple, they were now just another divisive force between X and me. I flashed back to the long-ago advice given me by a trusted tarot reader, whom I'd consulted when my marriage started going south years earlier: "Don't get any more dogs—X will use them against you." At the time, I hadn't believed those words could possibly come true; how could one dog-lover use a dog against a fellow dog-lover? Now I understood how, and how awfully accurate the psychic's prediction had been. Happily, as Sam grew stronger post-Vet-Stem, Britannia never made another assassination attempt on him—yet another compelling, if gruesome, endorsement of the procedure's success. She also got along famously with all the other dogs in the "woof pack," Sheba in particular; the two were best girlfriends. I'm also proud to report that Britannia was remarkably tolerant of the most recent arrivals in the animal house, Lupa and her best friend Dora, Angus's girlfriends. And so, after Sam's stem cell success, I felt OK about diverting my attention from him and the other dogs just long enough to rescue yet another pit bull. The house was already full to bursting with canids, but as X and I used to joke in happier times—referencing the justly famous "Twenty Two" episode of *The Twilight Zone*—there was "room for one more honey." That's how I brought home a honey-colored honey, a tan male pit bull facing untimely extermination in a rural Texas gas chamber.

But first, speaking of *The Twilight Zone,* indulge me a brief digression into that fifth dimension, "beyond that which is known to man." I thought I'd seen all of Rod Serling's mind-altering mini-masterpieces when, during one Syfy Channel New Year's Day marathon, I came across "Spur of the Moment." Scripted by none other than science fiction master Richard Matheson, this haunting tale of a woman who travels back in time, desperately trying to stop her younger self from marrying the wrong man, hit me where I lived. In the poem "I Go Back to May 1937," Pulitzer Prize winner Sharon Olds also imagines traveling back in time, where—alluding to the emotional carnage that bad marriages wreak—she contemplates urging her parents not to get married. One of the things the poet wants to warn them: "You will want to die." It may sound awfully bratty considering how lucky I was to have survived septicemia, but in the final years leading to the ultimate dissolution of my partnership with X, when things were so difficult at home yet I couldn't bear to leave my dogs, I often prayed for deliverance by death. But what always brought me back from the brink was God-spelled-backward. Rescuing another dog was my way of affirming life, positivity, and possibility in the face of abject marital misery. And that's how a dog named Lazarus entered my life.

He was on the euthanasia list at a rural Texas animal shelter. I arranged to have him flown north, and we met for the first time at the cargo area of New York City's LaGuardia Airport on May 18, two days before my birthday. Like the previous dogs I'd had flown to New York on Midwest, "Shorty," as the animal control officer had dubbed him, arrived calm, cool, and collected, as if he'd enjoyed a long, relaxing nap in the belly of the plane. Shorty's complete lack of stress upon exiting his Sky Kennel was an endorsement for Midwest's "Best Care in the Air" slogan. I took this cool canine customer for a quick relief walk before the drive home. He promptly showed his appreciation for the airline that flew him to safety by taking a leak on the Midwest sign. There was a lot I was yet to discover about my butter-bull birthday dog, but I wanted him to have a handle more dignified than Shorty, pronto. Before that unfortunate name could have a chance to stick, and he wouldn't respond to any other, I named him Lazarus in tribute to that very first pit bull I'd ever met back in '93, the brawny brindle male who belonged to one of my neighbors. It's not an

Lazarus and his signature shit-eating grin

exaggeration to say that the course of my life changed the day that Lazarus sweetly stood up in the elevator to give me a hug. From that moment forward I was a proud pit warrior. I became the pit reporter that day; the Pet Reporter six years later. An ancient Greek word meaning "God has helped," and the name of the man raised from the dead by Jesus Christ, according to the Gospel of John, Lazarus was a perfect handle for my little canine Texan. After all, dog-spelled-backward had seen to it that he would rise not once but twice: the first time, escaping the gas chamber, and the second, when the Midwest plane lifted off.

When I brought Lazarus to the Humane Society clinic to be neutered, a blood test revealed that he could not undergo surgery because he had an epic case of heartworm disease to match his epic new handle. He underwent treatment at the clinic, then came home to heal. The goal was to keep him calm, for too much excitement could literally stop his heart. Although initially he had a bit of a dog-aggression issue (which has since, happily, mellowed significantly), Laz had always been respectful and friendly toward cats. So I kept him apart from my other dogs, as reacting to them would surely raise his heart rate, by sequestering Laz in the feline wing of the apartment. As the bedroom had been Britannia's recuperative domain, the living room was Laz's healing haven, while his parasite-infested ticker evicted the worms that could have easily killed him in a heartbeat. Having read that eating a bit of the same organ that's afflicted can have a curative effect—liver for someone with liver disease— I periodically fed Laz beef hearts, which he loved. From nursing Lazarus, I learned a great deal about getting and staying heart-healthy—an important thing for all of us forty-plus women to think about, because heart disease is the number-one killer of women, and we are 15 percent more likely to die of a heart attack than men. To keep Laz's now-worm-free ticker toned, I supplemented his diet with heart-healthy hawthorn, CoQ10, and omega-3s in the form of fish oil. Liquid from cans of water-packed sardines was one of Laz's favorite snacks, along with the sardines themselves, which are a heart-healthy treat. This dog showed me that, with TLC, even a diseased heart could be restored to fine working order and maintained with heart-healthy activities and supplements. On the face of it, I had a heart-healthy lifestyle: going for vigorous dog walks, eating a diet free of fried or processed foods, taking supplements. But unlike Laz, I was still harboring a kind of parasitic infection: the stubborn belief that settling for a lifetime sentence of unhappy marriage was the only way to keep my dogs happy. They weren't happy, because X and I weren't happy. I'd put up an impressive wall to keep human love out and secured the keep with a platoon of Medicine Dogs. After a period of adjustment, Laz's heart was going to be just fine. Wasn't it high time I healed my own? First, however, something would happen to put a big tear in it.

On the morning of September 11, 2008, I was struggling with a couple of writing deadlines but took a quick break to run Britannia out to the sidewalk for a speed leak. Although she never had another episode of incontinence after her final acupuncture appointment two years earlier, I gave her frequent relief walks. Actually, we did this for all dogs over age twelve, Sam and Pepper included. That morning, Britannia dropped her butt into the pee position, but what came out wasn't urine; it was dark blood, and the flow seemed, as in a horror flick, unstoppable. When it finally did stop, I marched her back inside, made sure the other dogs were comfortable, and rushed Britannia to the Humane Society clinic. Figuring whatever this was could be fixed—just the day before, Britannia had executed her signature three-foot leap in the air for a treat!—I left my best-B-loved in the care of the Society's excellent doctors and vet techs, and raced back home to finish my deadlines. I'd wrestled death for Britannia before and won, so I was stupidly arrogant in my confidence that this latest development would be just a hiccup along the road to what I fully believed would be B's extra-extended, supplement- and healthy-food-powered long life. Besides, she was only fourteen years young.

A few hours later, Dr. Rubinstein, renowned for his brilliant diagnostic skills, called to give me the update. The vet who moonlighted as a cards-carrying illusionist and enjoyed kidding around with clients, treating them to tales of magic tricks and cracking jokes like "urine good hands" while drawing pee samples, was not his usual chipper self. In his most somber tone of voice, Dr. Rubinstein reported that tests had revealed the cause of all that blood loss was a splenic mass that had ruptured. Nothing could be done; Britannia was bleeding to death. I promised to be right over. Things were happening too fast for me to think about being sad, so I switched to hyper-efficient mode. Grabbing the portable CD player, pre-loaded with Susan Raimond's harp music CD—the celestial music that had been the soundtrack to my brindle girl's tetanic recovery effort—I stopped to realize that Sheba would forever fret over what had happened to her best friend. So I brought Sheba with me. We hailed a cab and made a mad dash back to the clinic, following the same route taken five years earlier when racing Britannia down Second Avenue to the emergency hospital. I took comfort thinking that Sheba could offer moral support to Britannia in her last moments, and come away with a sense of closure.

Wait a minute: Wasn't that me, a few paragraphs ago, warning about the dangers of anthropomorphizing dogs? You wouldn't have known it that day, when I loaded my own emotional baggage onto Sheba's frail little back. In moments of extreme emotional distress, common sense often flies out the window. The injection of pink liquid entered B's veins, and she was gone pretty quickly because, thanks to copious internal bleeding, she was already halfway dead. Sheba stared up at the table at her lifeless friend, and you could see the gears in her brain registering the terrible information. Then she abruptly pulled to get out of that exam room, as far and fast as her poor arthritic legs could carry her. Almost immediately upon returning home after watching Britannia depart for the Bridge, Sheba began having projectile diarrhea; she'd succumbed to a *Campylobacter* infection. Again, stress had caused one of my pack mates to experience an immune system collapse. Thankfully, after a brief stay at Fifth Avenue Veterinary Specialists, as recommended by the Humane Society, Sheba made a full recovery.

Permit me to pause for a moment. Britannia left me so suddenly that, despite a house full of dogs to care for, I'm still not over her passing. This is the first time I've written about that awful day, and it's as if she died all over again. I love all my dogs, but that little one staked out a special place in my heart, like a benign parasite I never wanted to evict.

By December 2008, things with X had finally deteriorated to the point of no return. There were so many unfortunate incidents: the one when he slowly drove the car over my left foot while I was taking the dogs out of the backseat . . . the one when, grabbing and holding hostage the galleys of my latest book, which were due back to the publisher, he said, "You're not going to make your deadline." Every day he told me one or more of the following: "You ruin everything," "You fucking idiot," "Try writing books people want to read," and "Who gave you the right to think?" But the incident to end all unfortunate incidents would focus on—I cannot lie—the loo. It happened when, one fine morning, X asked me if I needed to use the toilet, because he wanted to take a bath. Ah, the pleasures of two people having to share one bathroom. I was working at the computer and didn't have to "go" at that moment, but said I'd give it a college try. I tried, but nothing happened; we dog people know that when our best friends just don't have the urge to poop, no amount of coaxing will extrude a BM from their butts if they're not feeling it. I told X the bathroom was all his. It was a weekday, so I had no idea X was planning to set up shop in there, turning the tub into a work station complete with newspaper and coffee mug. I went about my verbal business, but about forty minutes later, my unpredictable, temperamental gut let me know it had its own job to do. Loath to disturb X—he did love his super-long soaks—I waited, but nature's call became wildly urgent, so I knocked at the door and asked if X would mind if I quickly used the toilet. I figured we'd just do what we'd often done in the past—deploy the shower curtain for the privacy of bather and crapper, so I could dash in and out with minimal disturbance to him. In such instances, I always kept my hand on the toilet handle during peristalsis, ready to flush the instant the action started; my handy bottle of tea tree essential oil was always at the ready on the toilet tank, so I could put a few drops in the bowl to disinfect it and mask lingering offensive odor.

But this time, all precedents were history as X started yelling and cursing, repeating, "I asked you if you needed the toilet!" He stood up to grab a towel and bolt from the bathroom as if I'd screamed fire. I told him there was no need, I'd be super quick. I got my business done and asked X if he'd like me to draw another bath for him; he said no. By the next day, X still hadn't washed his hands of the bathroom incident. I was finishing up my morning shower when the bathroom door flung open and X snatched the only towel. To my surprise, he then grabbed my arm and pulled me out of the tub and out the bathroom door. I'd just washed my hair, which was extra-long then, so I was extra-well-drenched, and the apartment was frosty. My pleas for X to hand over the towel were rebuffed: "Now you can feel how I felt when I had to jump up from my bath," he said.

I'd been dutifully taking my omega-3 fish oil and hawthorn capsules every day for heart health—the same supplements Laz took to support his heart. But all the supplements in the world weren't enough to counteract the negative effects of seeing sheer hatred blaze from the eyes of the man I loved, or hearing him berate me every single day. The water-torture incident was the final straw: This parasitic infection had to be evicted from my heart and home once and for all. For the first time in our strange history of breaking up and getting back together, I didn't repeat the motions of moving out. Instead, I told X it was *his* turn to move, and this time our breakup would be final. It didn't happen without a fight—lots of them, in fact, the petty arguments and confrontations that two incompatible people sometimes find strange solace in. X promptly located an apartment. The division of dogs was as follows: I would keep Lazarus, Tiki, and Sheba. X would take Sam, Pepper, Lupa, and Angus. X was adamant that Angus wasn't my dog—that Angus wasn't even a dog, but the reincarnation of X's horse from a past life. I believe wholeheartedly in past lives, but this new equine revelation was too much even for me. Angus: the dog whom X had once decreed we could only foster; the dog who appeared with me in the newspaper every week, and curled up every night close to my rib cage to cuddle me to sleep; my handsome canine date who posed so fetchingly on the red carpet for the paparazzi covering the New York premiere of the movie *Marley and Me* at the Tribeca Film Center.

"Don't fuck with me," X warned. "Angus is mine."

I didn't want to put this darling dog through a custody battle. I flashed back to the unfortunate day, years before in the country, when Sam was in the back of the Volvo and X and I were arguing vigorously. We'd arrived at our house and stepped out of the vehicle at the same time; both back doors were flung open and each of us was cajoling Sam to come out on our side. How idiotically symbolic: We were really asking him to make an impossible choice between us. That smart, sensitive dog was so infinitely more evolved than X or I was. Sam just sat there with his shoulders hunched, looking straight ahead, not wanting to hurt either of us by so much as glancing an inch in either direction. I was mindful thereafter not to place any dog in that awful position again. More to help myself cope than anything else, I consulted with animal communicator and author Amelia Kinkade. With her expert guidance, I learned that Angus felt his job was to protect X. I'd have to let him go; it was the right thing to do, because it's what Angus wanted.

What about Dora? What did she want? I consulted a different communicator, Dawn Allen, about who should get custody of this sweet pit mix from the animal shelter in Carrollton, Texas, whose soulful face had haunted me for one long, sleepless night the year before, after I received an urgent e-mail that finally moved me to have her transported up North along with her kennel mate Lupa, the white pittie. Right about now, you're probably thinking I'm nuts, and that consulting with animal communicators about a dog's destiny is "woo-woo" or worse. Call it woo-woof and think what you will, it worked for me. I've found that, whether you're pondering a life-or-death matter (such as when to put an elderly, ailing dog to sleep) or seeking insight into your pet's behavior, a psychic consultation can help understand animals in surprising new ways. Many skeptics have been converted by a brief consult with Dawn, and the astonishing insight she offered enabled me to make the best decision on Dora's behalf. Dawn got a loud-and-clear message from my little brown-eyed girl. Although Dora had a strong heart connection to me, I'd have custody of the cats—and this was a dealbreaker for Dora, because ever since moving in, she desperately wanted to eat one or all of the meowing menaces. Dora had resisted the urge thus far, but she conveyed to Dawn that she felt it was best for everybody if she stayed with X, who was catless and planned to keep it that way. I'd never suspected this—that's how successfully Dora had controlled her cat-killing urges just to please me. Sweet Dora, whose amazing eyes communicated volumes, couldn't stand the stress of living under the same roof with all those tempting tabbies, knowing I'd be very unhappy if she ate just one. And really, who could expect her to stop at just one? "Dora is a great dog, a leader," Dawn said. Ironically, the dog Dora had grown closest to, besides Lupa, was cat-loving Lazarus. I miss that little gal, and I know Laz does too, but am comforted to know that, with Dawn's help, I honored Dora's own wishes, just as I had in the case of Angus.

It's not unusual for strong medicine—the fever curer—to feel like it's going to kill you. X's leaving ultimately saved me, but I lost a great deal in the process: beautiful, loyal dogs I'd invested so much love and time in, and might never see again. I was especially concerned about Lupa; would X be diligent about her daily dose of Lepsilyte? The day we parted for the last time, X drove away with five substantial pieces of my heart. I wasn't sure I'd be able to compensate for that loss. But I knew that I wanted to heal, and having a partner whose presence makes you want to die is not exactly conducive to that goal. One of the principles of ayurveda (traditional Indian medicine) holds that even powerful medicine is of little use if the fundamental pillars of life are not strong and solid. The heart is the main support; without that support, the house collapses. Without peace of mind, even my formidable pack of Medicine Dogs was powerless to save me. Sometimes, the glass you try so hard to perceive as half full needs to be completely emptied out, then smashed to pieces.

CHAPTER 8

Come to Heal

When teaching a dog to walk by your side, the drill is called "come to heal." I confess I'm a pretty lax trainer, and I tend to let my dogs lead *me* on the street, to the consternation of many behaviorists who have worked with me and my dogs over the years in an effort to curb this bad behavior, which is really mine and not the dogs'. But as I came to terms with losing half of my woof pack, I began to understand that letting dogs lead me was perhaps the smartest move I ever made. I don't love the term "master" as applied to a pet owner, mostly because I believe the real masters—the masters of well-being—are dogs. The year 2009 went down in my personal history as the year I "came to heal" by consciously following my canine masters' lead. By this time, I'd worked with or interviewed numerous excellent veterinarians and arrived at the conclusion that vets, not human docs, are the health professionals most effectively raising awareness of wellness in America. Vets are potent healers because they work with animals. We know how healing dogs are, how it does a human body good just to pet them; now think about the healing power in vets' hands, and how it's boosted every time they touch their animal patients, which they do all day long. I believe it's not woo-woo—or woo-woof—to say that vets draw healing power from animals' therapeutic energy, because dogs foster an atmosphere of calm and wellness wherever they go. Medical doctors, on the other hand, don't have that professional perk to recommend them. In the musical *My Fair Lady,* Henry Higgins wonders, "Why can't a woman be more like a man?" To that I say, "Why can't doctors be more like vets?"

My canines are my own personal wellness watchdogs, but it's not an overstatement to say that the best American vets are boldly taking on that health-guardian role for our country as a whole. Consider Dr.

Marty Becker, who deserves his handle "America's Vet," and who gets extra points with me for adopting a little black pit bull named Amazing Gracie. Known to millions for his best-selling books and regular appearances on *Good Morning America* and in the *AARP* magazine, Dr. Becker's mission is to bolster the human-animal bond by educating us all about pet health. But what he's really doing when he discusses, say, the serious medical problem of overweight dogs, is getting us to care about our own health. He's doing what doctors are supposed to do, but don't always succeed at doing. The bond between person and pet breaks if one of us gets sick and dies—it's as simple as that. So, when Dr. Becker describes how obesity raises a dog's risk of diabetes, joint problems, high blood pressure, respiratory problems, and even cancer, he's tactfully but impactfully reminding us that those very same ailments could easily befall us, too, if we don't watchdog our own weight. Talking about issues many people would rather not think about while holding an adorable dog or cat in his arms, America's Vet makes bitter-tasting health topics cute, cuddly, and easy to swallow—subliminally and sublingually. And by getting people, especially kids, to care about wellness through pets, Dr. Becker performs a valuable and perhaps undersung public service that positively affects his fellow Americans' longevity. That's kind of genius.

What is it about the veterinary character that makes a pet doctor a compelling leader? Perhaps it has something to do with the oath a vet takes before embarking on his or her career. The Hippocratic Oath is a solemn promise to practice medicine honestly and humanely; it's been revised many times since being written in the fifth century BC, most significantly as the Declaration of Geneva, drafted to prevent heinous medical crimes like those perpetrated by Nazi physicians. Interestingly, there is no legal obligation for medical students to swear an oath upon graduating, yet an estimated 98 percent of American med students choose to do so anyway. However, nowhere in the oath is there a mention of a doctor's duty to keep pace with new information and developments in the field of medicine. Now, consider the Veterinarian's Oath, adopted by the American Veterinary Medical Association's House of Delegates in 1969, and subsequently amended by the AVMA Executive Board in 1999 and 2010:

Being admitted to the profession of veterinary medicine, I solemnly swear to use my scientific knowledge and skills for the benefit of society through the protection of animal health and welfare, the prevention and relief of animal suffering, the conservation of animal resources, the promotion of public health, and the advancement of medical knowledge. I will practice my profession conscientiously, with dignity, and in keeping with the principles of veterinary medical ethics. I accept as a lifelong obligation the continual improvement of my professional knowledge and competence.

That last sentence is key: Vets appreciate that part of their job is to stay on top of their game by keeping abreast of the latest scientific information and medical techniques. This respect for the new has proven critical for the dissemination of adult stem cell technology, for without vets seeking to learn about regenerative medicine for their animal patients, awareness of ASC's healing potential for all species, especially humans, would simply not have reached as many Americans as it has. As with Dr. Becker's healing message, the information was absorbed because it came in a package everyone could relate to: a formerly lame horse or dog who could now walk tall. (Incidentally, Dr. Becker is certified by Vet-Stem and has performed numerous adult stem cell procedures on animal patients.) Sadly, I had experienced firsthand how doctors on the human side don't always strive to keep learning and continually improving—how many of them are perfectly complacent with what they already know. And frankly, that doctor-like complacency turned me off from conventional medicine at a time when what I really needed and wanted most was to be healed in a modern, high-tech way. Happily, a doctor arrived on the scene who would become "America's Doctor" the way Marty Becker is "America's Vet"—Mehmet Oz. After five years as Oprah's popular featured guest, Dr. Oz landed his own show in September 2009. Skillfully navigating the tightrope between conventional medicine and integrative options like a Wallenda with a stethoscope, Dr. Oz presents his viewers with valuable health information we all can really use. Moreover, like the best vets, he keeps current with breaking medical news and often cedes show time to his healing colleagues, among them Dr. Andrew Weil, Dr. Tieraona Low

Dog, and Dr. Joseph Mercola. It doesn't hurt that Dr. Oz is a dog lover who often talks about Rosie, his black Lab. As if another reason to like this popular doc were needed, wouldn't you know he's good friends with Dr. Becker, who's a frequent guest on *The Dr. Oz Show;* it was, in fact, Dr. Oz who dubbed the animal doc "America's Vet."

There was one upside to losing custody of Sam, Pepper, Angus, Dora, and Lupa: With fewer dogs to care for, and all of them in good health, I suddenly had time to turn my remedial attentions to myself. I was the animal in the house most in need of healing, and here was my chance to get me some. I finally figured out that soy milk was not the food I should be starting my day with; switching to almond milk, I was able to ingest the morning meal without excruciating gut cramps. I also made sure my pantry shelves would be well stocked with the foods, supplements, spices, and oils I'd seen work wonders for my dogs' overall vibrancy.

Free of that hypercritical spousal presence, I began raising my self-esteem from the deep hole where it had been buried and left for dead. Lacking the superheroine abilities Beatrice Kiddo displays in the *Kill Bill* movies, I revived my inner fashion hound. First, I found a waxing techni-cian intrepid enough to help me keep the scar back there clear of hair. Natasha of Elizabeth Arden would turn out to be a healer in her own right. Almost always fully booked, "Doctor" Natasha is nice enough to text me, when I'm desperate for depilation, if an opening arises. Now that my legs were hairless, I bared them in shorts and skirts. People in my neigh-borhood began to notice a difference in my demeanor; many remarked on my more relaxed appearance and congratulated me on splitting with X, with whom they'd had unpleasant run-ins over the years. To celebrate my new nontoxic lifestyle, I decided to evict the mercury from my mouth, and made an appointment with Dr. Jablow to have my amalgam den-tal fillings removed and replaced. Still, such was the negative impact of dual asshole issues—fistula (i.e., pain in the gut) and ex-husband (pain in the butt)—that I felt compelled to do something out-of-the-ordinary to mark the final fade-to-black of the weird film noir that was my long, unhappy marriage. So I booked a phototherapy session with Circe Ham-ilton, a talented photographer whose specialty is nude and seminude por-traits of women designed to boost the sitters' self-image. It's an unusual

"Doctor" Circe's phototherapy Rx CIRCE

way to combat low self-esteem, and it works. In fact, phototherapy is so effective that I wish I'd thought of consulting Circe sooner, because her work has had enormously positive and long-lasting effects. After hearing some of my story, she focused on my posterior. Making love to Circe's camera was a tremendously freeing experience. By the end of our shoot, "Doctor" Circe's breezy, incredibly supportive bedside manner enabled me to peel off whatever I still had on and jump into the tub, allowing the last protective layers of makeup and hair products to dissolve away. She caught that on camera, too. Later, I tentatively showed the results to a few friends, and hearing their positive feedback was like taking a warm bath. My tail was nowhere near as disfigured as I'd been led to believe. In fact, it was still my best (ahem) asset.

I sat down on that asset and got to work figuring out a strategy to increase my income. I was now the sole breadwinner and caretaker of a pack of precious dogs. The safety and security of these sweethearts was in my hands, and it was a responsibility I took very seriously. Combining my two other favorite topics, decor and astrology, I devised a new monthly column: "Star Style," a feature about design and the zodiac, or "designastry," as I call it. It wouldn't be forecasts; after all, I'm not an astrologer making predictions about the future, I'm a zodiac aficionado focusing on the past and present. I studied astrology from several different angles, and one of the things I discovered is its historical use in diagnosing and being proactive about illness. My star sign, Taurus, is prone to throat problems, while Virgo, the zodiac tribe of many people I care about, tends to suffer a great deal of digestive upset from all the worrying Virgos infamously do. (Incidentally, Louis XIV was a Virgo, which might partly explain his vulnerability to PF: not just his digestive delicacy, but his infamous lack of personal hygiene, an extreme version of the common Virgo trait of, say, going unshaven.) Amazed that I'd never been aware of Nicholas Culpeper before, I acquainted myself with the life and work of the physician-botanist-astrologer, and that was a revelation. Boning up on the zodiac was more than a way to earn money; it developed into a passion, as it was starting to explain so many things. But most important, it explained why I value dogs and the natural kingdom as a whole so highly: That's a typical Taurus thing.

I briefly took in a roommate, ostensibly to assist with the rent, but really because I was terrified to be alone. I'd met P because she lived on my block and we'd had several lovely conversations. When she mentioned that she needed somewhere to stay for a few months, I offered my place. In her early thirties, P was a brunette beauty to rival the Venus de Milo: tall and slender, with long hair and dark eyes. Her style sense was spot-on (she's a Libra, the zodiac's most fashion-conscious sign), so she always cut a dashing figure, whether she wore flats and trousers or a long skirt with a tank top and flip-flops—this gal even looked chic in pajamas, with a towel on her head! Plus, she'd surprise me by adding lovely touches to our shared space. She was charming and fun to have around. P arrived at the apartment one Monday after a weekend spent with her boyfriend. In a freak accident, she'd managed to scald her forearm with the contents of a tea kettle; it was a very serious burn. At her request, I set about fixing it. Applying neem oil to her arm, I loosely wrapped the area with gauze and secured it with surgical tape. True to form, the neem went to work healing her skin, which was back to normal in a couple of days. Thereafter, P was devoted to neem, and applied it to her skin at every opportunity! For this garlicky-sulfurous-smelling oil, that's a huge compliment; Libra tends to favor fragrant, flowery scents.

One night, I received a frantic call from my friend A, who rescues Chihuahuas. Two of her fierce little friends had gotten into an epic battle over their dinner; reaching in to stop the hostilities, her hand was seriously bitten up. But A was loath to go to the emergency room because visions of her dogs being impounded made her terrified a doctor's interrogation might cause her to snitch on her best friends—and she didn't want to have to make up some story about some other dog having bitten her (we dog rescuers are loyal like that). I felt her pain, so I told her to give me a few minutes and I'd be right over. Into my Medicine Dog bag—what else should that be but a Crypton tote with a William Wegman dog drawing on it?—went my trusty bottle of povidone-iodine, Buck Mountain Botanicals wound balm (a concoction of echinacea, burdock, and yarrow formulated for animals, but I use it on my own cuts and bruises), plus a jar of olive-leaf extract. I packed light because A said she'd already raided the pharmacy for bandages, gauze, and tape. When I arrived, each of her fingers was already bandaged. After carefully removing each bandage to inspect the wounds, I cleaned and re-bandaged three of the four damaged digits on her poor hand (her thumb had, happily, escaped unscathed), then arrived at the fourth finger. I could tell this one needed stitches, pronto. Not surprisingly, A protested. I told her not to worry, they couldn't bust her dogs, it had been an accident—but I emphasized that this was her hand, and she needed both of those in good working order to continue her rescue efforts, and to take care of her own dogs in the style to which they'd become accustomed. That got to her, and we jumped in a cab to the nearest emergency room. After a few hours of waiting, I had to run back to walk my dogs. I offered to return, but A insisted that she'd be fine on her own. The next morning, A told me she wound up waiting until the wee hours to be told that, yes, that finger I was concerned about absolutely required stitches. She was instructed to return at midday, when the plastic surgeon was on duty. The ER doctor who looked at A's hand told her that whoever had treated her other fingers had done such a good job that they didn't need to be re-bandaged. All that experience tending to the Medicine Dogs' wounded knees and paws had apparently been pretty good training.

P left the country; following close on her departure was the arrival in New York of another brunette beauty looking for lodgings, this one on four legs. It was the dog days of August, and thanks to an urgent Facebook appeal, I became smitten with an adorable pup at risk in Ohio. She was pre-named Cupcake. Figuring that this little canine confection would be no problem to fold into my diminished woof pack—room for one more honey!—I reached out to the rescue volunteers at the Trumbull County Dog Pound in Warren, Ohio. Cupcake arrived on a transport with a virulent case of kennel cough; this was easily enough fixed with loving spoonfuls of raw honey plus a wonderfully effective homeopathic cough syrup for humans called Umcka, which I'd used on myself and on numerous rescue dogs. But Cupcake's poor eyes also exuded copious amounts of green goop the likes of which I'd never seen. As no stranger to pus, I gladly rose to this new healing challenge. A quick consult with homeopathic vet Dr. Michele Yasson revealed that the remedy for ocular discharge is the aptly-named eyebright, also known as *Euphrasia officinalis*. I began administering the tiny white pellets to my pretty pupcake— placing them onto the gum and gently holding her jaw shut, as I'd always done with arnica—and her eyes cleared up in about a week.

And then someone else arrived on the scene, another brunette beauty with a therapeutic tip just for me—not a dog this time, but a veterinarian. I received a message from one of the docs who worked with Vet-Stem, Dr. Julie Ryan Johnson; she'd been my point person during Sam's treatment. As had happened with so many people I've been lucky to "meet" and interview by phone, we'd bonded. Throughout the lows and highs of Sam's stem cell saga, Dr. Julie had been a constant, comforting voice— from her early reservations that Vet-Stem would be able to collect even one vial of viable cells from my elder statesdog, to the indescribable elation of discovering that we obtained fourteen viable vials, to the day in 2008 that Sam came home from the hospital a changed dog. The last time Dr. Julie and I had spoken was earlier that year, when Sam received a booster shot of his own cells, which had been stored on ice for him at Vet-Stem HQ. Dr. Julie said she was visiting New York on business, and invited me to join her for lunch. Although I couldn't wait to meet her, I hardly suspected that lunch would alter the course of my life.

It was friendship at first sight. I told Dr. Julie about my condition and my concerns about rejoining the dating scene at age forty-four; although I'd made peace with my scar, there was still the matter of the ongoing relapses, a less-than-romantic prospect for any long-term intimate partner. Cutting right to the chase as only vets do, Dr. Julie asked why I hadn't investigated stem cells to fix my problem? Lightbulb! It had simply never occurred to me. I'd come to accept that my condition was something I couldn't change because the sole option my doctor had presented—fistulotomy—was unacceptable to me due to the incontinence risk. So I focused my efforts on helping my dogs overcome their miscellaneous health hurdles, then writing about them to help others. It never occurred to me to question the judgment of the doctor who'd "saved my butt" back in 1999, or to seek out alternative modalities for myself. Now, I was intrigued. How would I find out more? Easily, Dr. Julie said: by going to ClinicalTrials.gov and typing "perirectal fistula" into the search field. So it was as simple as that? I was still trying to get my head around the idea that stem cells might cure what ailed me.

No sooner was our lunch over than I made a beeline for my computer to see which, if any, trials were recruiting patients. Right off the bat, I came across this:

Study #NCT00475410, "Efficacy and Safety of Adipose Stem Cells to Treat Complex Perianal Fistulas Not Associated to Crohn's Disease."

Bingo! It was precisely what I was looking for—astonishingly precise, to be exact. The sudden realization that my condition afflicted enough people to motivate doctors to perform such an investigation was profoundly empowering; PF *was* serious, and these physicians were giving it its proper due. The study involved three varieties of experimental treatment: In the first, subjects would be treated with a dose of twenty million ASCs and evaluated after twelve weeks. If needed, a second dose of forty million ASCs would be applied then. In the second version, subjects would receive a dose of twenty million ASCs plus fibrin glue, a surgical tissue adhesive, and evaluated after twelve weeks. If needed, a second dose of forty million ASCs plus fibrin glue would be applied then. Lastly, the third version involved treating subjects with a dose of fibrin glue alone—no stem cells—and evaluated after twelve weeks. If needed a second dose of fibrin glue would be applied then. According to the study description:

> *Perianal fistula accounts for 10% to 30% of coloproctological surgical procedures. Currently accepted conventional treatment is surgery intended to treat the tracts using different technical options. This surgery usually has a highly bothersome postoperative period and may involve two major complications: anal incontinence and recurrence. The biological properties of stem cells derived from adult tissues make them adequate candidates for the treatment of diseases in which tissues are damaged or the healing process is altered. This study will compare the efficacy of ASCs versus ASCs plus Fibrin adhesive versus Fibrin adhesive alone for closure of complex perianal fistulas not associated to Inflammatory Bowel Disease. Fistula closure is defined as absence of suppuration and re-epithelization of the external opening in the clinical evaluation and absence of collections >2 cm directly related to the fistula tract treated, as measured by MRI.*

Reading about this study did three important things for me: (1) validated my decision to refuse a fistulotomy out of concern of being left incontinent; (2) began my education in medical terminology—for instance, nobody on the team at the hospital where I was treated in '99 had ever used the word *suppuration* when referring to persistent drainage from my surgical site; (3) inspired me to start sharing the story of stem cells in the human medical sphere, to help others who, like me, might be helped. On that day, I diversified my advocacy, becoming my own patient advocate as well as my dogs' wellness watchdog. I began poring over medical abstracts the way I pored over urgent alerts about dogs in need of rescue. It was starting to feel as if I were taking a crash course in stem cell therapy by auditing classes at the most sophisticated medical school in the world.

To be eligible for the study, volunteers had to be eighteen years and older. Among the other criteria for inclusion, one had to have a complex perianal fistula (check) and at least one prior surgery for a fistulous disease (check). Being pregnant or lactating and having acute sepsis were among the exclusion criteria; I was neither, so I was good to go. The clinical trial would be taking place in Madrid, Spain. I e-mailed the principal investigator, Dr. Damián García-Olmo, as yet knowing nothing of his tremendous stature in the world of cell medicine or his rightful place on the timeline of fistula treatment technology. Little did I know that this was not unlike e-mailing one of the "Big Four" founding professors at Johns Hopkins Hospital, if electronic mail had only existed during their tenure. So, when the doctor e-mailed me right back, just two short hours later, I didn't fully appreciate the significance of this very busy scientist taking time to respond, so promptly and with such kindness:

> *Dear Julia,*
>
> *I'm sorry to inform you that the recruitment is now finished. I hope this clinical trial will permit the stem cells' use in all patients in a few months.*
>
> *All the best,*
> *Dr. García-Olmo*

I was launched on a mission: to get treated with my own stem cells just as Sam had been. I'd been an outspoken advocate for pet patients since the day I was denied the tetanus antitoxin for my dog. Now, six years on, I became my own health advocate. My goal was to be treated like a dog, by a doctor as competent and compassionate as a vet. Would that even be possible? I was determined—doggedly determined—to find out. Because the trial was completed, with a very encouraging 83 percent success rate, then surely I could receive the same treatment somewhere else? After all, it was proven effective at the prestigious Spanish teaching hospital, La Paz University Hospital in Madrid. All a doctor had to do was study Dr. García-Olmo's abstract—right? For the first time, I had hope that I would very swiftly find a solution to the medical problem that had vexed me for the preceding ten years. Yet ten years—ten *more* years—was how long the experts were saying it would take before stem cells would become available to American patients, and that was an optimistic estimate. Although my dogs could be treated with their own stem cells, I could not. My dog's cells could be expanded in the laboratory—cultured to multiply their strength in numbers—but mine could not. For dogs, the future of medicine was happening now in the United States, but American humans still had to wait. Wasn't that a crazy situation? It became abundantly clear that, in order to find effective relief from the condition that had cramped my style for the past decade, I'd be traveling abroad in the very near future—whether to Spain or to some other destination where such restrictions didn't hamper the progress of visionary doctors and their anxious and willing patients.

This prospect presented more than a philosophical challenge to wrap my head around. I'm a patriot, the only child of two brave people who left Europe for the United States in search of the better life all immigrants seek. I'd always assumed that here in America we have the best of the best medical care, and it pained me to realize that, sadly, we do not. Now that I was faced with the practical necessity of dusting off my passport and traveling in search of the care I needed, I'd have to find a safe, reputable place to look after my dogs for the duration of my eventual treatment, wherever in the world that was going to take place. My dogs had grounded me from long-distance travel for many years, as it was tough to find caretakers I could trust. Now, the hunt was on for a safe, solid place to board my dogs when the inevitable day would arrive—very soon, I was completely confident!—when I'd leave home to receive treatment.

Happily, just one month earlier, I'd learned of a brand-new establishment called Unleash Brooklyn, whose owners described as a "holistic loft for cats and dogs." The place looked and smelled immaculate and was constructed entirely of green materials. Offering doggie day-care and overnight boarding—completely cage-free—it was also the home base of Dog Habitat Rescue, where the refugees are treated as royally as the paying clients. Canine guests enjoy supervised play time in three roomy runs outfitted with shock-absorbing, recycled-rubber flooring.

Now that I was set on my healing path, with a safe haven to park my pets when the need arose, the next step was to determine my destination.

For that, I turned back to the Internet—but with an entirely new attitude. It was back-to-school time, the 'Net would become my next alma mater, and I had lots of studying to do. This homework would be fun, for it would enable me to research my disease to keep informed about the latest scientific progress. Upon matriculating at 'Net U, I undertook a course of learning that would take nearly four full years to complete—the same time it took to earn my B.A.—but this campus had satellites all over the globe. My stem cell scholarship would be the equivalent of an extended Junior Year Abroad. During my college years, regrettably, I never availed myself of the glamorous junior-year travel option; nor did I go on a single date. I was a certifiable tool—a "Black & Decker," in campus parlance. Now, for my self-styled academic concentration in stem cell studies, I would do things differently. Travel would be a requirement during this school session, not merely an option. As for love, perhaps it didn't have to hurt the way it did when I was married. Certain people, like certain pharmaceuticals, simply should not mix. X and I brought out the worst in each other; we were "highly clinically significant," like a major drug interaction in which the risk far outweighs the benefit. Every interaction between people carries some risk to the parties' physical and mental health. If love is a potent controlled substance, the safest thing would be to abstain from dating entirely, but I had no intention of going that route. Instead, I would assess and minimize risk, then do my utmost to—in the phrase of my defensive driving instructor—leave myself an out. Maybe, instead of being avoided, love could be a healthy, extracurricular activity one harnesses to heal, the way one leashes oneself to an unconditionally loving Medicine Dog. Maybe love didn't have to be a four-letter word. At any rate, as I was about to learn, looking for the L-word would definitely be part of my educational experience.

CHAPTER 9

Medical Tourist Traps

Welcome to Internet U, your virtual medical school, where you get around by surfing. Roam the campus freely to learn all about your illness, creative ways to cope with it, and the doctors working toward innovative cures. I'm a fool for a nice library, and the science libe of Internet U is an amazing resource that enables you to stay abreast of medical news that perhaps your physician isn't keeping pace with; this information is available to all web users, not just those with an MD degree. Plus, in this libe you're encouraged to chat; you'll find all sorts of people to commiserate and laugh with, and that's tremendously liberating—as comedian Ben Morrison, who has Crohn's disease, proves with his brilliant "Pain in the Butt" routine. Medical knowledge really is power, but first you have to know how to access it. Just because the information is out there doesn't mean it's ready to jump out at you on the first, or even twenty-first, search. Understand that reputable doctors and clinics don't always invest in advertising or other types of marketing—they are more concerned with treating patients than promoting themselves or courting publicity, so their sites probably won't be designed for maximum SEO (search engine optimization), the newfangled form of marketing that capitalizes on keywords and often-searched-for images. Or the doctor you need to find might not even have a site. To increase your chances of scoring new and useful data each time you surf the Web, vary the search's geographical location and web browser. Recruit friends to help you search. There have been times I've Googled something to do with stem cells while on the phone with someone clear across the country, whose simultaneous search yielded an entirely different informational haul. Incidentally, remember that Google is not the only search engine; there's Dogpile, Bing, Ask . . . use more than one, and vary your search terms. One way I ultimately learned to find stem cell stories was to pretend that I'm something I am not: anti–adult stem cells. Entering the search terms "stem cell snake oil" or "stem cell strip mall" yields useful information, because many vocal critics of ASC harp on the fact that its practitioners are located in strip malls, as if they should set up shop . . . where, in national parks, or landmarked town houses?

As it happened, a landmarked town house temporarily did become a healing haven for me, although there were no doctors on the premises. I'd become quite friendly with some neighbors, partners in a business located about ten blocks from my apartment. I'll call them V and The Babe. V was single and extremely eligible, huge into dog rescue, with primary custody of the four dogs he and The Babe had rescued over a period of years. Tall, pale, and handsome, V was a vegetarian with exquisite taste in clothing, art, and home furnishings. He was also gentle and evolved, a fan of philosopher Eckhart Tolle; so moved was he by *The Power of Now* that he'd bought numerous copies to hand out to friends and acquaintances. Ten years my senior, he stayed in excellent shape thanks to moonlight runs round the Central Park Reservoir; a skin-cancer scare made him shun the sun. With granny glasses perched on his nasal bridge, this catch of a man resembled a cute, contradictory cross between two of my Enlightenment heroes: Thomas Jefferson and Ben Franklin. Our values were in synch, for he fed his dogs premium food and thought nothing of driving several miles outside city limits for the best veterinary care. His place of business was a generously proportioned town house, one of the most beautiful in New York City, and he lived high above the store in a modest one-bedroom apartment.

I began to notice that whenever I'd arrive to visit The Babe, V would smile broadly and stand up from whatever he was doing to come over for a hug. One time, he ran out the door, then reappeared a few minutes later with a loaf cake from the bakery around the corner for us all to share. I suspected he liked me a little, but I was loath to rock the boat by being so bold as to ask him out without clearing it with The Babe; we were all friends, plus V and The Babe had been lovers some twenty years prior and were still very close. Finally, I overcame my trepidation to ask The Babe if I might please have her permission to invite V out for a date?

"I've thought of this," she said. The Babe thought of everything. "The two of you have so much in common."

I waited for a signal from The Babe; months went by, but nothing happened. Finally, I figured she just wasn't feeling that matchmaker motivation, and if a move was to be made, I'd have to make it. It was a few days before Christmas; The Babe and family would be spending the holiday upstate, which meant V would be in the city, alone with the dogs. I summoned the courage to tell her that I wanted to invite V to see Robert Downey Jr. do his Sherlock Holmes thing on the movie's Christmas opening. In short order, I received a phone message from V himself. "[The Babe] says you'd like to go to the flicks," he said, warmly welcoming me to call and make plans.

On Christmas Day, I stood in the movie line, reading the Tolle book, then grabbed two seats when the doors opened. The previews started; where was my date? The door to the darkened cinema flew open just as the movie started; V took his seat beside me, whispering that he'd lost track of the time because he'd been mesmerized listening to Bach. What a sweet and original excuse! After the movie, V took me for a lovely vegan dinner, then walked me home. It was a perfect, courtly first date. We swiftly became an item, and I couldn't have been happier. V had said he wanted to learn how to cook, and I gave him culinary tutorials in his enormous kitchen equipped with a Viking range that heretofore had been used for pot-and-pan storage. When V came down with the flu, I went into full Florence Nightingale mode, treating him with the same TLC I gave my beloved dogs. My combination of remedies—notably a curative tea made of lemons, ginger, cinnamon, cloves, and raw honey—fixed V in record time.

"I didn't know we had a white witch in the family," The Babe remarked, asking for my lemon-tea recipe.

V and I attended some glamorous events at a range of cultural venues, from the Brooklyn Academy of Music to the Metropolitan Opera; we got all steamy at the Russian-Turkish Baths; but those wonderfully homey evenings in his kitchen were my favorite times together. I remember putting the finishing touches on a curry as he made his nocturnal tour of the reservoir; he returned to remark on how the aroma had beckoned him from the street. Later, I would overcome my hatred of jogging to join him. We'd run across town, stop to enjoy dinner at a vegan restaurant, then return to his place by cab for more canoodling before I went home to my dogs.

It would take many long weeks before we became intimate, however. We'd have extended makeout sessions in his office and kitchen, with me becoming increasingly clear about letting V know how much I desired him. When, in utter frustration, I sneaked up behind him and pulled down his sweatpants, he gasped theatrically like a Catholic school girl auditioning for the lead in *The Sound of Music*. None of my overtures were refused—in fact, quite the opposite, he'd practically swoon—so I knew he was warming up to the idea of s-e-x. At long last, all indications pointed to Valentine's Day as the date we'd finally do The Deed. The day arrived and we proceeded to the elevator, then upstairs to his inner sanctum, the flat at the top of the building. Finally, I thought, pumping a mental fist. Reclining with me on his bed, V interrupted our embrace to make this confession: "I haven't been with anyone for nineteen years." V, you see, is for Vampire. I was about to free New York's most eligible undead bachelor from his coffin. Ever since overcoming drug addiction after a stay at a renowned rehab facility, building his business left him no time for a relationship. I told him not to worry, that we'd take it as slow as he needed. He'd helped me with my running, I explained—now, we could approach this as a different kind of workout, with me as his trainer! He laughed, but as things grew more heated, he kept crying out, "I can't!" To which I said he absolutely could—and he did. Austin had given me this healing gift; I was glad to pay it forward to V. Cuddling in post-coital contentment, I stared at my sleeping sweetheart. I'd never seen a vintage photograph of him but could now clearly picture him thirty years younger, as if a Photoshop chip were implanted in my brain. What I saw was not this bald head on the pillow, but its twenty-something version 1.0 with a full mop of tousled blond hair. We took a break for me to run and check on my dogs. I distributed snacks and gave relief walks to everyone, then walked Sheba back with me to V's.

It was now six months after my medical consciousness-raising, yet despite numerous attempts to locate a doctor somewhere in the world willing to duplicate Dr. García-Olmo's procedure, or a new clinical trial recruiting patients, I was having no luck. Luckily for me, Dr. Bob Harman was traveling to New York and agreed to meet for coffee and a visit to the Humane Society of New York. I explained my situation, and he promised to put me in touch with scientist-entrepreneur Neil Riordan, PhD, with whom Dr. Bob had coauthored a couple of stem cell research publications. Riordan's Stem Cell Institute operated two clinics, one in Costa Rica and the other in Panama. Since 2006, some 400 patients, most of them Americans, had been treated by local doctors at these two venues for arthritis, multiple sclerosis, and spinal injuries. The Institute did not use embryonic cells; like Vet-Stem, it used only adult (autologous) cells harvested from patients' own fat and bone marrow, and from donated umbilical cord blood. After Dr. Bob got on the case, things moved ahead with lightning speed: He introduced me to Neil via e-mail; we had a very productive conversation, and Neil graciously offered to treat me at no charge, in the interest of science. He would arrange for a GI surgeon in Costa Rica to duplicate Dr. García-Olmo's procedure so that more people with fistulas and other IBDs could find relief without risking incontinence.

I was thrilled that my procedure would benefit not only me but also my fellow fistula sufferers, who would soon have a place to go to find the most sophisticated form of treatment for our historically vexing malady. Dr. García-Olmo had kindly offered to answer any questions the surgeons might have, and weren't we in luck that there'd be no language barrier! As all medical professionals do, Neil inquired as to who was my doctor, so I told him the truth: I didn't have one. Although I regularly visited Dr. Jablow, my dentist, and my excellent doctor of chiropractic Joyce Nawy, I was not in the care of a gastroenterologist, or even a general practitioner—I was actively steering clear of physicians, preferring to deal pretty much exclusively with veterinarians, including the excellent holistic vet practitioner Dr. Michele Yasson, an Iron Man triathlete and model of wellness who moonlights as a health coach for people. To his credit, Neil did not laugh me off the phone. Instead, he referred me to one of the very best physicians in the country, his friend the board-certified gastrointestinal surgeon Leonard Smith of Florida, who agreed to a telephone consultation. So many times in my career as a journalist I'd made vital connections by telephone, forging bonds with extraordinary people that would last many years despite our never meeting in person. Yet I didn't imagine that telephony is how I'd find the real medical thing: a doctor I could believe in and trust. Well, here he was. Dr. Smith spent close to an hour patiently discussing my condition and its probable cause, explaining everything with perfect clarity. His bedside manner was straight out of a movie and later, when I saw photographs of him, it turned out that he has matinee-idol looks, too. His zodiac sign is Scorpio; enlightening me about Scorpios, he explained, "We make great hit men, spies, and surgeons!" Dr. Smith's rising sign, Leo, explains his commitment to teaching and generously sharing information, as the zodiac's regal lions instinctively do. Afterward, although we hadn't met in person, I felt confident and proud to say that I did, indeed, have a doctor—a great one who actually cared enough to help me find the most sophisticated treatment for my problem, and who kept up to date on the latest medical innovations, especially as regards the healing potential of stem cells.

Here, at last, was a specimen of the rare breed of healer I'd been seeking: a physician as dedicated to scientific inquiry as the best veterinarians. Whereas the default answer of the surgeon who had treated me in 1999 was "I don't know," Dr. Smith didn't deal in default answers. Instead, he explained how I came to have PF in the first place: It was the result of "chronic bacterial overgrowth," an unusually toxic buildup of bad bacteria in my gut. "Picture millions of little men in hard hats drilling away at your intestine," Dr. Smith said. "Those are bad bacteria, and they finally got through, creating a tunnel—the fistula." He could appreciate my refusal to undergo a fistulotomy; although he'd successfully performed the procedure many times, he confessed that he always "sweated bullets" because he never wanted his patients to emerge from surgery with incontinence. I pictured Louis XIV's surgeon sweating bullets while operating on the king; Dr. Smith treated all his patients like royalty, because that's what Olympian healers do.

After reading the abstract about Dr. García-Olmo's trials, Dr. Smith allowed that "this could be one of the most important breakthroughs in the treatment of IBD." When he asked if I had any other medical issues,

I mentioned my occasional bouts of Raynaud's Syndrome. Named after nineteenth-century French physician Maurice Raynaud, this disorder is the result of blood vessel spasms that block blood flow to the extremities, and it's triggered by cold and emotional stress. If you have Raynaud's, on cold days you might notice your palms looking beet-red, while your fingers, deprived of blood flow, appear yellowish-white and feel tingly or numb. This condition can cramp your style while out on a wintry dog walk. Dr. Smith reckoned that an intravenous injection of my stem cells would likely help alleviate my Raynaud's symptoms, too.

Ten years almost to the date of my emergency surgery, I finally had real answers and a real reason to hope—and all thanks to Dr. Bob, the veterinarian who'd pioneered the stem cell procedure that enabled my crippled dog to walk again. I was overcome with gratitude and excited that finding a cure with my own cells was now within reach. Dr. Smith promised that he would scrub in to my procedure, which about left me speechless. Prior to this conversation, I didn't have so much as a primary physician; now I'd found a consulting specialist and genuine patient advocate—and they were one and the same doc. An integrative practitioner, Dr. Smith was a big believer in probiotics, and recommended that I start taking RenewLife brand's Ultimate Flora Critical Colon BifidoMax supplement, which delivers eighty billion live cultures per capsule of fourteen beneficial bacteria strains. Until my stem cells could be deployed to repair the damage done by the bad-bacteria invasion, the good bacteria in those capsules would patrol my digestive borders, protecting the war zone in my gut from further devastation.

Although I identify as a Taurus, I was born at the tail end of the bullish sign, May 20, which sits squarely on the cusp of Gemini, the sign of the journalist. And the journalist in me knew I had a hot story on my hands, even if it was my own story. So I got to work pitching a first-person account of seeking stem cell therapy to a publication whose readers care about matters of health. Identifying the magazine I most wanted to carry the story of how my sentinel dog Sam had set me on the path to high-tech treatment, I worked up a proposal letter. I completed the pitch and hit "Send," receiving a response welcoming me to submit long-form writing samples. Now, all I had to do was sit back and wait for my treatment date in Costa Rica. I had something pleasant to distract me: I was in a committed relationship and very happy about it; The Babe, very much less so. V and I would be snuggled up on his sofa of a weekend evening, watching a DVD, and she'd call him to natter on about nothing in particular. One evening, V located an enormous tick on one of his dogs and immediately jumped on the phone to call The Babe for guidance, even though tick elimination is a particular talent of mine, and I'd already removed the blood-engorged varmint.

One morning, I needed to take two dogs to the Humane Society clinic: Tiki, for a checkup, and Cupcake, to get spayed. V kindly offered to drive us. I brought the dogs out and met V at the back of his vehicle. Both dogs were safely loaded in when, suddenly, something came down hard on the top of my head. As if expecting an avalanche, I dropped to the ground with my head in my hands. Looking up at V, I saw him staring down at me coldly. "You're joking," he said. The hatch was down; V had released it prematurely and my head had gotten in the way. Silly head! The top of the skull happens to be the softest and most vulnerable, so I asked V to please wait while I ran inside to get something: the homeopathic remedy *Arnica montana*, for bruising and trauma. I returned to the car and we proceeded to the hospital—the animal hospital. I have my priorities. Besides, as I'd learned years earlier, after banging my forehead on the edge of a propped-open glass door, there's little doctors can do for a concussion. At the next light, I tried to show V the impressive Wile E. Coyote bump on my head, indicating where it was so he could get a feel for its Looney Tunes proportions. To my surprise, he indignantly replied, "I'm not going to feel your head!"

We arrived at the animal hospital and offloaded the dogs, then returned to the car. V took me to an Italian cafe for hot cocoa and blueberry scones. "When I don't get enough sleep, I cock things up," he explained, by way of apology. So this accident was my own fault, for molesting the poor dear past his bedtime. "From now on, I must be in bed no later than 10:00 p.m.," he said. That didn't leave us much together time, as V was frequently meeting clients as late as 8:00 p.m. But I wanted to make this relationship work, so I practiced lightning-fast dinner-fixing then, like an X-rated Cinderella, speed-seducing my sweetheart before the clock struck 10:00 p.m. And because I'm a reporter with plenty of experience beating the clock for deadlines, I got pretty good at it. After a while, however, this routine grew exhausting and enervating; I asked V if I might please have access to the kitchen earlier, so I could prepare dinner ahead? No, he said; The Babe was concerned that I was an insurance risk in the kitchen by myself.

It was the first indication that The Babe openly disapproved of our relationship. And yet, ironically, the only one at risk in that kitchen was me; most of what I ate there was a recipe for digestive disaster. V was violently allergic to avocados, which agree with me; but I abstained out of respect for him, figuring it might not be good for him to be exchanging body fluids with someone whose cells smacked of a fruit that made him ill. A staple of V's diet was meat substitutes, so we were eating lots of "hot dogs" and "sausage" made of textured vegetable protein (TVP), i.e., unfermented soy, which doesn't agree with my digestive system. In meatless dishes, I prefer meaty mushrooms and a medley of toothsome veggies. V loved having fruit for dessert, which I later learned is a no-no for me. One evening after our meal, V noticed that my stomach looked quite distended. It was hard not to notice: The fast-digesting fruit was fermenting in my gut atop a pile of slow-processing TVP, so I appeared dramatically bloated, wearing the result of fruit-for-dessert. "Lookit Mummy's tummy!" V said, wide-eyed with amazement. It's tough enough to deal with IBD without your bowel getting all inflamed on you right there at the dinner table with your sweetheart. What could I say? "That's my intestine getting angry"? Isn't *that* romantic! So I made a joke—but my quip was more inflammatory than any bowel disease: "Maybe I'm pregnant?"

You could have heard a pin drop in Central Park. "Whaaaaaat?" V said, his jaw nearly dropping to the floor like Marley's ghost in *A Christmas Carol*. "A baby is the last thing I need!"

"Aw . . . what's wrong with a little baby?" I cooed. "That would mean my stem cells are healthy and vital!" V was horrified. He denied me sex until he felt assured that I was using a reliable birth control method. At around this time, something else was pregnant with possibility: I received a call from Costa Rica with wonderful news. The doctors at the hospital there were very close to locating a GI surgeon. My surgery would happen any week now, and all I had to do was arrange for someone to accompany me because, as Neil had explained, "A liposuction is not a cakewalk—you can't go it alone." The total time away would be five days. Feeling secure in my relationship with V, I assumed he'd join me on my stem cell pilgrimage. Over dinner, which I'd just cooked, I told V of the wonderful Costa Rica development. When I got to the part about a travel companion, he put on a worried look and said, "Well then, we must find someone!"

Crushed, I said I'd hoped that someone would be him.

"I can't just drop everything and go with you to the Dominican Republic."

"It's Costa Rica."

"Same difference!"

Somehow, my joyful health development had given rise to our first argument. The following day, I let V know how much it hurt that he wasn't even trying to consider coming with me—and how, if he should ever need surgery, I'd surely be by his side in a heartbeat.

"That's not fair," he said, frowning crossly. "Perhaps if you'd asked nicely . . . but you can't go around demanding that people drop everything to go with you to the Dominican Republic!"

"Costa Rica."

"Whatever! Besides, what's your hurry? You've lived with this thing for eleven years."

Whoa. I didn't think I hadn't asked nicely, for starters. In my opinion, what wasn't nice was his not bothering to remember the destination. Moreover, I was surprised and stung by the "what's your hurry" bit: *You've lived with this thing for eleven years.* Forgive me for jumping at an opportunity to find relief from years of pain—what was I thinking, how terribly gauche of me! Evidently, the world views us "medical tourists" as a selfish, wanderlustful lot. Our conditions must not be that serious, or we wouldn't be traveling; we just use illness as an excuse to see the world. The issue would turn out to be moot. I received another encouraging e-mail from the magazine, asking a few pertinent followup questions; I replied to all questions, only to receive this the next day:

Thanks so much, Julia. But jeez, what a difference a day makes. I was just Googling the Costa Rican Stem Cell Institute (I wanted to get some numbers—how many people have gotten stem cell therapies there), and saw that they're closing their doors today. Have you seen that? I'm sorry; I know that this is of much more than professional interest to you. Take a look at [link to Reuters article].

Let me know what you think of this (and whether you're still interested in pursuing treatment elsewhere—Spain?)

Best,

[Editor]

Of all the people you don't want to get this kind of newsflash from, I daresay the editor at the major magazine you'd just interested in your story tops the list. Happily, the news was not as bad as it seemed. I reached Neil Riordan by phone. The embodiment of grace under pressure, he was disappointed but not surprised by the way the media had reported the Costa Rica clinic's closing. He had not been "forced" to close it; faced with ever tighter restrictions, he simply decided to consolidate operations at the Panama clinic. Neil promised to do all he could to schedule my surgery in Panama as soon as possible. Once again, not surprisingly, the media had failed to report an adult stem cell story accurately. Shoddy reporting is largely responsible for the rise of the crisis public relations specialist, whose expert services are engaged to counteract the damage caused by just such journalistic blunders. Unfortunately, medical pioneers have more important things to do than joust with journalists who have an agenda, so they don't do the requisite damage control. Such careless reporting can actually hurt patients in need of treatment. Who knows how many people suffering with chronic disease were considering traveling to Costa Rica, but became permanently turned off by the Reuters story? This much I knew: I wasn't turned off; I was more eager than ever to receive treatment. And in an epiphany quite similar to the one occasioned when elevator pit stood up to hug me, I resolved to do my part in the media to counteract the negative press being heaped on adult stem cells and medical tourism.

A terminal case: Medical Tourist awaiting liftoff CATHERINE NANCE

This new inspiration arrived just as I was trying to get used to not having Sam for a living muse. Two months earlier, I'd written his obituary, which was also my last *Post* column, and the hardest one to write: "Sadness for Sam." After eleven years, the paper abruptly decided to "take the Pets page in a different direction." In our last collaboration as canine co-parents, X and I agreed that it was time to take Sam to the Bridge; our boy could no longer hold his head up and his wagless tail was firmly wedged between his hind legs. Compounding Sam's physical weakness was his obvious grief since the death of Pepper, his beloved companion, in January. X had insisted on letting her die at home, and I know her final moments were filled with the trauma of slow respiratory failure, which poor Sam witnessed, unable to help. Sam and Pepper had been a strong, solid item for eleven years. Like Britannia and Haus, they'd had the great marriage X and I could never work out. It was asking a lot to expect Sam to thrive without his sweet soul mate. By the third week of March, Sam was deteriorating terribly. I begged X not to let Sam go the way Pepper had. He finally relented, and on March 25, we took Sam for a drive, treating him to two cheeseburgers from J.G. Melon. Then we proceeded to the Humane Society for the lethal injection.

Shortly after I set my curative compass for Panama, V broke up with me—on the sidewalk, while walking his eldest dog, a hound mix named Chucky. The Babe called him in mid-breakup. The volume was turned up high on V's cell phone, so I could hear her pulling his marionette strings, as I'd suspected she'd been doing for weeks; she was going on about something burning in the kitchen. I was glad I couldn't be blamed for starting that fire, but oh, how I would miss noodling at that stove! I was touched that Chucky offered moral support by standing next to me.

"Please," I asked V while petting Chucky's head, "can't we just go home and make dinner?"

"No, my love—I can't do this anymore."

There was no more room in this *Dark Shadows* triangle for me. I turned and walked toward my apartment without looking back. That was a long block and a half. It was a stunning quadruple loss: No Sam, no surgery, no column—and now, no romance. How was I going to make ends meet? What would we do for dog food? The stress was overwhelming. Thankfully,

Poor Cupcake keenly felt my stress.

I had my best friends, the Medicine Dogs, at home. Cupcake and Laz tucked themselves into bed. Poor old Sheba's rapidly advancing arthritis meant she could no longer access the mattress; lifting her onto the bed, I applied the dogs and tried to sleep. I couldn't, I wouldn't, let them down.

CHAPTER 10

Political Animal

In August 2010, just four short months after my termination by the newspaper I'd served for a decade and a year, I was offered a new gig by the website Dogster. I would be their "Living with Dogs" columnist, producing one blog posting per weekday. This presented a wonderful opportunity to do what I love: help my fellow dog lovers with the latest wellness scoop, while chronicling the miscellany, major and minor, of my own dogs' lives. The workload was daunting; how would I fill that much space, and with what? Happily, I lived with a pack of dedicated news hounds. Whenever I hurt for material or inspiration, one of the dogs in my care—whether a permanent pet or a foster—would oblige by doing something out of the ordinary, and that would turn into a story. In their wordless way, the dogs were actively giving me valuable tips, so I learned to watch them closely for cues. I had only the woof pack to thank for enabling me to churn out the required number of articles per week! Truly appreciating the adage "health is wealth" as never before, I resolved to extend my dogs' lives as long as possible. Dogster soon named me its Health Editor and "Alternative Pet Health Guru."

Dr. García-Olmo's words had been so straightforwardly optimistic: "*I hope this clinical trial will permit the stem cells' use in all patients in a few months.*" But that was Spain. According to the doctors routinely quoted in the American media, here in the United States the possibility of stem cell treatment was still "ten years away," give or take. So now, not only was veterinary medicine ahead of human medicine in the United States but also European medical technology had officially surpassed its American counterpart. Our medical advances lagged seriously behind those of other countries—and failed to keep pace with the great strides made by veterinary researchers right here at home. It would take me some time to digest these shocking epiphanies; as a patriot and proud owner of *American* pit bull terriers, I was loath to accept this poor diagnosis of US health care. As a reporter, my beat had been veterinary medicine; now I was about to shift gears to focus on human medicine, and the contrast was striking. In America, vets were deploying stem cells to help their four-footed patients, while American people were being told that they couldn't receive the same type of treatment. What was the good of having an Affordable Care Act if the so-called care was inferior? But before I could really sink my teeth into this controversy, a new health crisis arose in the animal house: While I wasn't looking, my latest rescue sank his teeth into a highly toxic substance.

Redmond's red coat earned him the name of Ryan O'Neal's red-haired character in the movie *Barry Lyndon;* I'd pulled this magnificent mutt from an animal shelter in Louisiana, one of many that had become overwhelmed after the oil spill in the Gulf of Mexico, as thousands of

Redmond, the handsome troublemaker from down south ANNELI ADOLFSSON

pets were surrendered by people who'd lost everything. Somehow, Redmond managed to unearth a plastic squeeze bottle of Gorilla Glue I didn't even know lurked in the apartment. To the dog, this object looked like a fine chew toy. But Gorilla Glue happens to be one of the most hazardous home-improvement items; a polyurethane adhesive, it expands and hardens to form its famously tough seal. If ingested, it will bond to your insides and cause gastrointestinal blockage, which could prove fatal. There was no way to tell if Redmond had eaten any of the glue; the container looked close to full, but I didn't know whether it had been unopened before Redmond found it. His fangs had left impressive perforations in the plastic bottle, plus he was wearing the sticky stuff on his fur. We raced to the Animal Medical Center, where the ER doc explained how she'd once had to remove hardened Gorilla Glue from the GI tract of a Labrador retriever; if Redmond did have glue in his gut, he'd have to be operated on to the tune of four thousand dollars. But it wasn't clear from the radiograph whether the gray matter in his gut was glue, or his still-digesting evening meal. After clipping off the sticky fur patches, the vet advised me to take Redmond home and observe him for changes; his subsequent bowel movements were perfectly normal, as were his appetite and energy level. Crisis averted; it was time to put my nose to the ground and resume reporting on adult stem cells.

Discussing health care in America means talking politics. My politics can be summed up like this: Nothing is more important than every American's right to have the dog he or she wants—and every American's right to receive the best, most sophisticated medical treatment right here on US soil. I'd always viewed political issues through a filter of animal welfare; now stem cells determined my criteria for competence in a candidate. And the politicos who "got" the stem cell debate, who were in the right as to the critical distinction between embryonic and adult cells, were *on* the right. So, in a poignant irony, just as I was fired from the ultra-conservative *New York Post*, the right-wing tabloid my liberal friends gave me endless grief about, I came around to conservatism. One year later, when Rick Perry—a vocal supporter of adult stem cells since 2009—entered the presidential race and I publicly endorsed him, the liberals in my life reckoned the unglued one was not Redmond, but me.

To fully appreciate this ideological 180, it helps to know that I received my formative education at the hands of left-leaning Democrats, at a prep school where New York City's blueblood limousine liberals parked their daughters, and where my hard-working immigrant parents scraped together whatever they had to secure me a good education. After Spence, I went on to graduate from a college whose student body is well known for its liberal activism. Three years before I started my academic career at Vassar, its students made headlines by vehemently rejecting the proposed commencement speaker, conservative commentator William F. Buckley Jr. The naysayers had circulated a petition that was signed by a majority of the class's 555 students, 301 of them to be exact. Buckley had no choice but to withdraw, but he hit back, hard. In a letter to Virginia Smith, then-president of the college, he called Vassar students "a fearfully ill-instructed body," adding, "I have spoken, I suppose, at 500 colleges and universities in the past 30 years and nowhere have I encountered that blend of ferocious illiteracy." I admired the agitprop attitude of that class's graduating seniors who, under their commencement robes, wore "ferocious illiterate" T-shirts custom-printed for the occasion.

Most of my closest friends are die-hard liberals; I have only ever voted a Democratic ticket. For the historic 2008 election, my polling place was the lobby of a building housing a dry cleaning establishment; inhaling those chemical fumes and knowing just how toxic they are, I nonetheless stood in line for well over an hour to cast my vote. I was enraptured with the candidate who, upon winning, promised to visit an animal shelter when looking for the dog he'd promised his adorable daughters, because, as he explained, shelter dogs are "mutts like me." It was the most endearing political promise imaginable and I believed he'd make good on it. I managed to stay employed as the *Post*'s Pets columnist for eleven years by adopting a "bi-pawtisan" approach, diligently keeping my editorial focus on something red and blue constituents agree on: Animals make excellent companions. So how did my politics go to the dogs? The short answer: stem cells. They make strange bedfellows. Now, what if you're blue, politically speaking, but the one doctor who has the cure to what ails you or your child, spouse, or parent happens to be red? Would you refuse treatment based on ideological differences? Maybe you would, but I wouldn't.

I'd already written a few articles about pets for the conservative politi-cal site PJMedia, including one about (surprise) the pit bull. Now, I was about to dive off the deep end of the polemical pool, launching headfirst into the two topics most unfit for polite society: politics and religion. Always a sucker for an underdog and an underreported story, I took up the cause of adult stem cells as vocally as I'd championed pit bulls. Both had been unfairly misrepresented by the mainstream media, and the way I saw it, the consequences of the resultant misunderstanding were harm-ful to the public. I sincerely believe it's doing people a disservice to deny them Medicine Dogs by categorically portraying pit bulls in the media as snarling demons. Happily, other journalists were taking up the pro-pit cause (notably *Sports Illustrated*'s Jim Gorant, who authored the book *The Lost Dogs,* about Michael Vick's canine victims) and filmmakers were harnessing the power of the documentary to raise awareness of anti-pit prejudice. I felt OK relaxing my grip on the pit bull polemic's leash han-dle to come out swinging as a staunch supporter of adult stem cells—and a critic of the mainstream media's relentless demonizing of them.

In July 2010, I marked my conservative coming-out in a PJMedia story titled "The Pro-Life Case for Adult Stem Cell Treatment." It started like this:

> *The mainstream media rarely misses a chance to point out that animal medical care in the United States is almost on par with the best in human health care. But the reality is that the level of animal medi-cal innovation has actually surpassed that of human medicine—and mainstream media bias is partly to blame.*

I described Sam's success with his own stem cells, and how seeing my old dog walk never failed to raise the question, "Can they do this for people, too?" I quoted Dr. Bob Harman:

> *Vet-Stem has received hundreds of comments in the past few years from dog owners lamenting that they cannot get the same treatment that their pets are getting. They also ask frequently for recommenda-tions of where to go to get treated overseas. After* Nightline *did a story*

on Vet–Stem, many of the comments on the ABC website were from people who were frustrated that pets could get stem cells and they could not. I believe our data are helping people understand that adult stem cells from fat tissue really work. Our client veterinarians have treated over 6,000 animal patients with great success and great safety.

Incidentally, as of Vet-Stem's tenth year, 2013, the animal patient count rose to 10,000.

My article went on to describe the Institute of Cellular Medicine in Panama and its expansion to accommodate patients in the wake of the Costa Rica clinic's closing. I described one of the patients who had undergone treatment in Costa Rica:

As for proof, albeit anecdotal, of the Institute's treatments' effectiveness, conspicuously absent from the Reuters article of June 2 and its June 7 follow-up story was the curious case of Juan Carlos Murillo, 30, one of Riordan's satisfied customers. A commercial pilot, Murillo had been confined to a wheelchair, paralyzed from the waist down in a 2008 airplane crash. Today, after several treatments with adult stem cells harvested from donated umbilical cord blood, Murillo can walk without assistance. He was evaluated by a neurologist at the University of Miami; in spinal cord injury cases, spontaneous neurological restoration rarely happens, and spontaneous restoration of bladder/ bowel/erectile function virtually never happens. In Murillo's case, all of the above happened.

Murillo would later pass his flight physical and resume his career as a commercial pilot. Reuters' follow-up story interviewed a couple of Americans who, having undergone treatment in Costa Rica, were "outraged" to hear of the clinic's closing.

Curious to hear from Americans who would dare to book passage to Panama even after such a media "scandal," I interviewed one of them for PJMedia: Texan Sam Harrell. A high school football coach who'd been diagnosed with multiple sclerosis in 2005, he was fulfilling his coaching duties from a golf cart and dreading early retirement due to his worsening condition. After watching videotaped testimonials from the Institute's patients on YouTube, Harrell converted his very observant Christian community—which, like many communities, had assumed that all stem cells are embryonic simply because those cells get so much more press:

> *The initial response of Harrell's friends, neighbors, and fellow worshipers at the Creekside Church of Christ was disgust; but after he got done making the distinction between adult and embryonic stem cells, his community responded by raising the funds needed for their coach to be treated at Riordan's institute. Says Harrell, "Just the mention of stem cells, and people look at you like, Aren't we in America against that?"*

My article concluded with what I hoped would be a call to action:

> *Harrell's circle of supporters has a definite interest in helping him overcome MS; he's coached some very talented athletes, including his own son, Graham Harrell, who now plays for the Green Bay Packers. Keeping him on the field coaching young players ensures that the school's team stays on the athletic map. But all Americans should care about getting adult stem cells on the fast track for FDA approval. Doctors who use adult cells are not charlatans or faith healers; they are medical crusaders. Let us pray that the MSM can drop its bias, so more Americans with no other treatment options can learn about adult stem cells and reap the health benefits, right here at home—as our pets already can.*

That last sentence was a cry from my heart. As one of the "Americans with no other treatment options" my article described, I was awaiting treatment in the Panama City clinic, where Neil's team was working to locate a gastrointestinal specialist willing to duplicate the Madrid procedure on me. It was taking longer than expected, but Neil was confident they'd have success soon.

We bloggers are often obliged to recruit friends to comment on articles that could use the backup; that wasn't necessary in this case because, in the ultimate blogosphere validation, folks I didn't know were coming out to support my story unsolicited. Several comments came from Richard Humphries, who had undergone treatment for MS. Considering how debilitating Richard's condition had been prior to treatment, I was impressed to observe that he was now typing numerous fast, well-formulated comments—and swift replies to comments. To wit:

> *In April 2008 I basically went bedridden resulting from Secondary Progressive Multiple Sclerosis. After exhausting everything the US had to offer, I went down to Costa Rica for a stem cell treatment. With the lack of coordination, over 600 seizures, loss of cognition, fatigue, loss of hearing, numbness in feet and hands, muscle stiffness, tremendous pain, stumbling with occasional falls, using a cane and even my wife was forced into feeding me, I flew to Cell Medicine. Being the first patient to receive the adipose treatment along with the umbilical cord stem cells my life is only 85% improved.*

"Only" 85 percent improved! I appreciated the poetry of Richard's phrase "flew to Cell Medicine," encapsulating both medical tourism and the idea of the leap of faith needed to embrace the new and different, in medicine or anything else. This was a case of the comments actually making the story, and I watched with gratitude and gratification as they quickly accumulated.

One "Phillep Harding" wrote the following, in response to another comment that read, "I thought the US had the greatest health care around the world":

> *The US is best—overall—for many routine treatments. Other countries place fewer barriers in the way of new drugs and treatments. Sometimes good, sometimes it's bad (note "thalidomide"). A notable bit of foolishness is how the FDA requires an entirely new set of experiments before approving a drug or treatment for use in the US. Tests and experience outside the US mean nothing to the FDA, so we are not exactly "cutting edge."*

Another comment, accented with vehement capitalization, Gorilla-Glued my faith in adult stem cells and the doctors and scientists making them medical reality. I would gladly wait however long it took to undergo regenerative therapy, because to judge from this comment by "MDarty," it would be SO VERY WORTH IT:

> *I have also been one of the LUCKY ones to receive stem cells at Neil Riordan's clinic. Before, I was BED BOUND and HOUSE BOUND most days. I had horrible cognitive problems and was unable to even do most daily LIVING activities. Exhaustion was my middle name. After going to Costa Rica I am now feeling SO much better. I am able to do ALL that I want/need to do. I am NOT reliant on others for care. I walk for 30 minutes every day, I clean and do laundry and have even been able to go back to work. My cognitive abilities are so strong I am back in a "prestigious" position of my work. I can socialize with friends that I haven't seen in 8 years. Placebo? I think not. Amazing and simply a Godsend? YOU BETTER BELIEVE IT. I got my life back, and a BIG thank you to Neil for that . . . if not for him I do not know where I would be. THANK YOU NEIL for helping me find life again.*

No article about a medical procedure could be credible without input from a doctor—and along came Charles Horn, MD, with the most compelling comment of all:

> *I am a retired physician who has known Richard Humphries since we were kids. When Richard reached the point of barely being able to walk because of his MS, it thrilled me that he had decided to go to Costa Rica, his last hope for help, as the MS medicines were no longer of benefit. Am I a believer in stem cell therapy? Without any doubt. I have seen Richard return to not only walking but also running. He has returned to his love of playing golf and shooting sub-par rounds again. More importantly, his ability to think and express himself has returned to normal. His seizures may occur rarely now but they are minor in intensity and better than the 400 per month he was having*

before his therapy. Amazingly, some of the hearing frequencies he lost have returned. In short, Richard's life has returned to about 90 percent normal, if not better. I have met Dr. Riordan and he is a brilliant and caring individual. There are many physicians that feel stem cell therapy should be used in this country. Research can only be done with private donations. It is time for Americans to speak up and take the politicians out of medicine. Embryonic stem cells do not have to be used. That is the point that most people are missing. Adult stem cell therapy research should be allowed and it is time that distinction is made. Caring about the human being, relieving suffering, and improving one's quality of life is what medicine should be. I have witnessed too many people who were against something change their minds in an instant when someone in his or her family was involved. We should not judge. We should all have the right to decide what is best for each of us.

Now, what if an American doctor were to do more than leave a positive comment on an article about the merits of adult stem cell treatment—what if he were to travel to undergo treatment himself? That's exactly what Stanley Jones of Houston, Texas, did. A respected orthopedic surgeon, Dr. Jones suffered from rheumatoid arthritis so severe he was unable to operate. He flew to South Korea for harvesting and culturing of his own stem cells; because injecting the cells is illegal in South Korea, Dr. Jones then traveled to Japan to receive his injections. While still abroad, the well-connected Dr. Jones called a close personal friend back home: Governor Rick Perry. "I told him, I'm in Korea seeing miracles, and something needs to be done for our fellow Americans," Jones told the *Texas Tribune*. Perry, who hadn't yet become a household name outside the Lone Star State, suffered from lower back pain, a major cause of disability in America and all over the world. By the time Perry achieved national renown, in 2011, he boldly underwent spinal fusion treatment with his own stem cells; the operation was performed by Dr. Jones, who was back in action in the OR thanks to his own life-changing stem cell procedure.

Medicine and health care are politically divisive issues. Sports, on the other hand, have the power to bridge vast philosophical divides and bring people together. Throughout history, athletes have served as national heroes—think of the fighter Joe Louis, or the track star Jesse Owens. Now, four-footed athletes were models of sports diplomacy, and living proof of the power of regenerative medicine. Vet-Stem success stories started to galvanize the attention of medical doctors—especially sports-medicine specialists treating patients who, like horses, are natural athletes. In late 2006, a National Champion purebred Bay Arabian named Merritt began limping at the canter; then he started limping at the trot. The cartilage in his right hind fetlock had deteriorated. Pretty soon, the splendid dark-brown steed was reduced to a pained walk. In August 2007, he underwent the Vet Stem procedure in Texas, then resumed training in October. By 2009, his public saw a glimmer of Merritt's old self when he placed in the top ten in Purebred English Show Hack. Today, the bona fide Vet-Stem success story razzle-dazzles 'em in dressage; horse doctors who've manipulated Merritt's joints are amazed at their fine working condition. Many more success stories followed on Merritt's handsome heels. Surveying their owners, Vet-Stem learned that impressive numbers of sport-horse patients—race horses as well as performance horses—had returned to full work after treatment: 76 percent of those with suspensory ligament injuries; 77 percent with tendon injuries; and 57 percent with arthritis. And each of those rejuvenated horses strode forth to capture the public's imagination as stem cell special envoys.

Human athletes were among the first to seek the treatment that had helped their equine counterparts. In 2010, Bartolo Colon played for the New York Yankees; the power pitcher's famous fastball flew at ninety-three miles per hour and sometimes faster, more than twice the velocity of a racehorse's top running speed. But Colon was underperforming due to ligament damage and a torn rotator cuff in his hurling arm. In the bluntest baseball lingo, he was a "has-been." Then he underwent successful treatment with his own stem cells in his homeland, the Dominican Republic. The media got wind of this one year later—by which time Colon was confidently back in the game, his fastball fast and his strikeout rate high. By then, a couple thousand more racehorses had been treated by Vet-Stem with their own ASC, resulting in a 50 percent reduction in repeat leg injuries. Colon had put himself in the care of Florida physician Joseph Purita, who flew to the Dominican Republic to perform the procedure. Dr. Purita told the *New York Times* he combined ASC from Colon's fat and bone marrow, injecting them back into the pitcher's elbow and shoulder. The controversial specter of human growth hormone was raised, although Purita said he did not give Colon HGH treatment. Numerous media outlets, predictably, echoed doubts as to the ethics of the stem cell procedure, reporting that Major League Baseball was "actively investigating." The investigation turned up nothing.

Of course, lacking Colon's connections and financial means, or those of Rick Perry, I couldn't keep up with the Dr. Joneses, and was still awaiting a treatment option. But my life's twin focuses—dogs and the stem cell debate—conspired to turn me into a political independent with conservative leanings. Yes, Virginia, there are sincere pro-animal folks on both sides of the aisle—starting with Pat Buckley, Bill Buckley's wife, who was seated beside me at a dinner and earned my eternal respect by graciously inviting me to enlist her support with the pit bull rescue effort! Would you believe the late Mrs. Buckley graduated from (gasp) Vassar? One of history's most humane political animals was Republican President Gerald Ford, a devoted dog lover who holds a special place in my heart. When my parents left Hungary for America in 1956, part of President Eisenhower's Operation Safe Haven, they were concerned that passage on a Navy ship would be rough on my mother, who suffers terrible seasickness. My aunt, then living in Grand Rapids, Michigan, asked her Congressman, the Navy hero, whether he might please arrange for her sister and brother-in-law to travel by air. Representative Ford graciously obliged, and Mom and Dad arrived on a military plane.

Dogs taught me to think for myself about political matters, to use compassionate canine sense rather than slavishly adopting a hard party line. They made me aware of the issues that really matter—not just to four-footed citizens, but to us all. This was not a matter of trying to be contrary; it was a matter of facing up to colorectal disease and the fact that, apparently, only Republicans were displaying stem cell savvy. I still have a blue heart, but if a Republican does right by animals or stem cells or both, I will vocally support the red individual in question. When Governor Perry ultimately did become a household name, in 2011, it was for his epic blunder during a presidential debate. But what he should be known for is his support of stem cells. Liberals insist there's nothing between the ears on either side of Governor Goodhair's perfectly coiffed head, yet he sees adult stem cells' potential to return America to our rightful place as a global medical leader. Reestablishing us as a medical top dog would help our citizens who struggle with illness and cure our economy by creating jobs and keeping patient spending on these shores. However IQ-endowed you think Perry is or is not, consider how stem cells achieve healing improvement all over the body, not just at the site where they are injected. I'll wager that his debating skills have sharpened since his spinal fusion procedure. If he ever makes another presidential run, he'd be the darkest of dark-horse candidates—but, as the dusky, cell-enhanced equines Jantastic and Merritt prove, a dark horse can also be a beacon.

CHAPTER 11

Cellbound

In February 2011, I received a call from the Stem Cell Institute in Panama City. Over the preceding seven months, Neil had periodically checked in by e-mail to report that his team was encountering unexpected delays in locating a gastrointestinal specialist willing to duplicate the Madrid trial on me. It had been almost three years since Sam's Vet-Stem procedure, and with each passing year it became more absurd that an American dog could receive an injection of his own stem cells right here on US soil, but the dog's human could not. And now, even the sure-thing offshore option I'd eagerly anticipated was looking elusive. In the months leading up to the closing of the Stem Cell Institute's San Jose clinic, the Costa Rican government had displayed a cautionary, "not invented here" approach. Now, it seemed that the Panamanian medical establishment also preferred not to engage in so-called "experimental" treatments that they themselves hadn't devised and perfected. Having been performed successfully in Spain, my procedure was not experimental; it was, rather, investigational, with an 83 percent success rate among the Spanish patients recruited for the trials. The only difference in my case was that I would be the first American to receive it. But that "first" distinction is what doubtless made the Panamanian doctors extra wary. Although Panamanian doctors were already working at Neil's clinic to treat patients with arthritis, MS, and spinal cord injury, my procedure required a gastrointestinal surgeon—and the available gastrointestinal surgeons simply could not be convinced that the procedure in question was anything but experimental. Because only a Panamanian surgeon can operate in Panama—nobody could fly in to perform this procedure on me—it was beginning to become evident that I wouldn't be treated there after all. And so, when Dr. Andres Caballero finally telephoned at Neil's request, I sensed this would be the outcome even before I heard the disappointment in his voice. He broke the sad news to me as gently as he could.

It was a particularly painful breakup, yet I knew this was not the end of my journey—far from it. The more I wrote about stem cells, the more fascinated I became with their astonishing healing potential, and the more determined I was to undergo this treatment at any cost. In my own riff on the classic Siouxsie Sioux song "Spellbound," I became cellbound—as "entranced, entranced, entranced" with the curative capability of ASCs as one would be with the most captivating love object. Every day, I took a capsule of Stem-Kine, the nutritional supplement Neil formulated to increase circulating stem cells. Then I decided to give the New York doctor who had performed my emergency surgery in '99 another chance. I wanted to believe that American medical technology might yet offer me some kind of relief right here in my home town, a center of medical innovation (or so I'd always believed). After all, it was now more than a decade since my near-death experience. Surely some advances had been made in the area of helping people with a condition like mine? Perhaps my doctor could tell me of possible new options, and I could gain new insight into my twelve-year-old problem, which was starting to behave, as befit its age, like an awkward adolescent. I made an appointment with Dr. Schmerz and hoped for the best.

Certain science-fiction narratives have always carried real weight with me. As a child watching *The Bionic Woman*, my idol, I had no doubt that fully functioning body parts would be engineered by the time I reached adulthood, and cyborgs like schoolteacher Jaime Sommers and Max, her bionic German shepherd, would walk among us even if they might not outrun automobiles. I fully believed that American doctors would make all this happen, because they could do anything. In most sci-fi scenarios, doctors were good guys on the order of the Starship *Enterprise*'s Bones McCoy, or Rudy Wells, the doc who rebuilt Jaime Sommers and Max the dog. Even if the docs weren't, technically, good guys—as in *Planet of the Apes*—they knew the answers to the big questions. Just before the breathtaking finale of the original *Apes* movie, medicine orangutan Dr. Zaius withholds the cause of human civilization's demise from Taylor the astronaut, but he knows what it is. I'd heard about the 1968 movie *Charly* but didn't get around to seeing it until shortly after Sam enacted a real-life sci-fi story on my stoop. Adapted from Daniel Keyes' novel *Flowers for Algernon,* the film stars Cliff Robertson as Charlie Gordon, a mentally challenged man who receives an experimental operation that transforms him into a genius. But Algernon—the sentinel mouse who receives the procedure before Charlie and eventually becomes his pet—reverts, then dies. Despite the high caliber of the medical minds on Charlie's case, the only one who can decipher his precarious fate is Charlie himself. Now, my own story had shades of *Charly* plus Marley, the canine icon made famous by my journalist colleague John Grogan. Like a dog with a bone, I'd put my reporting skills to the test to find a cure for what ailed me. Now, would I find a physician willing to implement that cure, a doc as savvy about stem cells as Bob the vet?

It was time for my appointment with Dr. Schmerz. In he walked, trailed by an entourage of some three interns in their twenties. Time had added gray hairs to his head and a reserve of stem cells to his midsection. It had been just over a decade since our last interaction, but he indicated that he remembered me, which was reassuring. I suppose you remember the patient you hauled yourself out of bed at two o'clock in the morning to perform life-saving surgery on; we'd had a one-night stand of sorts, and unless one really has no heart, one doesn't forget an encounter like that. The hospital had undergone a redesign; the exam rooms were bigger and cleaner than the ones I used to have my rechecks in, but that was about all that had changed. This was still a teaching hospital, so mortification was still the order of the day. I gulped upon hearing that I'd be undergoing not just a rectal exam but also a recto-*vaginal* exam. Only one of the interns was a woman; registering the look on my face, she placed her hand on my leg in sympathy. A cannula—a narrow metal tubular instrument resembling a straightened-out paper clip—was inserted into the fistula on my butt-cheek to see whether the tunnel in my flesh was still open. Of course it was, but it had been dormant; this primitive probe succeeded in inflaming it and making me bleed. I asked Dr. Schmerz whether he'd followed the clinical trials being performed in Spain with stem cells. He just looked at me with a blank expression that clearly said, not only had he not followed them but also he hadn't heard about them and wasn't interested in hearing about them now. In that case, I continued, could he please recommend any other treatment modality besides the fistulotomy, that might improve my condition, hopefully something less invasive? Negative. Fistulotomy was the only way. Five hundred dollars, please.

After my cordial communications with some of the world's finest medical minds, this was particularly disheartening. A friend of a friend recommended a GI specialist for a second opinion, saying he had a reputation for being refreshingly un-doctorlike. I made an appointment. Following another rectal exam and a review of my hospital records from that fateful night in '99, this doc gave me a very concerned look. Shaking his head, he observed, "You were very sick." But as we discussed my condition, he let me know that he didn't think I understood it, showing me an anatomical model of the GI tract to back up his belief. When I expressed concern about developing colon cancer, he told me not to worry—squamous cell, maybe, but not colon cancer. Then he offered to recommend me to his friend the plastic surgeon, who could probably help me better than he could. Evidently, the one who didn't understand my condition here was not me. I told him about the adult stem cell trials in Madrid. "How come you don't have a job?" he asked.

"Because," I replied, "my job is to raise awareness of stem cell regeneration therapy."

He nodded. "Warning: Live one," read the thought bubble over his head. And with that, he walked me to the reception area and wished me all the best. Five hundred dollars, please.

If medical doctors could be this willfully clueless about my condition and the latest medical developments that address it, then my madcap, multidisciplinary approach to self-healing was starting to look downright respectable—yep, even the astrology part. Hurting for healing but blocked at every turn, I craved the therapeutic benefits of witnessing sci-fi-in-real-life. So I turned once again to the experts in that department: Vet-Stem. It was high time to get Sheba treated with her own stem cells. My beautiful border collie, who never had a health problem before the day I idiotically took her to witness B's passing, had stood patiently, stoically by as almost everyone else in the animal house received special ministrations. In fact, like a dedicated vet tech, she often tended to her pack

My beautiful Sheba, pre-Vet-Stem ANNELI ADOLFFSON

mates by regularly using her tongue to keep their ears clean. She was taking an arsenal of joint-support supplements, yet still I needed to lure her to the park with meaty treats, because her aching back and creaky joints made getting there a serious effort. It was Sheba's turn to experience cell therapy and the Benjamin Button effect. As a fringe benefit, witnessing her walking tall could only have a beneficial effect on me. So I called Vet-Stem and began making the arrangements.

Permit me a few words of Sheba appreciation. Here was a creature as modest as she was magnetic, who could walk confidently up to Howard Stern and Richard Belzer and interrupt them at the North Shore Animal League gala without so much as raising either one's eyebrow, then turn the tables on celebrity, getting the stars to fawn over her! How many humans could claim the same? Equally smart and sweet, with a gorgeous sable coat, she exhibited the border collie trait of extreme intelligence, with a strong independent streak that would compel her to wander off our property in search of adventures. Her theme song was "Babe, I'm Gonna Leave You"—which, although made famous by the men of Led Zeppelin, was in fact written by a woman, Anne Bredon, who perfectly captured the rambling sheepdog spirit. Several times over the years, my heart jumped out of my chest when Sheba would go missing; I'd call frantically for her, and she'd wait just long enough—until the moment I was ready to collapse in panicked tears—to return with a gleam in her eye, her ears bouncing up and down and her plush tail swishing merrily from side to side. "OK," she seemed to say, "I came back this time, and you know I'd like to stay here, but . . . that highway's calling me to travel on alone."

The gentlest creature on four legs, she carried the healing touch in her tongue and was generous in applying it to a tear-streaked human face. By now, arthritis had slowed down Sheba's gait while old age had frosted her face white. Although she hadn't collapsed on the street as Sam had, our walks to the park were taking longer and longer, even with those treat lures. I knew she'd be an excellent Vet-Stem candidate: She had new incentive for rejuvenation, having made fast friends with a puppy named Piggy, a three-legged border collie mix who could pick up remarkable speed despite his "disability." Piggy's owner was an animal activist named Tod. While Piggy attached himself to Sheba upon their first meeting,

Sheba and me, 1998

like a foundling pup to his long-lost mother, Sheba fell hard for Tod, who described her as a perfect hybrid of dolphin and fox. I knew Sheba wanted to be able to keep up with these two on walks to the park. To make that possible, on April 11, she underwent a liposuction at the Humane Society of New York, in the expert care of Dr. Higgins. Once again, a sample of fatty tissue was FedExed on ice to Vet-Stem in San Diego for processing. Two days later, vials of her stem cells were overnighted back to New York, ready to be injected into her hips and bloodstream. Knowing from experience how those injections would change our life for the better, giving Sheba longed-for arthritis relief, I anticipated the precious package containing those three doses of stem cells like a Christmas care package. The morning her cells were scheduled to arrive at the clinic was one of those chilly, rainy April days that make Mr. Arthur's invasive visits more

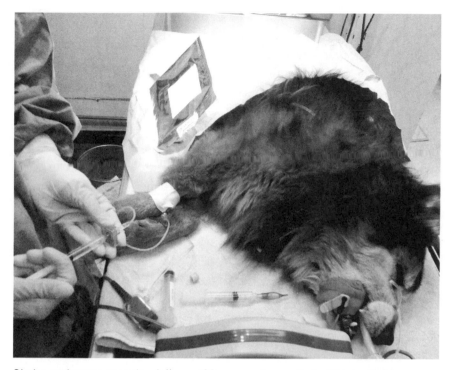

Sheba undergoes vascular delivery of her own stem cells by IV injection.

excruciating than usual; Sheba's pinched, crouching posture was a dead giveaway that she resented his presence keenly. Descending the steps outside our building was a slow process, and the effort clearly exhausted her. I dropped her off at the Humane Society and returned home. Around 3:00 p.m., I received a call from Dr. Higgins that Sheba was about to go under. The doc conferred a rare privilege on me: permission to come and observe the procedure! Luckily, I'd charged my trusty digital camera, so I was ready to record this exciting moment in my family history.

When I arrived, Sheba was lying on her left side with her tongue hanging out of her mouth, in that deathlike limbo state that anesthesia induces. Sterile blue OR toweling covered her midsection, exposing a small field of flesh where the needle would go in. Both hips had just been injected, each with one dose of Sheba's own stem cells—about four million cells per vial. Now it was time for vascular delivery of her stem cells, via the IV injection. The doc expertly installed a catheter in Sheba's foreleg, then attached the third vial to it and pushed in its contents. The Vet-Stem procedure was done! It was time to revive my dog. As Sheba came to, her tongue tucked itself back inside her mouth where it belonged. I left my groggy sweetheart so she could emerge from anesthesia fully and safely, but before I went, I told Sheba how proud I was of her and promised her all the lamb shawarma she could eat as a reward for her act of valor. Shortly after 6:00 p.m., I returned to collect her. No sooner was the gate to her kennel unlatched than she charged out of it, then led me all the way down the long hallway, through the waiting area, and out onto the sidewalk. In a hurry, she stopped just twice—to relieve herself of number one, then number two—then continued her forward march until we reached the getaway car. Once home, she climbed the stairs to our building faster than she'd been able to do in some time and made a beeline for her recovery crate. She happily devoured the promised lamb and took a long drink of water. Three hours later, it was time for a quick relief walk. Sheba hopped down the steps with surprising speed—a dramatic difference from that morning's snail pace.

By May, I still wasn't willing to give up on Panama, and I hoped that an opportunity would arise for me to persuade the doctors there to treat me after all. In the meantime, I stumbled on the Twitter feed of another offshore option, and some of my diversified hopes were now riding on it. I'm a huge fan of the microblog. I don't just "like" Twitter—to borrow Facebook terminology—I love it. Twitter is the fastest way to get the most sophisticated information about any given topic, especially stem cells. It's also great for connecting with fellow animal advocates and IBD sufferers all over the world. I can pinpoint the exact date I fell hard for Twitter: May 12, 2011. That's the day I sent a direct message to StemCellMx—the handle of the Stem Cell Center of Excellence in Tijuana, Mexico—and received a direct message back from the center's publicity director, an extremely savvy PR strategist. Hearing my story, she expressed confidence that arranging treatment in exchange for media coverage would be no problem and e-mailed me a contract to sign. It should be fine, she surmised, for Dr. Smith to scrub in. Thrilled at this promising new development, I upheld my end of the bargain, starting with giving her a radio interview about my experience. But months went by and nothing happened. When I'd call or e-mail to check in, she'd promise that the doctors would be in touch, they were just very busy, and so on. A couple of months after we'd initiated contact, during which the date of my procedure was continually pushed back, she got around to telling me that the doctors would not permit Dr. Smith to scrub in. It wasn't an encouraging sign, so I suppose I shouldn't have been surprised when, after our radio interview had aired and she'd retweeted it several times, weeks would pass before I'd receive a return call from her. Finally, she called me back and helpfully suggested I seek treatment in Asia—perhaps Thailand? I'd resolved to go to the ends of the earth to receive stem cell treatment, but I refused to travel for treatment to any country where dogs are on the menu, which pretty much puts Asia out of the running.

While I awaited treatment with my own stem cells, my interim therapy would have to be the medicine of love. I resolved to actively nourish and communicate with my cells, encouraging them to do their best job of helping my body heal. And I would draw on every healing trick I ever used on my dogs, combining cutting-edge contemporary modalities with herbal remedies that have been around for centuries. Incidentally, the marriage of conventional and alternative veterinary medicine is dramatized in the 1964 Disney movie The *Three Lives of Thomasina*, which tells the story, penned by author Paul Gallico, of a marmalade cat and a little girl named Mary. Patrick McGoohan of *Secret Agent* fame plays Mary's father, a country vet with a compassion deficiency. The doc crosses paths with Lori MacGregor, a "witch" who heals animals with natural remedies, plus what the vet calls the "medicine of love." Naturally, vet and witch are happily wed in the end. Of course, things in real life don't work out the way they do on screen, even when you meet someone online and you travel, movie-style, to meet that person. That's what I learned when a unique opportunity to visit Panama presented itself, and I leaped. How far would you go to receive a novel cure for an ancient malady? To get my PF repaired with my own stem cells, I was ready to go as far as necessary. Of all the so-called perils of medical tourism the media relentlessly warns readers about, the real hazards remain unreported; these are the risks incurred by traveling when one cannot afford the costs. Which brings me to my temporary gig as an international escort.

In August, I met a potential new client, an independently wealthy man in his thirties looking to hire a remote assistant to handle his affairs while he traveled the world. The only male heir of a very wealthy philanthropist, Richie wasn't just rich, he was filthy rich and, I would later learn, quite smug about having no obligation to work. He was not unlike many of the girls I'd grown up with on planet private school. In fact, he'd attended a nearby private boys' school. I have been a workaholic since childhood, always looking for ways to supplement my income. And yet, in a classic case of opposites attracting, a strong attraction developed during our Gmail chats. His birthday was coming up, and he offered to fly me to Central America, where he was traveling, as his gift to himself. Flattered, I accepted. When he asked where I'd like to meet, I replied, "Panama!" Finally, I'd be able to visit the Stem Cell Institute and hopefully talk them into giving me treatment. I was in luck: Panama was on Richie's short list of places to visit. He sent me the money for a round-trip airline ticket.

Never mind medical tourist traps, how about a medical tourist death trap? What if Richie were actually a sophisticated serial killer, using information he'd found online to hook me into meeting him abroad? I could find no footprint of the guy anywhere online; either he didn't exist, or he worked diligently to remain under the radar. To his credit, Richie did want to meet in person. That's no small thing: I had chatted with so many people on Facebook or OkCupid, people who were right in my home state or within two hours' drive, yet who couldn't make time to meet. New York to Panama is a long distance to travel for a first date, but, hey, why not? On the ride to the airport, I discussed the details with my friend the professional driver, who had discreetly borne witness to his share of shocking incidents while ferrying folks with money to burn; he almost didn't allow me to leave the vehicle. But I was on a mission and couldn't be stopped. "Am I going to read about you in the newspaper?" he asked, only half kidding. Of course, I replied: "But no reports of my untimely death. You'll read all about how I eventually got my stem cell procedure!"

Some stress was occasioned by a communication blackout, during which I didn't hear from Richie the entire day leading up to my evening flight and wasn't entirely sure he'd be at the other end to meet me—in a fine example of how the rich stay rich, he refuses to own a cellular phone, conducting his calls by Skype. When I arrived, he was waiting for me at the airport as promised. "Look at me with the hottie," he proclaimed.

We were driven to Panama's picturesque Old Quarter, Casco Viejo, and enjoyed a late-night dinner. From there, it was a short walk to our hotel, a luxury property owned by a transplanted New Jersey native. Upon landing in our room, I was desperate to use the restroom—fecal urgency alert!—and excused myself, hoping my bowels wouldn't embarrass me on our first night together. I minced to the bathroom in my silver high-heeled Jack Rogers Navajo mules and was about to close the door to the bathroom when Richie held it open. Maybe he needed to go even more urgently? I was about to cede the seat when I remembered that our room had a second full bath. "I thought we had two bathrooms?" I said.

"I don't have to go," Richie said.

"OK," I said as cheerily as I could, as peristalsis got under way and I felt myself about to morph from high-heeled hottie into panting, grimacing Ms. Hyde. "Well then, I'll be out in a few minutes—just need a little privacy for a bit!"

"You should be able to do it with me standing right here," he said, crossing his arms, leaning back against the bathroom door frame and standing firm in the bathroom doorway, looking right at me. Uh-oh. Talk about boundary issues! I'd never had someone watch me take a crap before; it takes all kinds, apparently. Trust me, Richie's voyeurism was not a turn-on. I was a little afraid that this was only the tip of a hideously kinky iceberg, but there was no time for debate; nature was calling and I couldn't ignore her summons. For privacy, I covered my face with my hands. Happily, despite the usual physical discomfort I experienced with every bowel movement—now compounded by this thoroughly unwelcome bathroommate—everything came out clean. Also happily, Richie didn't do anything that outright weird again.

He was, however, shockingly tight with money—even tighter than the jeans he wore, so cheap he squeaked. Over the next few days I found myself increasingly mortified, to the point of tongue-biting outrage, as

Richie would refuse to pay three-dollar cab fares, insisting on handing over only $2, until one driver smartly threatened to call the cops. An elderly gentleman who gave us a non-touristy tour, which he'd said upfront would cost ten dollars, was paid only seven. Taking Richie aside, I begged him in a discreet whisper to please pay the whole ten, reminding him that we'd been shown the authentic Panama, as promised. Richie stood firm at seven. And yet, he wasn't the type to go near a cheap eatery or B&B; he only stayed at four- and five-star hotels. Still, the most persistent source of outrage for me on this trip wasn't my skinflint travel companion and shit chaperone, but the heartbreaking sight of stray dogs and cats everywhere the eye could see: There were too many to count, let alone save. Sending dispatches to Dogster, I reported on the efforts of SPAYes (Spay Panama's Animals Yes), a nonprofit started by a group of volunteers and vets with the noble mission of making Panama a "No More Homeless Pets Country" through spay-neuter initiatives intended to reduce the exploding animal population. I wrote about the Organic Chocolate Company, a cafe that sold handmade dog biscuits known as "doggie crack." All proceeds from sales of these "Drool and Devour" treats were dedicated to providing low-cost sterilization of dogs and cats in nearby villages.

Going on a walkabout after a day of taking in the breathtakingly beautiful churches of Casco Viejo, Richie and I passed two men sitting in chairs on the sidewalk with a couple of dogs. A pendulous-breasted brown female, evidently recently delivered of pups, thought we were up to no good and started walking toward us with menacing intent. I deliberately slowed my pace but kept walking as if not afraid, carefully avoiding eye contact with her. I turned around to see Richie staring the bitch down. Concerned for our safety, I used my friendliest voice—so as not to upset the mama dog—and called to him to please keep walking with me. He walked toward me, put his hand on my upper arm, turned me around, and tightened his grip.

"Don't ever undermine me like that again," he said.

Ah, now we were dealing with serious control issues—as if that weren't already self-evident from the hotel toilet incident. I tried to explain that the way he was challenging the dog could have resulted in serious harm to us both. The owners of the dog were hugely entertained by this scene of a gringo love spat. Meanwhile, their unfriendly dogs were still circling uncomfortably close by.

"Can we please walk away now?" I asked.

As he had in the bathroom doorway, Richie stood firm.

"You've never been to a Central American country," he said so disparagingly I thought he might spit.

"True," I countered, "but I do know a little bit about dogs, and what you were doing could have gotten us both hurt."

"I know how to kill a dog if I have to," he replied, his eyes narrowing.

Boasting about killing dogs is no way to get on my good side. So now I was traveling long distances to find the choicest creeps! Why did I stay? Because I simply did not have the available funds or credit to fly myself out of there. And so, I endured this man's most unpleasant company in the hope of securing my stem cells. Happily, not every encounter with Panama's native animals was cause for distress. Our visit to Cerro Ancon was delightful. Hiking up this 654-foot hill overlooking Ciudad de Panama, adjacent to the township of Ancon, one is transported to an urban oasis, thriving with orchids and jungle wildlife, including toucans, sloths, coati, armadillos, tamarins, and deer. Its history is as rich as its flora and fauna. Before the pirate Henry Morgan sacked Panama City in 1671, his scouts climbed Ancon Hill to scope out the local defenses; later, the hill was the headquarters of the US Southern Command. Although light years apart, Cerro Ancon and a very different Panamanian oasis, the Stem Cell Institute, are separated by a short distance. Many people had expressed concern about my determination to seek treatment in Panama because, well, it was Panama and not Europe or Asia. I suppose folks were picturing some kind of third-world M*A*S*H unit complete with thatched roof, mosquito netting, and creaky ceiling fan, not to mention polluted water and air. Yet here was a streamlined facility as high-tech as anything in a sci-fi film, like sick bay on the Starship *Enterprise,* and more meticulously clean than any hospital, emergency room, or clinic I'd seen in Nueva York. This place was cool in every sense of the term: painstakingly climate controlled, well worth recommending to friends and family and inspiring nothing but absolute confidence in its doctors and staff. Before undertaking a walk-through of the super-sterile laboratory where mesenchymal stem cells are harvested from patients, then cultured and cryopreserved, I was asked to outfit myself in a sterile blue gown, mask, and booties. Touring this facility, and the tremendous care taken to protect its absolute cleanliness, would change even the most skeptical critic's mind about traveling outside the United States for stem cell treatment.

I had a meeting with the clinic director, and we discussed other options for injecting my cells that wouldn't require the participation of a GI surgeon, including a rejuvenating beauty treatment. This last hope was squashed when he followed up by e-mail to let me know that the doctors didn't think the rejuvenating treatment would give me the therapeutic result I sought. My breakup with Panama was final. The good news was that I was flying out in two days. It was time at last to return to my dogs and bid adieu to the spiritually impoverished Richie. Picking up Sheba from her extended sleepover with Piggy, I delighted to hear Tod describe their daily trips to Central Park, with my young, old girl happily keeping pace. Just as Sam had done, Sheba was overcoming the pain of crippling arthritis that had made moving her hips and hind legs a slow and painful effort just three months earlier. Once again, everyone in the animal house was healthy. There was room for one more honey.

CHAPTER 12

Déjà Doo

It had been almost three years since I lost Britannia, but someone up there saw fit to send me another sister-soulmate. On Sunday, July 3, 2011, I received the latest series of alerts from my local animal shelter, Animal Care and Control of New York City, Sam's alma mater. The e-mails described, as they always do, the dogs at high risk for euthanasia. I wanted to help all of them, but one in particular caught my eye: Jassy, described as a geriatric German shepherd. Dogs deemed "less adoptable"—the ones with easily treatable mange or kennel cough or orthopedic injury—are put in the care of the shelter's New Hope program, which diligently reaches out to rescuers who might be able to pull them. Of course, my eyes saw nothing "less adoptable" about this dog—I'd always, always wanted a German shepherd, ever since my teenage days when, glued to the TV set, I worshiped the Bionic Woman and her bionic dog Max. Thanks to the fictitious canine cyborg whose running speed reached 90 miles per hour with low-tech special effects, I was confident that science fiction would be a matter of fact by the time I'd become an adult, and that American technology would surely bring prematurely deceased people and dogs back to life and make us all "better, stronger, faster." I also fully expected that I'd have a German shepherd of my own someday, but after becoming an advocate of shelter dog adoption and rescue, I knew I could never justify buying one from a breeder. So when I saw this dog's sweet face and soft eyes, I knew I'd won the lottery, and I pounced. Figuring it would be a piece of cake to incorporate this sweet, mellow, aristocratic senior into my woof pack, I hit reply and typed, *I'LL TAKE HER!* I was glad to give her the nice retirement home she deserved.

I was eager to begin the extreme-makeover process I'd applied to several other dogs from the same shelter. It was almost as dramatically

My darling Desiree

gratifying as watching my senior canines morph from lame to limber with stem cell therapy. I reckoned that by the time I got done with this German shepherd, she'd be unrecognizable from her "before" photo, in which she's pictured pitiably holding up a sprained forepaw. The July Fourth holiday weekend had begun, however, and the New Hope staff of dedicated dog rescuers was out of the office and not responding to e-mails, so I didn't hear back about whether my German shepherd had escaped the euthanasia run. It had happened once before that I'd put my name on a dog, a small female pit bull, only to find out that there had been a communication misfire at the shelter; the computer was down, the euthanasia command was already in place, and the rescue memo arrived too late. The dog I'd wanted to save was killed. So needless to say, July 4, 2011, was a nail-biting Manic Monday as I fretted for twenty-four solid hours about the fate of the German shepherd I'd already renamed Desiree, after Desiree Armfeldt, the femme fatale at the center of the Bergman film *Smiles of a Summer Night* and the Sondheim musical *A Little Night Music.* I was overjoyed to receive an e-mail the next day, Tuesday, that my new dog would be delivered to me later that day, so July 5 became my Yankee Doodle Doggy's birthday. Her transport was coordinated by the Mayor's Alliance for NYC's Animals, a coalition of 150-plus nonprofit shelters and rescue groups working to end the killing of healthy and treatable dogs and cats at the city shelters, Animal Care & Control of NYC. The Alliance's goal is to transform New York City into a no-kill community by 2015. Until that noble mission is accomplished, the Alliance's efforts are helping make my hometown a less-kill city. As always, I closed my eyes in silent prayer for the other dogs I couldn't take that day—and the ones that wouldn't enjoy the exhilaration of the freedom ride.

Stepping outside to meet the transport van, I was greeted by a frantic kangaroo impersonator. Making vertical leaps high in the air, this was no geriatric canine, but a skinny puppy in a state of severe neglect. It's understandable how, upon first glance at intake, shelter workers estimated her to be geriatric; there was a gorgeous dog in there somewhere, but she was in such sorry shape that she appeared much older than her actual age (which, to judge by her perfect pearly-white teeth, was under one year). She was thinner than a social X-ray and very ribsy. Her dull, grayish coat was shedding like mad and emitting a putrid, yeasty odor, as if she'd been kept in a damp basement and fungus had begun proliferating on her skin, which was exposed all along her forelegs thanks to a bad case of demodectic mange. Step one in this makeover would have to be a bath, stat, but I knew this dog's copiously shedding hair would clog my bathtub drain within seconds. So I marched her to the nearest grooming establishment, where, as I'd suspected, mounds of hair came off her. I took over grooming duty after that, performing frequent sudsings with neem-enriched shampoo, to which I added several drops of straight neem oil. Desiree's now-clean coat revealed giant bald patches from mange; her chest was pretty much entirely bare of fur. Good thing this was summer in New York City, so she wouldn't freeze. Yet I quite deliberately opted not to subject Desiree to the conventional mange treatment, which involves concentrated doses of ivermectin, the active ingredient of oral heartworm-preventive medication. The toxic chemical assault would have had a huge impact on Desiree's cells, especially those of her liver, and I wanted that important organ to stay vital so it would continue to serve her for a very long time to come.

To help heal Desiree's sprained forepaw, I took her to Dr. Jill Elliot for cold laser treatments, which the vet explained would also help eradicate her mange. To put meat on Desiree's bones, I began feeding her all the fortifying foods and supplements I could think of. Proving quite a challenge, the poor thing was so far gone that she resisted my best healing efforts—the tricks that had worked wonders for all her predecessor patients. Desiree's immune system was in total collapse. After a few days, she would lie down on the sidewalk during even the shortest relief walk, completely exhausted from the effort. A visit to the Humane Society clinic revealed she had pneumonia, which soon resolved with a course of antibiotics. As I always did, I administered a probiotic two hours before or after the prescribed antibiotic, to help maintain a healthy balance of intestinal flora and support her immune system. Later, Desiree developed an uncontrollable itch. Figuring it was an allergy to fleas, the Humane Society docs urged me to let them administer one dose of parasite control, but I respectfully refused. Determined to tough this out the natural way, I gave Desiree daily baths in neem shampoo and dabbed straight neem oil directly onto the points of her body fleas gravitate to—head, neck, chest, and under the tail. To no one's surprise, the more effort I put into this dog, the more attached to her I became. As Desiree's health hurdles required a great deal of effort, my attachment to her grew exponentially. She was as yet intact, because each time I was about to make the appointment to have her spayed, some new health issue cropped up to prevent the operation from taking place.

I'd been smitten at first sight of Desiree's photo, but now I was living my childhood fantasy with my very own, real-life German shepherd, and she was even cuter than the Steiff shepherd pup I always bought at FAO Schwarz as a baby gift for expecting friends. Sometimes, Desiree didn't even appear real; she was more like a deluxe, life-sized plush toy come to joyful life, and I half expected to see the signature Steiff button appear in one of her gravity-defying ears. Except Steiff toys aren't tormented by violent itching. Desiree's itch wasn't caused by fleas after all; it was caused by severe food allergies. I tried just about every type of kibble and canned food, and it would agree with Desiree for a little while—until it wouldn't. When food didn't agree with Desiree, she'd vomit or have excruciating rounds of black, projectile diarrhea, waking me in the middle of the night, desperate to be taken out. It was déjà vu all over again. Make that déjà doo: *Don't get diarrhea* wasn't just my mantra; now it was Desiree's, too. Doing my utmost to prevent it, I tried every premium food option: frozen raw, frozen cooked, freeze-dried raw. Then I started serving Desiree steak cooked in coconut oil or grass-fed beef hearts with a side of oven-baked, organic sweet potatoes. This worked for a while— and then it didn't. Nothing stuck to my girl's ribs; the only food that didn't cause her digestive distress was oven-baked sweet potato, to which she became so attached that she'd swipe raw ones from the shopping bag if I wasn't looking and start munching away. At my wits' end, and afraid that she'd wind up severely malnourished, I stuffed the potatoes with supplements. Desiree seemed, just like Julia Roberts's Julia Roberts-esque character in the movie *Notting Hill*, "hungry for a decade," constantly on the hunt for things to eat, including—yuck—other dogs' poop. It was making me heartsick, because I understood exactly how she felt. When my own gut was at its most inflamed, I too would experience hunger like a burning hole in my stomach. Folks were stopping to admonish me in the park, on the street, at the bank, in the Sprint store: "Miss, you need to feed your dog."

It's often said that people are drawn to dogs that resemble them. Ever since taking up the cause of pit bulls, I've been told I am a pit bull (and I'll take that as a compliment, thank you). But in one respect—one that's not evident on the outside—I'm very much like a German shepherd. Not only do Desiree and I both have delicate digestive systems (and that's putting it delicately), we are both poster girls for inflammatory bowel disease. Wanting to know which diseases German shepherds are prone to, I researched the breed thoroughly. As it turns out, shepherds get several breed-specific ailments, one of which I know all too well. Yes, dogs get perianal fistula disease too, and of the canine population suffering PF, also called anal furunculosis, some 80 percent are German shepherds. Because they carry their tails low and close to their bodies, these dogs' anal areas are poorly ventilated, resulting in conditions ripe for unhealthy bacterial overgrowth. (Unfortunately, tail amputation is a common surgical solution.) As with people, more male dogs are affected than females.

But just as it does with canine osteoarthritis, stem cell regeneration therapy offers hope for dogs with inflammatory bowel disease and PF, two conditions at the top of Vet-Stem's list to study once grant funds are secured. If there was ever any trace of doubt that Desiree had come to the right place, it vanished when I learned this. If and when she'd ever manifest PF, I'd be ready to help Desiree as few others could. On some nights—notably the one when the poor dear woke me every hour on the hour to be taken outside—I wondered, did I really need a dog with a digestive system as troubled as my own? But the answer was always, clearly, yes. Caring for Desiree was precisely what I needed to help me stay the course in caring for myself. So everything really does happen for a reason. For such a graceful, feminine creature, Desiree has comically large paws, like a drag queen. I came to understand that's because she had big paw-prints to fill: Sam's. She officially inherited his position as pack healer, and she was now my main Medicine Dog. We shared everything, even the same malady! And just to make sure I got the connection, she would perform her version of the laying-on of paws by applying those oversize feet to me at every opportunity. She likes to stay in close physical contact, which is charming. At bedtime, with her head on my pillow or shoulder, she'll place a foreleg on my arm; or, if lying with her back facing me, she'll place a rear paw on my thigh.

Close observation of Desiree's eating and pooping habits helped tame her gut and helped me tame my own. It dawned on me that the grain-free diet was working for all my dogs. And so, in solidarity with them, I signed up too, evicting not just wheat gluten but rice gluten, too. Bread and pasta are like crack for me, but they cause inflammation. And while I've always loved rice, and could happily eat it by the bowlful seasoned with coconut oil and sea salt, it's tough on a compromised digestive system, because rice—not just the processed, white kind but healthy, brown rice too—expands in the gut. In the history of seafaring, many shipwrecks happened because the vessel was transporting shipments of rice; water leaked in, expanding the rice to the point where the hold was sealed shut, and the boat sank. So rather than risk shipwrecking my GI tract, I substituted rice with Desiree's favorite baked sweet potatoes and learned to love gluten-free quinoa, the grain-like food that's classified as a pseudocereal and was a dietary staple of pre-Columbian civilizations.

I also became strict about food combining. After all, the dogs were taking their proteins without grain, so I wanted to try this for myself. Of all the admittedly strange things I've done in my life, adhering to a food-combining regimen proved to be one of the most socially controversial. My mom took personal offense when I explained why I couldn't partake of her greatest culinary hits—at least, not all at the same sitting. Meanwhile, at restaurants, my dining companions all thought I was practicing some strange form of food voodoo as I abstained from delicious bread and pasta (not easy to do if you're eating in a trattoria). I'm a big fan of Japanese food, but just try dining Tokyo-style and avoiding rice or noodles—the waitstaff gets weirded out.

After a while, I became really good at explaining, briefly but effectively, that I'm allergic to certain ingredients; when you do this, folks want to help. One evening, I was enjoying Italian food at the invitation of a friend and her husband, who happens to be a physician and pharmaceutical entrepreneur. Both halves of the couple were lamenting the fact that they'd become overweight. I was tempted to indoctrinate them in the finer points of food combining, but hesitated. During our stem cell discussion, the doc had remained tight-lipped until I got to the part about patients with Duchenne muscular dystrophy seeing impressive results with stem cell therapy. This prompted him to exclaim "Impossible!" in his most outraged, dismissive tone. While all three of us were still at the menu-scanning stage of the meal, I presented a quick rundown of the principles of food combining, shortest possible version: I explained what I was ordering for myself—*insalata tricolore* to start, then broiled fish with a side of sautéed broccoli rabe—and why I was abstaining from the highly enticing bread basket, loaded with fragrant slices of *pane di casa*. When I finished, the doctor remarked that, of all the things I'd described thus far, this seemed the most scientifically sound. Ha! And yet, instead of giving food combining a whirl, he proceeded to eat the bread, then order breaded veal parmigiana with a side of red-sauced pasta. I felt a twinge in my gut just contemplating the heavy burden he was putting on his.

The longer version of the food-combining regimen takes a little effort to get the hang of, but once you do, it becomes second nature, and so simple you'll wonder why you didn't eat this way before. This diet also enables you to really taste your food, and to appreciate individual flavors and the sublime ways they interact on the palate. If you weigh more than you'd like to, you'll also start to see pounds melting off that you thought you'd never lose—how's that for incentive? Here's how to do it: Before tucking into a meal, decide if you're having a protein platter or a starch special. With food combining, it's either-or, never protein and starch together, because your gut can only digest one at a time. While the protein, say, is being digested, the starch you misguidedly consumed with it just sits there, undigested and fermenting, releasing gas and sugar, and causing bloating and stomach upset. Lovely! Fettuccine with creamy sauce is fine, but just say no to spaghetti with meaty Bolognese or risotto with seafood and cheese. Remember, cheese is a protein, so don't mix it with pasta, rice, or bread. The great news is that all vegetables combine with proteins as well as starches, so embrace those leafy greens whether you choose meat or go meatless. Butter and cream blend well with both proteins and starches, so opt for a pat of butter over your pasta instead of cheese—or ask for a plate of plain pasta and season it to taste with olive oil, butter, salt, and your choice of veggie sides. Say *si, grazie* to black pepper—it's great for the digestion. Incidentally, dining at a vegan establishment is no guarantee that you'll come home with a calm, satisfied gut; soy and nuts are protein, so if they're mixed with rice or pasta to simulate cheese, you may still experience digestive upset after a mostly veggie meal.

Drink water before your meal, to prime your gut. Who doesn't love a refreshing glass of European sparkling water, especially Pellegrino? But I opt instead for its non-bubbly equivalent, Acqua Panna, because the bubbles contribute to gas buildup in the gut, which I definitely don't want. Salad may be liberally enjoyed with both starch and protein meals, as the green leafies' chlorophyll and water content are great digestive aids. Starchy foods digest optimally in an alkaline environment versus an acidic one, so add a squeeze of lemon or lime to your water to alkalize it (contrary to popular belief, citrus fruits are alkalizing, not acidic). If you're having a starch meal, dress your salad simply with olive oil and lemon juice, and skip the vinegar (unless it's alkalizing apple-cider vinegar). But if you're eating meat, fish, or cheese, your meal will digest best in an acidic environment—so vinegar is exactly what you want in your salad dressing, to help your gut process those complex proteins. If you're having alcohol with your meal, choose the right drink for your food selection. Beer and sake are basically liquid starches, and best paired with starchy, non-protein meals; wine and Champagne are fancy forms of vinegar, so they help digest protein.

Finally, let the fruit stay in the fruit bowl. Do not—repeat, do not—have fruit for dessert, including fruit that's been cooked, such as pie filling. (Pumpkin is a veggie, so pumpkin pie is fine.) If you do, it will sit in your gut like a Maserati blocked by a Mack truck, idling and emitting fumes to cause you digestive distress. Fruit digests very quickly, so it should ideally be eaten in the morning, fifteen minutes before your a.m. oats (the breakfast treat, alas, I had to abstain from in the years since 1999, because delicious oatmeal caused me to spend even more time agonizing on the john than usual). Melon doesn't even digest—it moves like a bobsled straight down the alimentary canal, so it's best eaten by itself, even moments before a meal. Don't combine melon with other foods. The world's most creative chefs are introducing a cornucopia of fruit to savory dishes, so if there's something irresistible in your order, such as a fruity condiment, ask for it to be served in a separate container. Enjoy it by itself as an appetizer, and talk with your friends for ten or so minutes (or "paws" to digest by petting the dog) before tucking into the other items on your plate.

Here's the best perk of food combining: Cacao and vanilla both combine well with all foods, and—as the ancient Mayans and Aztecs knew—are both antioxidant, good for your digestion, and sexy! If you're having Mexican food, by all means order *mole*. For dessert, choose chocolate or vanilla gelato or sorbet whenever possible—have a double scoop on me—and skip the fruit garnish in favor of a sprig or two of mint; this delicious herb happens to be a digestive tonic, and it combines well with everything. (Of course, keep anything with chocolate in it far out of dogs' reach, as it's highly toxic to them.)

Although my new dietary regimen enabled me to feel lighter and less full after a meal than I had in years, I was still experiencing painful PF relapses, and each one left me more exhausted and drained than the one before. Gravity and the aging process conspired to make me feel my digestive disease the way wet weather still magnified Sheba's arthritis. By October, Sheba would receive a booster injection of the cells that were cultured for her in Vet-Stem's lab. With winter on its way, I wanted to be sure she'd be able to move with ease through the snow. After the booster, she trotted around like a teenager, even in cold, damp weather. Having just acquired an iPhone that month, I was able to record footage of Sheba, to prove that this fifteen-plus senior dog was displaying an astonishing youthful vitality. An infectious zest for life overtook all of my old girl's movements, both indoors and out on the greenway near our apartment. The videos proved how, once again, Vet-Stem had harnessed the built-in healing power of a dog's own cells to do their remarkable healing work. A Halloween snowfall caught unsuspecting New Yorkers by surprise, but Sheba was ready to romp through the powder, apparently getting younger with every step until she was positively prancing.

Dogs are my medical sentinels, and my preferred guides through labyrinthine health scenarios have been vets. But for a lot of people, those roles are played by actress-turned-health advocate Suzanne Somers, whose best-selling books enlighten millions about important medical advances, such as bioidentical hormone replacement therapy, the subject of her book *The Sexy Years*. Who could ever have predicted that one of the legacies of 1970s TV would be ditzy Chrissy of *Three's Company* fame undergoing a *Charly*-like metamorphosis to spread the gospel of leading-edge medicine? The woman doesn't even like dogs! In November 2011, I received a copy of the December issue of *Life Extension*, the magazine published by a dietary supplement company I'd purchased a membership in earlier that year. The cover's model—a very familiar blonde actress—and main cutline grabbed my attention: "Suzanne Somers Uses Novel Stem Cell Therapy During Breast Rejuvenation." Inside, Somers gave a Q&A interview about her decision to reconstruct her breast, which had been treated by oncologists with a lumpectomy and radiation therapy ten years earlier, in 2001, and had subsequently become disfigured and painful. After learning about combination cell-assisted lipotransfer—an innovative take on the plastic surgery technique of autologous fat grafting, or fat transplantation, pioneered in Japan by Dr. Kotaro Yoshimura and his colleagues at the University of Tokyo—Somers convinced Hollywood Presbyterian Hospital to let Beverly Hills reconstructive surgeon Dr. Joel Aronowitz perform the procedure on her as a clinical trial of one, obtaining IRB (institutional review board) approval. The FDA would not permit Somers to use the stem cells she'd banked with NeoStem, a company featured in her book *Breakthrough;* she could legally use only stem cells taken from her own fat during the liposuction. A liposuction yielded her own adipose-derived stem cells, which were then combined with the fat intended for transplantation in her disfigured breast, with the aim of creating a reconstructed breast that would keep its appearance significantly longer than with fat grafting alone. Somers couldn't be happier with the results, telling *Life Extension*, "If I can brag a little, it is beautiful—high and firm and real and soft and unscarred. Talk about reverse aging. My breasts look like they're from a young woman." I couldn't understand why this exciting protocol wasn't being publicized for a more strictly therapeutic purpose. I'm glad Suzanne Somers loves the way her breasts look—but what about patients who want access to their own stem cells so that they can walk, breathe, or live free of gut pain and incontinence? Now, that's my definition of sexy.

Romping with the rejuvenated Sheba, 2011 WYATT MARSHALL

By this time, I'd had enough of being sick. I felt ill more than I felt well, and no wonder—continuous reinfection was keeping me in a constantly inflamed state. It looked as if, after my nearly three-year-long quest, Europe would be my only option to receive the treatment that would help me enjoy life again. I viewed and re-viewed the iPhone video of Sheba romping through the snow a few dozen more times. That moving image of my beautiful red dog, rejuvenated with her own stem cells, was all I needed to see. I drafted a pleading e-mail to Dr. García-Olmo, explaining how he was now my only hope, held my breath, and hit send. The good doctor wrote back with his usual promptness to say that he and his team were undertaking clinical trials related to Crohn's fistula, but that they were already treating non-Crohn's fistula patients through "compassionate use," i.e. free. It was another case of déjà doo all over again—the caring, altruistic spirit of Victorian London's Fistula Infirmary, where poor patients were treated for free, was alive and well in millennial Madrid! Only an examination could determine whether I was a candidate for this treatment, the doctor explained, so I'd have to schedule an appointment. Could I be in Madrid on the afternoon of December 15? Could I ever! I grabbed the nearest dog—a very surprised Sheba— and drenched her fuzzy shoulder with tears of joy. Pulling myself together, I sent the doctor a reply e-mail, then began researching flights to Spain.

CHAPTER 13

Cure What Ails Me

Feeling celebratory, I gave OkCupid another shot. My earlier explorations of this popular online dating site had been a disappointment. Rebooting my account was a snap and, after scrolling through the available talent, in short order I stumbled on someone who seemed, at first glance of his profile, as nice as he was nice-looking. His zodiac sign said Taurus, which is my sign. I e-mailed him to see if we should give Taurus + Taurus a try. He replied quickly, introducing himself as Peter and making a remark about how much he "hate, hate, hate[d]" my profile photo. Peter seemed to have an adolescent boy's sense of humor, mentioning an impending visit to the 11th Precinct to see about a traffic ticket, and how he'd be sure to have his mug shot taken there, to match my profile photo. He claimed to be six-foot-two and a marathon runner. He certainly looked to be in great shape—that is, if his photos were not outdated by several years. I hoped he wasn't lying about his height; I like a tall drink of water but had caught a few naughty OkCupid users misrepresenting how tall they weren't. Although normally I prefer to speak to any prospective date by phone first, I thought it was encouraging that Peter didn't insist on speaking—he wanted to meet and invited me out for drinks. In my experience, such a bold move is rare among OkCupid users, many of whom are only too happy to carry on e-mail conversations for weeks, even months, without ever meeting. At this point, I was at the tail end of battling the flu, and although no longer contagious, still had a rasp to my voice. So naturally, my friends were surprised that, what with my long-anticipated trip to Spain looming in a matter of days, I should be making time to schlep to Manhattan for . . . a date?

On the subway ride to Manhattan, I deliberately dialed down my expectations. Arriving a few minutes late, I was pleasantly surprised to see that Peter was, indeed, tall and handsome, if much older than his out-dated photos had led me to believe. Wearing a suit and trench coat and carrying a brief case, he was leaning casually against a lamppost outside a Champagne bar, smiling most fetchingly, like a lanky Irish wolfhound, with gray hair and chocolate-brown eyes. I expected to shake hands, but he kissed me quite continentally on each cheek, then told me that the bar was booked for a private event, so we'd have to find another place to get acquainted. He had a velvety voice. I suggested the Hudson Hotel just a few blocks away, and we started walking in that direction.

"Dark hair and blue eyes," he said, approvingly, glancing over at me.

I explained how my recent participation in a makeover on TV's *Today* had necessitated the transformation of my plain, brown hair into its current shade, that of a dark bay horse, which master stylist Louis Licari had assured me would complement my eyes. Evidently Louis was not wrong. Once in the hotel, Peter and I occupied a leather sofa. I told him about my trip to Madrid; he was curious to know why I was traveling, so I got my full-disclosure PF routine out of the way, expressing my sincere hope of being cured with my own stem cells. Then I sat back and waited for my truth-telling to take its toll. Not only was Peter not grossed out but also he knew a bit about the nascent medical technology and the difference between embryonic cells and ASC—plus he told me that the younger of his two sons had once experienced a health problem similar to mine, and he'd helped nurse the boy through it. He told me he was separated and in the process of finalizing his divorce from his wife of twenty-six years. My living in the Bronx was not a dealbreaker, as it had been for so many OkCupid swains; he lived just minutes away, in Westchester. Here, it seemed, was a first for me: a truly wonderful guy. Handsome, successful, kind, loving, a grownup despite his boyish sense of humor. I was thrilled when he leaned in and gave me a kiss. He did this despite my voice becoming raspier and raspier as our conversation went on, to the point where finally I was croaking in a hoarse whisper. His eagerness to insert his tongue in my mouth told me he kind of liked me—which made me glad, because I kind of liked him, too. We canoodled some more, then he abruptly announced it was time for him to leave for dinner. "It's just a business thing," he said. "Wish I didn't have to go." We walked out of the hotel, and he took my hand and asked if I needed a lift. I opted to walk. He kissed me good night and said he'd call. Then his cab disappeared.

He e-mailed that night to report that he had a big smile on his face and how glad he was that he'd kissed me. A couple of days later, he invited me to the New York Botanical Garden, one of several beautiful landmarks in my new home borough. We had a magical afternoon of walking, talking, and kissing against the landscape designed to transport visitors far from present-day New York City and into a timeless magic garden that could easily pass for a European monarch's backyard. At one point, in mid-embrace, I remarked that I was tempted to disable my OkCupid account. Peter was silent, but we continued kissing. Eventually, he said he had to get going, but that he'd really like to see me before I left for my trip, which was just three days away. We walked to his Jeep, and he drove me home. When we arrived at my building, we began making out again, the smoking point in the vehicle mounting until we almost repaired to the back. He told me to go and walk my dogs before he'd lose it; I did. He kissed me goodbye and said he'd call. I walked the dogs and puttered around the apartment, trying to come down from the surprising high of that date. As the hours wore on, however, I kicked myself harder and harder for blurting out that business about disabling my OkCupid account—*Congratulations, loser, now you'll never hear from him again!* As it turned out, I didn't need to worry. I went online and found an e-mail from Peter asking if everything was OK. About an hour before that, he'd sent me an e-mail letting me know that he'd disabled his OkCupid account! Thrilled, I replied to tell him that I was doing the same.

Two days before my departure for Madrid, Peter took me out for lunch. He mentioned that he suspected X had written some harsh lies about me online. I stopped, took a deep breath, and warned him that I was about to let my closeted skeletons out to dance. That wasn't my ex, I explained, that was the work of my stalker—yep, I had one of those, too. He was unfazed, and I was profoundly impressed that here was a guy man enough to judge me for himself, and to see that the stalker's poisonous words were just that—words, not truth. Had I just won the lottery, or what? We kissed goodbye and he asked me to please stay in touch while I was in Madrid. My friend the photographer Heather Green was flying in

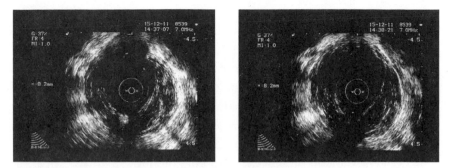

"The ocular proof": Two ultrasound views of my fistula

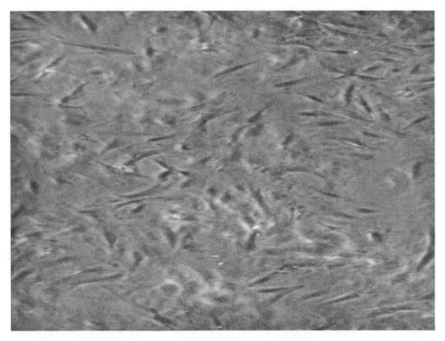

Stem cells extracted and cultured from fat DAMIÁN GARCÍA-OLMO

from Denver to accompany me on the Madrid trip; she'd always wanted to visit Spain, and I was grateful that she'd be there to support me and chronicle this leg of my medical odyssey. After years of nothing going right, I found myself in the unusual position of having everything go my way, all at once. We arrived in Madrid and checked in to our charming hotel on the Plaza de Santa Ana. Across the street, actor-poet Viggo Mortensen was starring in Ariel Dorfman's play *Purgatorio*. Aragorn from *Lord of the Rings*—who in real life adores dogs so much he wrote an elegy for one of his canine beloveds in *The Bark* magazine—was just a few feet away! I took even more comfort from the proximity of another benevolent literary-dramatic presence: the marble monument to the "Spanish Shakespeare," Calderon de la Barca, a few yards away, right in the center of the Plaza. Calderon's *La Vida Es Sueño* (*Life Is a Dream*) is my mother's favorite play. Life was starting to resemble a dream, a sweet one.

The next morning, I reported for my appointment with Dr. García-Olmo and received an exam unlike any I'd ever received in New York City: thorough and state-of-the-art. I was given a rectal ultrasound; the probe was expertly inserted and I did my best to relax as it navigated my inner space. It was the first proper, high-tech exploration of the fistula that had nearly killed me twelve years earlier. Despite so much research on the subject, my condition had always been something of a mystery to me. I never saw an image of my fistula—never, in fact, saw an image of anyone's fistula in any of the medical literature I'd read—so I had a hard time envisioning how it must look. It was my own personal Loch Ness monster: Was it even real? Dr. García-Olmo showed me the ultrasound picture, incontrovertible proof that the tunnel in my gut was no mythic malady—it really existed. Upon reviewing the image, the doctor gave me the great news that I was, indeed, a candidate for the stem cell procedure. The next morning, Dr. García-Olmo gave Heather and me a tour of the impressive stem cell lab at La Paz University Hospital. We looked at cells under a microscope—and it was thrilling to see the enormous potential of medicine's future taking the shape of these tiny, stem-like entities, all being cultured within the walls of the very same hospital where they'd be deployed to help the patients they'd been extracted from. Wow! *La vida es sueño*, indeed.

Walking and note-taking with stem cell superstar Damián García-Olmo, Director
of the Cell Therapy Unit at La Paz University Hospital   HEATHER GREEN

Damián García-Olmo moves with the speed, efficiency, and purpose of the cells he champions; you have to work to keep up with this dynamo doc, as I learned racing along those hospital hallways and jotting his running commentary in my reporter's notebook. I tailed this fast-moving medical target, scribbling notes as fast as I could write. Ever the precise professor, he peeked at my notebook to ascertain that I was spelling *mesenchymal* correctly. He introduced his team of doctors who had previously been his med-school students, and had—understandably—been inspired to follow their prof into the field of *terapia celular,* cellular medicine. After our tour, it became evident that this very busy man was being pulled in fifty directions and had run out of time, so he warmly hugged Heather and me goodbye and presented each of us with the volume he'd edited and coauthored: *Cell Therapy.* The famed scientist who literally wrote the book on *terapia celular* was handing us our very own copies. He promised to be in touch about my treatment date, which he hoped to arrange as soon as possible. I was floored by his combination of warmth and professionalism. He's the global stem cell guru and preeminent promoter of regenerative medicine for a reason, and stem cells couldn't have a more distinguished ambassador.

We returned to New York, and Heather flew home to Denver. By now, I could hardly wait to see Peter, who had kept in touch by e-mail and phone. He invited me to dinner, and we melted into each other's eyes all through the meal. "I have a confession to make," he said, ominously. Uh-oh, here it comes, I thought—he's not separated, he's married and seeking a midlife-crisis affair.

"I'm not a Taurus," he said, playfully bracing for my reaction. Apparently, he'd selected the wrong sign on the OkCupid zodiac questionnaire and never bothered to correct it.

"What sign are you?" I asked with some trepidation, fearing that it might be a spectacularly incompatible one.

"Cancer."

I breathed a sigh of relief—by all zodiac accounts, Cancer and Taurus are a match made in astrological heaven.

This time, it was Peter's turn to leave town. He was departing the next day for a Christmas trip with his kids. He promised to write every single day, and he kept his promise. Finally, shortly before New Year's, we were reunited. He'd said that he couldn't wait to have me all to himself for one solid day after his return. We agreed to meet at the clock in Grand Central Terminal, romantic rendezvous point for so many couples, actual and fictional; then we took a cab downtown to a swanky hotel on the Lower East Side and proceeded to make love five times in the ensuing six hours. Not bad for a couple of middle-aged folks, and I hadn't even received my stem cell treatment yet. The clock struck 5:00 p.m. and Peter informed me that he had to leave to dine uptown—this time it wasn't a business engagement; he was meeting his son and mother-in-law for dinner. I was taken aback and, frankly, disappointed. I'd pictured us having dinner together after such a momentous day—at the very least, sharing some kind of snack in bed—and falling asleep in each other's arms and had planned ahead for this eventuality by engaging the services of a dog walker. Instead, Peter and I showered, dressed, and shared a cab uptown. Kissing me goodbye, he promised to pick me up the following morning with his car, so we could speed back to the hotel to enjoy a few more hours of togetherness. The next morning, Peter was right on time. We made love twice this time, whereupon he took me out for lunch. Seated across from me at a French bistro, he grinned and blurted out, "So, think you can do this for the next thirty years?" I told him no, I could do it for forty—and I'd supply us with all the supplements we'd need to enjoy every decade to the fullest. He leaned across the table and kissed me. My oxytocin levels were skyrocketing to make up for years of lost time. Some weeks later, Peter took me for lunch in midtown in between business meetings. Standing one step below me on the stairs leading up to the dining room, he said, "The answer is yes."

"I didn't hear the question," I said.

He was silent. Later that day, I received an e-mail that read, "The question is . . . are you falling in love?" Thereafter, he'd say "I love you" at least once a day, whether in person, on the phone, or via e-mail or text. Sometimes, he'd come to visit me at my apartment; other times, we'd meet at different hotels around town. Each time, he had to leave abruptly, like Cinderella trying to beat the clock before the coach turns into a pumpkin. We never spent a night together. One time, he came over to my apartment on a Saturday—and left me slack-jawed by jumping up immediately after climaxing to announce he had to run to Manhattan to have dinner, this time with one of his guy friends. It was becoming quite apparent to me that this man was very much married, and this was very much an affair. I confronted him on the topic numerous times; each time Peter promised that he was just working out the way to make his divorce final without damaging what he held most dear, his relationship with his daughter and two sons. "Every time I see you, I light up," he told me. "The only other time I feel that way is when I'm with my kids. Please, be patient—we'll be together, I promise." Against my better judgment, I suspended disbelief because the guy made me so happy.

Peter happened to excel at every sport one can do on the water. When we met, I didn't know how to swim. I suspected this would be an obstacle to enjoying time together once the weather was warmer, especially after he mentioned his plan to take me to Florida, where we'd finally sleep *and* wake up together. Not wanting to wave to my sweetheart from the shore, I signed up for swimming lessons at a quaint little 1950s-era health club just a few blocks from my apartment. I never felt better than after those watery workouts; moving myself across the pool gave me a tremendous feeling of security. For many years, I had a recurrent nightmare in which I was standing on a tall, outdoor stairway made of slick marble. In the dream, suddenly the steps below me would turn into a sheer wall. With the steps behind me vanished, I had nowhere to go but down. I would often awake from this dream with a start. Now, for the first time, I resolved the situation while in the dream. When the steps morphed into a straight wall, I reached my arm back and out, as if doing the backstroke— and my hand grasped an unseen metal railing. I pulled myself to safety, then awoke to a newfound sense of calm. Calling Peter the next morning to describe this pleasant new twist on a scary old nightmare, I said that I strongly suspected I had him to thank for it. "It's my job to make you feel safe," he said warmly. "I love you." Between my relationship and my newfound aquatic exercise regimen, plus all the running and walking I was doing with my dogs, I felt better than I had in years. My immune system boosted as never before; I didn't feel sick for almost five months. Happiness and emotional fulfillment really can make the difference between sickness and wellness; the endorphins released when one feels happy can put a long distance between relapses.

At about the same time as I finally conquered my fear of swimming, a very sick little dog in Florida was taking a very different kind of dive—and reaping even bigger health benefits. In March 2012, a five-month-old Yorkshire terrier pup named Sofie emerged from a routine spay procedure blind and deaf, with no chew reflex and brain damage that caused her to stumble and bump into things (the medical lexicon calls this *ataxia*). A veterinary neurologist gently broke the news to Sofie's devastated owner, Corinne Scholtz, that euthanasia might be the kindest option. Luckily, the vet also suggested that Scholtz consult Dr. Andrew Turkell of Boca Raton. Turkell's expert recommendation was for Sofie to spend time in his hospital's recently installed hyperbaric chamber. Enclosing a patient for therapeutic exposure to oxygen under pressure higher than normal at sea level, the chamber breathes new life into all the body's tissues, reducing swelling and inflammation, stimulating blood vessel formation, and helping all the body's cells proliferate to promote regrowth. This extraordinary device resembles a submarine, down to its see-through portholes; its design is a pet-specific adaptation of hyperbaric chambers for people, which are enclosed in Plexiglas to minimize feelings of claustrophobia, something people experience more often than animals do. The vet was confident that Sofie would be helped tremendously by spending sessions in the hyperbaric chamber—colloquially termed "dives" because oxygen under pressure can simulate scuba conditions.

HBOT is Medicare-approved for the treatment of trauma; already, five months since installing the chamber, Turkell had observed how HBOT had spared many of his hospital's patients a lot of pain, and their owners a lot of heartbreak. He became a champion of the modality, and hyperbaric medicine is lucky to have such a dedicated spokesperson. In fact, Turkell was such a believer in the healing power of hyperbaric medicine that he'd renamed his practice Calusa Veterinary Emergency and Hyperbaric Center. After some thirty sessions of HBOT, Sofie was back to her old, young self, her motor function restored and her deafness and blindness reversed. Beyond grateful for this medical miracle, her overjoyed owner said, "I think Sofie is healthier now than before she was injured. She's a functioning, happy dog. HBOT saved my dog's life; I would recommend it to anybody." Digging deeper like my canine role models, the journalist-terriers I live with, I learned that HBOT has been proven to mobilize stem cells eightfold after twenty sessions. Dr. Turkell is so thorough in his multi-modality healing approach that, to ensure the best possible outcome for his patients undergoing regeneration therapy, he routinely recommends sessions in the hyperbaric chamber to clients whose pets, like my Sam and Sheba, seek healing relief with their own stem cells.

The person who'd tipped me to this story was veterinarian Dr. Diane Levitan, another champion of hyperbaric veterinary medicine and a friend from way back who'd treated several of my animals. Knowing something of my long struggle to find perirectal relief, Dr. Levitan asked why I didn't investigate hyperbaric oxygen therapy for myself. On the short list of Medicare-approved conditions treated by HBOT is chronic nonhealing wounds, and a fistula certainly answers that description. Intrigued that Dr. Schmerz had never mentioned it, I figured perhaps the hospital where I'd been treated didn't have a chamber, but a quick Internet search revealed that yes, in fact, it did. When I called the hospital's hyperbaric unit to inquire as to whether they treat perirectal fistulas, the answer was, "All the time." It wasn't stem cell therapy, but it was a viable cure for what ailed me, and it had been right there under my nose all this time, in my hometown—yet the doctor hadn't suggested it. Once again, I was astonished at Dr. Schmerz's compromised bedside manner. There was a hyperbaric chamber in the same hospital where he worked—yet he didn't make the connection between my chronic nonhealing wound and the chamber's potential to help it heal. I wonder what Hippocrates would think of that? Maybe, as a career surgeon, he just couldn't look past surgery as the answer to all medical problems. Whatever the case, his way of thinking was the polar opposite of holistic. Unfortunately, as I would learn, a session in the hospital's chamber costs in the four figures, and I was still uninsured. And besides, the hyperbaric nurse informed me, I'd have to revisit Dr. Schmerz for another $500 checkup, because he'd have to determine my eligibility for treatment. Argh! Talk about a curative Catch-22 and a sad indictment of health care in America. In my humble nonexpert opinion, I felt we needed a clinical trial, right here in the United States: The study's goal would be to prove the efficacy and safety of HBOT in combination with adult stem cells in treating PF. One group of patients would receive adjunct treatment with HBOT, while the other group would receive only their own stem cells. I bet both study groups would emerge from this trial feeling a lot better than when they went in.

Oh well, I still had the L-word as my adjunct therapy. But happiness, like Medicine Dogs, can only do so much, as I discovered one morning when I got the scare of my life. I was scheduled to tryst with Peter at a hotel on the Upper East Side; due to his hectic schedule, we hadn't been together in almost two weeks. The day before, I'd enjoyed a swanky business lunch, falling off the food-combining wagon by selecting risotto with salmon. Big mistake: It had been a long time since I'd enjoyed rice, formerly one of my favorite foods, but for the past several months, I'd reduced my consumption of this grain to the occasional bite of nigiri sushi. My system just wasn't accustomed to processing rice any longer—especially not the extra-sticky Arborio rice used to make delicious, creamy risotto—and it let me know that in no uncertain terms, in the most painful way possible, the morning after that luxurious lunch. Feeling the urgent need to go as never before, I sat down on the john; peristalsis began, but nothing came out. The cramps were excruciating. I was beyond constipated, doubled over and weeping with pain. I panicked, fearing that this was the end and I was going to be found dead right there on my toilet. As I cried and called out for my mommy—so loudly it's a wonder she didn't hear me nine miles away—my dogs and cats must have thought I'd finally lost it. Standing up to retrieve a handheld mirror from my bathroom cabinet, I checked back there, and saw my sphincter stretched wide open; the sight almost caused me to pass out. I climbed into the bathtub to irrigate my rear end with warm water, then climbed back out for another go on the john. This yielded just one paltry, raisin-sized segment of the gobstopper that clogged my plumbing, not the torpedo formation that signals a complete, healthy bowel movement. Far from relieved, I got up and stumbled all the way to the kitchen, fully crouched forward and unable to stand up straight. Somehow, I managed to reach the shelf where I keep the loose-leaf green tea—the extra-potent organic stuff from Japan—and brewed myself a cup.

Taking this beverage with me back to the bathroom, bent over like an upside-down and sideways letter L, I drank it down, then waited for the caffeine to take effect. I contemplated my solitary state; in one sense it was good that I lived alone, so no one had to be grossed out by these goings-on. But boy, it sure would be nice to have someone to fetch me a strong cup of hot green tea if an emergency called for one. Alas, I couldn't train my sweet Medicine Dogs to do tricks like that. Thankfully, the tea worked its magic within a few minutes, and I was able to empty my bowels completely. What came out was the size of a submarine. The sheer terror of that ordeal, and my very real fear of being found dead on the toilet days after the fact, had exhausted me to the point where I was obliged to take a cat-nap with my dogs. By the time I left for my date, I felt enormously improved, walking tall in my high heels. I brought along a couple of Eater's Digest tea bags. Despite its cloyingly cute name, this stuff works to keep my GI on the straight and narrow with its healing blend of peppermint and ginger. Peter and I had a lovely time together—he never suspected that I was anything but perfectly OK—but I resolved never to combine rice with protein ever again and haven't fallen off that wagon ever since. In fact, I've pretty much sworn off rice altogether.

Soon after, Peter took me with him when he looked at apartments with a real-estate broker on the Upper West Side, and we spent several afternoons deliberating over a variety of places until she finally showed us The Perfect Pad, in a brand-new, glass-walled high-rise. Then, suddenly, there was no further discussion of Peter's moving from the suburbs to the city. The weeks passed, and it became increasingly evident that he had no intention of leaving his family. As I worried over losing him, my stress began to take a physical toll. I experienced the first serious relapse I'd had in several months, with fever, diarrhea, pus, the works. I wasn't alone in having a health breakdown: Sadly, Sheba suddenly began to exhibit signs of rapidly accelerated aging. She'd been diagnosed with hypothyroidism just a few months earlier, and the underactive butterfly-shaped gland in her throat was giving up its valiant fight. We'd enjoyed thirteen wonderful months of rejuvenated mobility thanks to Vet-Stem, and many fun off-leash romps along the Pelham Parkway, but now, she could barely walk or hold her urine. Heartsick, I put my sweet old girlfriend to sleep on, of all dates, Mother's Day. Tod came along and brought Piggy. Surrounded by her favorite friends, Sheba was admirably calm and relaxed, smiling her dolphin smile. It was surreal déjà vu to watch the pink liquid enter her vein and take irreversible effect. Just the other day—last year at this very hospital—we'd revived her from the deathlike slumber of anesthesia after her successful Vet-Stem procedure. Today, injected with a lethal dose of pentobarbital instead of healing stem cells, she wouldn't be making a return trip. I could almost hear her whispering those familiar Anne Bredon lyrics: *"Babe, I'd like to stay here, you know I'd really like to stay here . . . "*

Dr. Higgins listened for a heartbeat. My rambling rose was gone, trotting confidently along the highway that had beckoned her all her life—trotting all the way to the Bridge, every white hair in her coat restored to glorious sable as if by Louis Licari himself. Sheba would soon be romping with the rest of my ghost pack—Britannia, Haus, Tiki, Sam, Pepper, and Daisy—in an unfenced evergreen field where cars are off-limits, it's always a perfect spring day, and nobody needs to wear a collar or start a fight. Still, even with that image, plus four very real, very big dogs

Farewell, sweet Sheba—till we meet again. WYATT MARSHALL

filling every corner of the small apartment, my home and heart echoed with emptiness. "She will continue to bring you gifts beyond description," promised dear John Bartlett in a sweet condolence message sent the next day via text. The fashion designer and animal advocate had been one of Sheba's biggest fans and still treasured a photo of my girl with his canine muse, the famous fashion hound and "tripawd" Tiny Tim. The quotable Mr. Bartlett was not wrong: Days after Sheba passed, I received the first of her gifts when an e-mail from Dr. García-Olmo arrived. It was time to return to Madrid for an examination at the private hospital. My procedure was finally about to happen, for real.

CHAPTER 14

The Stem Cell Cafe

You couldn't ask for a lovelier destination than Madrid in late May, and that's where I was headed. To get the approval for treatment, Dr. García-Olmo was obliged to reexamine me at the private hospital where the procedure would now be taking place, Fundación Jiménez Díaz, and to confer with the plastic surgeon who would be performing my liposuction. On Saturday, May 26, my plane touched down at Barajas Airport and I headed directly to the home of my host, a high school friend I hadn't seen in decades but had reconnected with on Facebook. After a shower plus a catch-up chat and dog-walk, it was time to get to the clinic. I was grateful to Dr. García-Olmo and his team for graciously agreeing to examine me on a Saturday; this saved me a lot of money, as airfare was significantly less expensive on the weekend than during the week.

Walking around Madrid on a Saturday morning gave me plenty of quiet time to think. Six days earlier, I'd turned forty-seven. A little knowledge is a dangerous thing, and I happened to know a bit about a handful of people who'd died at forty-seven, starting with Judy Garland. I was shocked to realize that the little old lady with the huge fan base, her body wracked with the pain of addiction, was just forty-seven when she OD'd. And Edith Piaf—what was it about torch singers dying young? It wasn't just female icons in the forty-seven club, either; Jack Kerouac passed in his forty-seventh year, and, just a few weeks before I left for Madrid, Adam Yauch of The Beastie Boys also left us. I'm not presuming to compare myself to these amazingly accomplished people, but we all know them, or feel like we do, so it's shocking to realize that they were just forty-seven when their lives ended. The final time I spoke to X, he made this unsolicited forecast: "You will die alone, and you will die of cancer." Talk about a scorched-earth farewell! I thought of X's cancer curse and

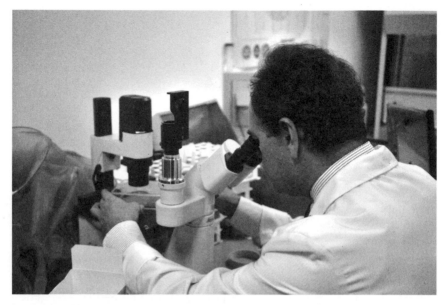

Dr. García-Olmo examines stem cells at La Paz University Hospital.
HEATHER GREEN

renewed my resolve to protect my cells so his poisonous prediction would never come true. We all die alone; this is a fact of life that my darling husband refused to accept. But I had no plans to die of cancer. Far from it! In fact, I would fight cancer preventively, and I'd fight it with all I had. The proactive battle would begin with protecting my cells from anything that wasn't natural—but especially the toxic assaults of abusive people; atmospheric pollution; and chemically "enhanced" foods, beverages, and personal grooming and household cleaning products. I looked forward to doing what I could to stave off cellular oxidation, getting past this land-mark year, and receiving the long-anticipated healing assist from my own stem cells. I could clearly envision this procedure enabling me to enjoy the second half of my life to the fullest, with my health problems receding in the rear-view mirror.

With half an hour to go before my appointment, I walked along the Avenida Reyes Católicos (Avenue of the Catholic Kings), location of the hospital named for an earlier Spanish medical pioneer with a double surname, Carlos Jiménez Díaz, who is justly renowned and beloved in his native country. Outside, there's an impressive monument to the great doctor, featuring three slender naiads surrounding a plinth on which is inscribed AL MAESTRO DE LA MEDICINA—CARLOS JIMÉNEZ DÍAZ—EL HOMBRE— LA CIENCIA—LA PATRIA—LE RINDEN HOMENAJE (TO THE MASTER OF MEDICINE—CARLOS JIMÉNEZ DÍAZ—MAN—SCIENTIST—PATRIOT—PAY TRIBUTE). With a commitment to his calling that's the stuff of legend, the good doctor more than deserved such a tribute; he showed up for work on crutches even after sustaining injuries in an automobile accident! It was time to go inside. Visitors were milling back and forth in the sun-filled, retro-style lobby, but the hallways, lavatories, and examination rooms upstairs were dark and empty. Everything was impressively clean, as if transported by time capsule directly from the 1950s, complete with the cleanliness we associate with that more innocent time. I kept walking until I heard voices. There was Dr. García-Olmo, together with Drs. Herreros and Guadalajara, plus one of the Fundación's plastic surgeons, who would be performing my liposuction. All had graciously taken time out of their weekend for me. On a pristine examination-room table, I received a quick, efficient rectal exam and was pronounced a candidate for the surgery I'd waited so long to have. I pulled my pants back up and reconvened with the doctors in the consulting office adjacent to the exam room.

Dr. García-Olmo proceeded to explain to me how the procedure would go: In the morning, I'd be anesthetized with propofol for the liposuction, to harvest adipose tissue from my thighs. The fat would then be processed for my stem cells at the cell medicine unit of La Paz University Hospital, seven kilometers away. Later that day, I'd be put under with propofol once again, so that the gastroenterologist could administer the injection of my cells directly into my fistula. To save money on an overnight stay, I could be discharged from the hospital in the care of a friend. The next day, I'd be free to return home to New York. Ideally, the liposuction would yield the number of cells needed, twenty million, but if not, increasing my cells' strength in numbers would happen in the La Paz lab, where they'd be cultured and cryopreserved for one year. In the event a booster was needed, I could return for a second, or even third injection of millions more of my own cells, without having to undergo another liposuction. The simple expansion and storage of my own cells—the very same culturing and deep-freezing that dogs' and horses' cells routinely underwent at Vet-Stem's lab—was par for the course for human cell therapy patients here in Madrid. Yet this enormous technological benefit is precisely what the FDA denies human patients in America, with the justification that a person's own cells, once cultured, become a drug that must be regulated in the interest of public safety.

Thrilled that this was finally about to happen, I had just two questions for Dr. García-Olmo: (1) Would I receive an intravenous injection of my cells as my dogs had? and (2) Would the procedure involve the use of fibrin glue, which had been a control in some of the clinical trials? The answers were, No and No. While I was glad that we wouldn't be using glue—who wants glue in one's gut?—I was less thrilled about not receiving an IV, or vascular delivery of my own cells. After all, per the Vet-Stem protocol, Sam and Sheba had both received intravenous and intra-joint injections—plus booster IV shots—of their own cells and experienced great success. Who knows how my best friends' outcomes would have played without those injections of healing cells directly into their bloodstream? But I respected that Dr. García-Olmo did not wish to veer from the protocol he'd established in the clinical trials and gratefully acquiesced. We said goodbye, and Doctora Herreros walked me down the hallway toward the exit. Upon arriving at the glass-fronted admission desk, I was presented with a bill. What was this? I was being charged 300 euros for the examination—except I'd been given to understand that my exam and treatment would be "compassionate use," therefore free of charge. There'd been no charge for the previous visit in December. Handing over my Visa card, realizing with no small amount of relief that my bank account had just the amount to cover the charge (approximately five hundred US dollars) but not much more, I grew very concerned. I asked Doctora Herreros whether I should expect to incur any further charges going forward. She explained that, yes, I'd have to pay for the procedure—only the culturing and preserving of my cells could be donated. Noticing my look of complete surprise, Doctora Herreros kindly advised me to address further money questions via e-mail to Dr. García-Olmo and to copy the rest of the team.

I was in shock, although, given the state of the Spanish economy—
which was at that point, like my own financial picture, on the verge of collapse—I shouldn't have been. At this point in its illustrious history, Spain,
birthplace of so many generous medical maestros, simply couldn't afford
to extend free treatment to a foreigner. I e-mailed Dr. García-Olmo to
thank him for his time and to inquire how much I might expect to pay
for the procedure. A few hours after hitting Reply All, I received a reply
from Dr. Guadalajara. The estimate was 19,000 euros—about $25,000. I
broke down in tears; I didn't even have $2,500. I'd come so far, but now
there was no way I could afford to have the procedure I'd waited for so
long to have. I walked around the beautiful Spanish streets, bawling like
a baby. Then I pulled myself together and hailed a cab to take me to the
Mercado de San Miguel, Madrid's mouthwatering gourmet food market.
The Mercado was packed with happy, hungry customers, many slurping
oysters and sipping sparkling wine. Being surrounded by exquisite edibles
always provides comfort and food for thought. Large spaces filled with
food vendors tend to do that, whether an open-air farmers' market, such
as the four-times-weekly one at Manhattan's Union Square, or Macy's
Cellar, the renowned food emporium in the basement of New York City's
legendary department store. And what I took in at the Mercado, with my
eyes and taste buds, helped to clarify a few things.

Consider paella, the rice dish that originated in Valencia, on Spain's
eastern coast. Paella's popularity across Spain might be one reason there
were enough Spanish fistula sufferers to warrant sophisticated clinical trials investigating ultramodern cures: Eating this classic example of a poor
food combination might be the culprit. Years of not just mixing rice with
protein on the same plate, but cooking them together so they become
inseparable, can devastate a delicate digestive system. And yet, paella
is inarguably delicious—*muy rico,* as the Spanish say—and a national
comfort food. Sometimes, familiar flavors—what the food critic Mimi
Sheraton, describing Thanksgiving, once wisely termed "the thrill of the
expected"—are the only cure for what ails us at a given moment, even
if they might later give us a spectacular tummy ache. And right now, I
craved edible comfort. But although I proceeded to break almost every
food-combining rule in the book, I stopped short of having rice, which

I'd promised myself I'd never do, not even here in paella central. Reason prevailed; my rational side knew that, in the absence of surgery, I'd have to really watch my diet now, turning my tiny kitchen in the Bronx—itself not much bigger than a stem cell—into a laboratory of sorts, where I would devise nutritious foods to keep my cells in peak condition. Why can't healthy food also be sexy and exciting and *muy rico*, as good as it is good for you? This was the kind of recipe I was determined to create, designed to optimize cellular health as well as delight the taste buds.

At times like this, it pays to eat dessert first, especially one as dense and delicious as the justly famous Sachertorte, a two-layer chocolate cake (*Torte* in German), accented with apricot jam, that was a sweet highlight of my childhood. All I could think about was mainlining a slice of the exquisite Sachertorte specimen I'd so enjoyed on my first Madrid trip back in December; I could taste its deliciousness on my mind's tongue. However, the Austrian pastry stall wasn't where I'd remembered it to be. Walking around looking for it, I circled back to where I started, then learned from a neighboring stall attendant that the Austrian pastry purveyors were no longer at the Mercado. They'd packed up and gone back home. *Auf wiedersehen.*

Early the next morning, I flew back to New York. There was plenty of time to think on that long journey home. At the airport, I'd managed to find a slice of Sachertorte—nowhere near as good as that peerless specimen I'd had five months earlier, but a serviceable substitute. Contemplating it, I had to accept—once again—that we really are what we eat. This got me thinking about what history's two most famous fistula patients ate. According to Susan Rossi-Wilcox, author of *Dinner for Dickens: The Culinary History of Mrs. Charles Dickens' Menu Books,* Mr. Dickens ate meat and lots of it, his favorites being mutton and pork, but he didn't care for vegetables or salad. Veggies and lettuce, of course, are a huge help when digesting complex proteins, especially pork, which can take as long as four hours for the gut to process. So most likely, Dickens's explanation for what had caused his fistula—that it developed from us writers' unfortunate occupational hazard of sitting for long periods—was spurious. The real explanation had to be that diet of his. The Sun King, meanwhile, was not a benevolent ruler where his GI tract was concerned.

Again the theory of what had caused a famous fistula—too much time in the saddle—was doubtless incorrect. The culprit had to be his decadent diet. For the 2010 exhibition "Louis XIV: The Man and the King" at the Palace of Versailles, sponsored by Moët Hennessy, parent company of Dom Pérignon (Louis's preferred Champagne), the Michelin-starred chef Jean-François Piège re-created a typical *grand couvert* (or king's dinner) down to the last historically correct crumb. Two of the dishes were garnished, accurately, with sprinkles of gold leaf. Looking at the menu, it's no wonder Louis suffered a fistula; the royal dining habits were a gilded recipe for digestive disaster. After four hors d'oeuvres, four soups, five *rôts* (scallops, wild duck, hare, roast beef, *and* wild salmon), plus a service of *entremets* (sides) including "Rice Salad à la Royale," the meal's last service was—I shudder to say it—fruit! But never mind the king-sized portions and poor combinations of food—how about the fact that dinner began at 10:00 p.m. and lasted about an hour and a half? Plus, the king's preferred pre-bedtime snack was boiled eggs and glazed fruit, not an easily digestible combo in any circumstance, but certainly not as a chaser to all that went before it! I wonder if Louis's grumbling stomach ever permitted him a decent night's sleep during his seventy-two-year reign.

Arriving at my apartment the next morning, I received a text message from Peter. This was the Memorial Day holiday, and he was weekending at his place in Massachusetts—the one he'd said he planned to give outright to the Mrs. as part of their divorce settlement. She was there with him. It was finally apparent that he was never going to be divorced and available. I'd given him so many opportunities to tell me the truth, even asking him point-blank if he'd changed his mind about leaving her. And each time he'd replied, most reassuringly, "Not right now—but very soon!" Peter called and asked how my trip had gone. I told him what had transpired. When he heard the sum that my procedure was estimated to cost, he balked: "That's way too much." Ah, comparative economics: I flashed back to the day, just two months earlier, when we'd found the "perfect" apartment after a month and a half of looking, then strolled hand-in-hand through Riverside Park, the trees bursting with pink and white flower buds that herald spring in New York City. Eager to impress Rula, the ravishing real-estate agent who'd shown us so many promising pads, he'd grandly assured her that it would be no problem at all for him to pay an entire year of rent up front to secure a very desirable $6,000-per-month apartment. My life-changing surgery was one third of that sum, but now it was "way too much." Well, it wasn't too much to me; I was already trying to figure out ways to raise the funds and make it happen.

I understood that it was only a matter of time before Peter would break off our relationship. He did it by inviting me to meet him for lunch on an unusually broiling day in late June. Strangely quiet throughout the meal, he asked if I had time to take a walk—except once outside, the sweltering midtown heat was oppressive enough to turn a stroll into a stress test. We walked west toward the Hudson Hotel, the scene of our very first date. Every indoor seat was filled with patrons seeking air-conditioned respite from the heat outside. For privacy, one had to repair to the deserted outdoor lounge, which was hotter than the inside of a tumble dryer. Once seated, Peter proceeded to tell me—calmly, quickly, frostily—that his wife had begged him not to go through with the divorce, so he was going to do everything possible to make his marriage work. His chilly demeanor was such a bracing blast of cold air that it could have air-conditioned that entire steamy outdoor space. Floored by his ability to maintain such corporate cool in such sweltering heat, I reminded him of the many times he'd assured me that "[His] marriage is broken and can't be fixed." So, I wanted to know, was I the fix?

"Come *on*, you always knew I was married," he said testily.

So he was revising history. The apartments we saw, his promises that we'd be together, I must have imagined them all. I rose to leave; the heat had expanded my feet, which were chafing in my high-heeled Christian Siriano for Payless sandals. Peter followed me indoors, then forlornly took my hand and asked me to please sit down with him. Like a dutiful dog, I sat. He was quiet, so I filled the silence by explaining that this was not the way our story was supposed to end. He insisted that he just couldn't risk alienating his kids; incidentally, the little ones ranged in age from twenty-one to twenty-six. "You went back to your husband many times," he reminded me. "I thought that you, of all people, would understand."

Sucker punch! He'd missed the moral of my marital fable—that returning to the spouse who makes you unhappy is never a smart move.

I'd made this sad mistake many more times than I should have, and now he was about to repeat it. Again, I stood to leave. I was crying by now and must have looked a spectacular mess. I had a long ride ahead of me, back to the Bronx and my beloved dogs. My contact lenses were fogging over from the tears, which stung like hell, and I had a hard time finding the escalator leading to the hotel exit. Peter just stood there watching me stumble around. No offer was made to put me in a cab; I was on my own now. I made it home and cried for a solid week, my right eye becoming so bloodshot that the white part, the sclera, turned bright red and remained that way for days. Not only could I not afford my surgery but also I couldn't even afford an ophthalmologist visit. So I stopped wearing contacts—the eyeball was so inflamed it couldn't support the lens—and really lived up to my old "GalWithGlasses4U" OkCupid handle. One night, Cupcake came over for a cuddle, and in a show of solidarity, she sweetly offered me her paw, which I lifted and kissed. That's how I remembered that I might fix my red eye with the same homeopathic remedy I'd used to heal her goopy ones: *Euphrasia officinalis*, also known as eyebright. I tried it, and it worked like a charm.

For the ensuing three months, I split my focus between writing and toning my cells the way I'd toned those of my dogs, confident that soon I would have my surgery, one way or another. Meanwhile, on Facebook and Twitter, I followed the excellent doctors Alejandro Junger, Julian Whitaker, and Marty Makary. I streamlined my supplement regimen, ordering several online as a cost-saving measure. When you check e-mails first thing in the morning, whose name do you usually see in your in-box first? Thanks to my supplement orders, every day I have several solicitous doctors competing with each other for in-box priority the way my Medicine Dogs joust for my attention, all checking in with helpful hints, special offers, and new formulas: Dr. Whitaker, Dr. Mercola, Dr. Sinatra, and Dr. Lark. Also offering excellent advice and supplements for pets is Dr. Mercola's excellent vet, Dr. Karen Becker. Then, after a few weeks, my in-box delivered a message from the most important healer of them all: Dr. García-Olmo, who kindly e-mailed me that he'd managed to pare down the cost of surgery to 8,500 euros—about $10,000 US dollars. It was far from an unimaginable sum, and I resolved to raise the money somehow.

The weeks flew by as I worked long and hard, writing as fast as I could in an effort to sock away funds. In previous years, this MO worked. But now, no matter how many Dogster articles I churned out, after rent plus utilities, it just wasn't adding up. There was no way to accomplish my self-healing goal without asking for help. In October, Hurricane Sandy struck New York City, and once again things were put in proper perspective. Life is a gift; I wanted to enjoy it free of health problems, now. No more waiting! I identified two people to whom I might appeal for a loan to cover the cost of surgery in Spain (and no, neither one was Richie, my Panama paramour). The first, billionaire brother of a high school friend who suffers from colitis, said no but wanted to know the name of my doctor; the second surprised me by saying yes, no questions asked, and sending me a promissory note to sign. The check arrived in the mail a few days after that, whereupon I sent Dr. García-Olmo a jubilant e-mail: *dear doctor, i have the money!* And the good doc replied that he would e-mail me forms to complete, so that we could schedule my procedure for January. As a pack, all the Medicine Dogs I'd ever nursed to optimal health had led me to this moment. I'd be following their healing lead, the better to continue being their wellness watchdog for as long as humanly possible.

Tearing open the package of information when it arrived from Madrid, I noticed something quite out of place and ominous: a warning about the possible risk of myocardial infarction. I'd been apprised that I'd be undergoing general anesthesia twice in one day, but it didn't make sense that propofol might cause a heart attack. Reading the fine print, I noticed that my procedure would involve the use of Tissucol Duo. A quick Internet search revealed that this is a widely used brand of fibrin glue comprised of bovine and human tissue. Had the doctor changed his mind about not using glue in my procedure? One of the main reasons I'd worked so long and hard to find healing with my own stem cells was that they were my own and carried no risk of rejection. Who knew how my body might react to the components of a sealant made of proteins derived from a person that I didn't know and wasn't related to? The extreme form of rejection is myocardial infarction. This wasn't much different from, say, receiving the transplant of a cadaver's joint, which I vowed I'd never do, or engaging in unsafe sex with a perfect stranger. And it goes without saying that the idea of being treated with a product made from a dead animal was ethically abhorrent to me. Even if I didn't encounter complications from rejection of the glue, how would we know whether what closed up the fistula was my own cells, or the glue? I was by now my own medical experiment, and I wanted to give my cells a chance to repair my fistula on their own, without fibrin-glue backup. I wanted to be treated, as my dogs had been, with my own cells and nothing but my own cells. This was my experiment, my clinical trial. It was certainly costing enough; let's please do it my way—Sam's way, the Vet-Stem way.

I e-mailed the doctors about Tissucol Duo. Dr. Guadalajara responded, *Hola Julia! In our experience, we have reported results are better with fibrin glue, so it will be used.* Despite my immersion course in science and medicine, my scientific thinking (if such it may be called) works like this: Basically, I look at things in terms of animals. I was suddenly reminded of the scare two years earlier, when Redmond turned that container of Gorilla Glue into a chew toy and the emergency animal hospital into our Saturday nightclub. Redmond turned out A-OK, but the medical moral was keep the glue out of the gut! Combining my cells with surgical sealant just didn't sound right. If the ASCs were like microscopic hunting hounds, how could they do their healing work when trapped in the equivalent of those awful rodent glue traps that doomed their victims to a cruel, sticky death? I was indeed cellbound, but Tissucol Duo was not the cellbinder I had in mind.

It was back to Internet U for a quick study session. On the NIH website, I found this article from 2007, on "Safety of the use of Tissucol Duo S in cardiovascular surgery: retrospective analysis of 2149 patients after coronary artery bypass grafting," authored by doctors at Germany's Hannover Medical School. "Fibrin sealant is widely used in almost all fields of surgery and has proved to be an effective therapeutic tool in cardiothoracic surgery," it began. "Nevertheless, there have been concerns about early bypass graft occlusion associated with the use of fibrin glue." I was satisfied to stop reading there; when doctors express concern, that's enough of a red flag for me. Then I registered the results of the study: Of the 2,149 patients studied, "879 (40.9 percent) were intra-operatively treated with Tissucol Duo S fibrin glue, 1270 (59.1 percent) did not

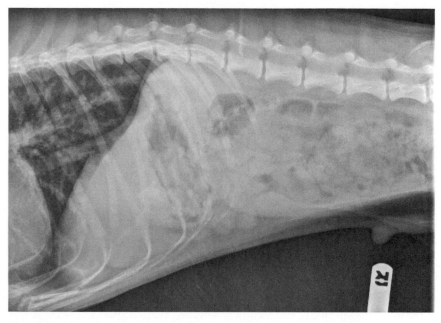

Mercifully, there had been no glue in Redmond's gut, and there wouldn't be in mine either. ANIMAL MEDICAL CENTER

receive fibrin glue (control group) . . . [and] there was an increased mortality rate in the Tissucol Duo S group compared to the control group . . . multivariable adjustment did not reduce the risk of fibrin glue below an odds ratio of 2.2."

Now I knew for certain that—with all due respect to Dr. García-Olmo and his team—Tissucol Duo was the last thing I wanted. After weighing the potential risks and benefits, it was with a heavy heart that I decided not to undergo the procedure in Spain. España had been my medical dream destination for so long that, inspired by that beautiful country and by my dogs, I'd developed a new motto, a Spanish riff on "Godspeed": *Vaya con Perros,* "Go with Dogs" or "Dogspeed." Now, "Going with Dogs" would have to mean not going to Spain. I sat down for a good cry. Brushing away my tears, I called the one person who could be counted on to give me the precise, expert, second opinion a situation like this called for.

CHAPTER 15

Treatment Day

Amazingly, the globe-trotting Dr. Bob wasn't away giving a presentation at a clinic or speaking at a cell-medicine conference; he was in his office and took my call right away. Bringing him up to date on my stem cell saga, I mentioned that my physician was none other than Dr. García-Olmo. The super-well-connected Dr. Bob was impressed: "Wow! He's THE guy!" And yet, the vet confirmed my suspicion that fibrin glue was not the best way to go. "It might actually prevent your cells from differentiating," he explained. Then he dropped a bombshell: "Did I tell you about my stem cell procedure?" It had been over a year since we'd communicated. Memo to self: Don't lose touch with Dr. Bob for too long. He proceeded to tell me about the long-term, chronic degeneration in his shoulder due to a torn rotator cuff and a tear in the labrum, and how the condition reached a crisis point when his shoulder froze in searing pain. He described his chance encounter with a plastic surgery salesman on a flight home from Florida in October 2011. The salesman was returning from the same conference where Dr. Bob had mentioned his painful shoulder during his presentation and recommended that he consult a Beverly Hills aesthetic surgeon named Mark Berman, who had performed the human equivalent of the Vet-Stem procedure on the salesman's knees. Dr. Berman did something that few doctors do: transition from the hugely lucrative cosmetic side to therapeutic practice, because of his confidence in the healing power of adult stem cells. Together with urologist Elliot Lander in Rancho Mirage, CA, Dr. Berman cofounded the California Stem Cell Treatment Center (CSCTC) in Rancho Mirage, CA, dedicated to the investigational use of stem cell deployments for degenerative conditions. In February 2012, Dr. Bob was treated by Dr. Berman and three months later had first-hand appreciation

Dr. Bob Harman and his canine alter ego, Ben the border collie

of the relief he'd made possible for so many animals: "I had my strength back, and full range of motion," he said. "No pain."

With his usual lightning speed, Dr. Bob introduced me via e-mail to Dr. Berman and Dr. Lander. I heard back from them within the hour. Dr. Lander's assistant scheduled phone time with the doc, during which I explained my medical history. When I got to the part about my menstrual period and the surgical incision, the doctor reckoned that I must have had a recto-vaginal fistula, but that it likely resolved on its own. I described my concerns about fibrin glue, and how the Madrid team, after assuring me there would be no glue, had changed their thinking. Imagine my shock to hear Dr. Lander say, "We only use material taken from your own body." The main material we were after was the stromal vascular fraction (SVF), a protein-rich segment from my processed adipose tissue. SVF contains a mononuclear cell line (predominantly autologous mesenchymal stem cells—ASCs), macrophage cells, endothelial cells, red blood cells, and growth factors that facilitate the stem cell process and promote their activity. CSCTC's technology allows its doctors to isolate high numbers of viable cells. To simulate the fibrin glue and help my cells "stick" where they'd be injected, so they could do their healing job, Dr. Lander explained how he would create a custom cell sealant for me using platelet-rich plasma (PRP), the centrifuged product of my own blood: "It's rich in growth factors and will help activate the cells and thicken the SVF for injection." I asked whether I would receive an intravenous injection. "Of course," Dr. Lander replied. "That's the whole point."

Of course. That's the whole point. After four years of red and yellow lights, of hearing doctors and administrators tell me maybe and no, here was the first physician to green-light my procedure precisely the way I'd imagined it: The way Sam and Sheba had experienced it, right here in America. This would be the first time the technique pioneered in Madrid would be combined with vascular delivery of cells. There could be no cell culturing or storage, because this is America, and those practices are verboten here; this would be a closed surgical procedure, meaning my own fat would be removed via liposuction, then my own stem cells would be extracted from my fat and reinjected back into me—all on the same day, in the same surgical setting. Although not FDA-approved, the procedure was FDA-compliant and perfectly legal. It was very similar to the autologous fat-grafting procedure Dr. Berman had been performing for years on his satisfied Beverly Hills clientele. Except now, instead of just aesthetic benefits, the transfer of cells from a patient's fat would yield a therapeutic effect. Now I had one last question for Dr. Lander. Did he have a dog? Yes, a rescued labradoodle; Dr. Berman had two dogs, a cocker spaniel and a poodle. That was the icing on an already-perfect cake. Wasting no time, Dr. Lander swiftly e-mailed the expert, Dr. García-Olmo: "We are planning to deploy SVF stromal vascular fraction (with PRP) into a perirectal fistula on Julia. Can you tell me exactly how you perform the injection? Thanks."

Sam and Sheba were my medical sentinels. Finally, I would follow their healing lead, down to the exact way their cells had been intravenously deployed. For the second time on this long, strange trip, I cried tears of joy, this time burying my face in the now-silky-haired chest of my German shepherd. I tried explaining to the dog I thought I'd never have that now, finally, I was about to receive the surgery I thought I'd never undergo. The cost would be eight thousand nine hundred dollars, slightly less than the Madrid procedure; even if I'd had insurance, it would not cover this. Setting the date for my procedure, I had the choice of January 9 or January 16. Not wanting to wait a minute longer than necessary, let alone a whole week, I opted for the earlier date. I called Dr. Smith; he was already booked to teach that day and wouldn't be able to scrub in to my procedure as we'd discussed, but he promised to send his love and positive thoughts. So, after all my diligent Internet research, how had I managed not to hear of the California Stem Cell Treatment Center? It had opened in December 2010, fully two years earlier, but there had been no media coverage, and the doctors don't advertise—they're too busy treating patients. So this treatment option managed to stay under my radar until the very last minute. If not for Dr. Bob, I might never have found it. And speaking of Dr. Bob, just a few months earlier, Vet-Stem began offering a new service called StemInsure. While a dog is undergoing a spay, neuter, or other elective procedure under anesthesia, any vet surgeon can easily collect a small sample of fatty tissue. With culturing in Vet-Stem's sterile lab, that small tissue sample will yield millions of the dog's young, vibrant stem cells, to be cryopreserved so they are ready to be deployed by the time the canine patient eventually needs them. With this option, when it's time for a healing injection of stem cells, even many years down the line, Desiree wouldn't need to undergo anesthetized surgery to collect her cells—they'd be ready and waiting to be deployed. Happily, her diarrhea had ultimately resolved thanks to a prescription dog food, which I faithfully supplemented with probiotics. Now, with StemInsure, her cells would stand ready should Desiree ever present with PF, osteoarthritis, or an orthopedic injury, and the peace of mind that provided was priceless. I called the Humane Society and arranged for Desiree to be StemInsured while undergoing the routine spay procedure she was finally cleared for. We'd be treated on the same day! Dogs had brought me this far; I wasn't about to undergo this without a canine companion by my side. OK, so Desiree would be on the opposite coast in New York City while I was in California. But she'd be spiritually by my side, where she belonged. And knowing that we'd be treated simultaneously—or just about, give or take a few hours—was as reassuring to me as sleeping with the *pudli* used to be decades ago.

Finally, after four long years of waiting, I had my desired date with destiny—and it was three short weeks away. The pressure was on to eat and drink only the most good-for-me menu items and to boost my intake of supplements that would support and jump-start my cellular health. As a writer, I appreciate words and often scrutinize them once I've written them down, looking for inspiration or hidden messages. Call it an occupational hazard; my trusty old-style chalkboard, salvaged from the trash heap outside an elementary school, comes in handy for this purpose. Well, just look at the word *menu*—it's me + nu. Me, new! I took this as a sign that the bill of fare I was about to dine on would rejuvenate my system and renew my cells. I would eat my way to a new me. My goal was to nourish my stem cells so that, together, we could achieve the best possible outcome in Rancho Mirage. I wasn't just feeding myself and my dogs now—I was feeding all of our cells to keep them in optimal condition. Dr. Lander had gamely agreed to take on my case; I wanted to partner with him to make our procedure the best success it could be, so that many more people suffering with IBD would benefit.

This was like cramming for the biggest exam of my life—except this time, I was cramming food as well as data. My kitchen became stem cell support central, the mess hall where armies of my cells could fuel up for the skirmish ahead. I christened that tiny cooking space The Stem Cell Cafe, because it was now the laboratory in which I would develop the *muy rico* health foods I'd envisioned in Madrid, to help ensure the success of my pending procedure. Of course, Stem Cell Cafe also has another meaning because, at 88 x 50 inches, my kitchen is practically microscopic. My refrigerator became the most up-to-the-minute medicine chest I could make it, stocked with jars of my multivitamin for women over forty, vitamin D3, L-carnitine, curcumin, various omega-3s, ubiquinol, astaxanthin, milk thistle, and Juvenon. I asked Dr. Lander what supplements I was missing; he recommended boswellia. Great call: I'd given this ayurvedic medicine staple to my dogs for its anti-inflammatory effect on their arthritic joints, but overlooked its long-documented benefit for the digestive system. For Dr. Smith, I made sure to replenish the RenewLife probiotic supply. In addition to Neil Riordan's Stem-Kine supplement, I started popping a blue-green algae supplement called StemPlex. Meanwhile, I had to gain weight so Dr. Lander wouldn't have a hard time extracting fat from my belly. I know what you're thinking: That's a nice problem to have! But it's not, really, when your metabolism, normally high anyway, is now adrenaline-charged, plus dog walking and food combining keep you on the svelte side of zaftig. I have to hand it to the lovely actress Renee Zellweger; nothing separates the women from the girls quite like expanding to the challenge of gaining weight on a deadline, in anticipation of a big performance. My mother did her very best to pump fattening food into me, baking batch after batch of buttery cheddar-cheese cookies, which I inhaled. As for her other valiant cooking efforts, at that point, she and I weren't seeing eye-to-eye on the genetically modified organisms (GMO) debate. She'd offer me steamed spinach, I'd ask her if it was organic, and a disagreement would ensue over the high price of organic produce, with me trying to explain that eating genetically modified food carries a much higher hidden cost. I knew I had to be careful not to expose my healing cells to harmful substances in this final home stretch, so I consulted fellow organic foodie Celia Kutcher, a nutrition expert for dogs and people whom I'd interviewed numerous times. Here's the easy-to-follow regimen she prescribed:

Eat loads of greens, like kale, collards, broccoli and bok choi; you'll need the chlorophyll to heal and strengthen your immune system. Daikon radish, cauliflower, and burdock root are great, you can find burdock in health food stores near the carrots.

Try to get in at least 8 servings of veggies daily; one veggie is one serving, like 1 carrot = 1 serving.

You want to alkalize a bit after surgery so start your day off with a hot (not boiling) glass of water with one whole lemon squeezed into it; lemons alkalize the body.

Brown rice is excellent for a few reasons—it's alkalizing, plus it's got silica to help heal. It's also great to detox from the anesthesia.

Root vegetables are super good, but eat yams instead of white potatoes, don't go overboard on them. They do have sugar but it's different. Beets are great for your blood and cleanse it. Ginger's very healing too; I grate some up and put it in hot water with raw honey and lemon juice—lovely.

Onions and garlic are wonderful, eat lots, either cooked or—if you can handle it—raw.

Reduce your white sugar intake as it stresses the body; best to have none. If you need a sweetener, go for stevia, the best is the green powder. Keep away from Truvia, it's got sugar in it. Also avoid white flour, it's acidifying.

Beans are wonderful, also garbanzos. Keep away from tofu unless it's organic, most soy is GMO these days, even edamame.

Raw, fermented sauerkraut is full of healing probiotics. I'm sure you can get some at Union Square Greenmarket or health food stores, make sure it's raw. Eat at least a tablespoon daily.

If you eat meat, only have pasture-raised, grass-finished beef. Organic chicken is better than conventionally raised, but it can mean they're eating GMO corn. Best are the pasture-raised so they can eat bugs. Try to avoid pork as it's really hard to find some that's eaten well. I love Grazin' Angus Acres, they're at Union Square on Saturdays; their eggs are fantastic if they've got any, super healthy. If you're into fish, only go for wild caught, farm raised are like eating fish from a filthy fish tank.

Keep away from alcohol, caffeine, sodas, fluoridated water, and black tea (which also has fluoride). No dairy either, and nothing processed—no junk food! Try to get some good spring water in a glass bottle. Coconut water is also good for you, look for Harmless Harvest's 100 percent raw brand, which comes in a green-capped bottle, it's not heat treated. Drink tons of water, half your weight in ounces (so if you weigh 100 pounds, you'd drink 50 ounces daily). Herbal teas are fine, so is green or white tea. I go for water decaf green, which is pretty easy to find.

Probiotics are great, see if you can find the yogurt made from coconut, it's called "So Delicious"—it's good stuff and will get you the needed nutrients.

Another friend, the French composer Alain Amouyal, reminded me of advice he'd offered many times: "*Ecoutez vos cellules,*" Alain wisely counseled in his native language; listen to your cells. Our cells speak to us in a kind of musical code that may be instinctively understood. To get in tune with our microscopic healing forces, all we need to do is open a healthy dialogue with them—just like talking to our dogs. Someone else referred me to the Oregon-based medical intuitive Jennifer Kaye Dickinson. During a Skype session, Jennifer predicted that my surgery would bring me much relief but cautioned me to remain calm and avoid upset at all costs in these weeks leading up to the big day. I mentioned my frantic attempts to eat only organic food, and the occasional tiffs that kept erupting between my mom and me over my orthodox organic food faith. Jennifer explained that if food was made with love—as obviously Mom's food is—then I should just swallow it with gratitude. So, it's OK to overlook the occasional pesticided ingredient? In a word, she replied, yes. Wouldn't you know, mother really does know best.

Made with love. Ah, words again, scribbled and scrutinized in my reporter's notebook. Subtracting the preposition, the phrase becomes *made love.* I didn't need to be reminded: It had been a while. People, dogs, armies of stem cells . . . nobody thrives on food alone. Play and enrichment must enter the equation, too. I'd been celibate for too long; without providing my cells much-needed enrichment, how could I expect the microscopic army within to merit a Purple Heart on treatment day? There was no time to waste. Sex was the all-important vitamin S1, as essential to the health and vibrancy of my stem cells as food, hydration, exercise, rest, and sunshine. A consultation with Drs. Clement and Clement wasn't necessary to let me know that I was now officially S1-deficient. I almost flew into a panic. Unless I could get laid, pronto, my procedure might not be completely successful, because my cells wouldn't be fully energized! Amazing, isn't it, how the unleashed, overstressed mind can freak itself out, like a frightened dog spooked by thunder or fireworks? I reactivated my long-disabled OkCupid account, and in short order, hooked up with Last-Minute Man. He gave me and my cells a serviceable send-off: Orgasms were achieved, oxytocin was released. Finally, I could relax; all would be well. Then I did better than disable my OkCupid account—I deleted it. "There's no going back!" the site's resident robot mascot warned. Well, thank dog for that. The last piece of the puzzle was in place: My bag was packed, and I was ready to go.

On the afternoon of January 8, the day before my date with stem cell destiny, I was Rancho-bound, driving with Stan, the cameraman I'd hired to videotape the next morning's proceedings. The goal was to scout the location prior to shooting. Although I'd be conscious for the entire procedure, I knew I wouldn't be able to take proper notes. Having the procedure filmed would enable me to review and transcribe everything that happened in its entirety, so I could do my journalist thing and write about it all with accuracy. Arriving around 4:00 p.m., we drove along roads named for famous people who'd been Rancho regulars: Gerald Ford Drive . . . Dinah Shore Drive . . . Frank Sinatra Drive . . . Bob Hope Drive (Mr. and Mrs. Hope donated eighty acres of land for the building of the Eisenhower Medical Center campus). By the time we reached the California Stem Cell Treatment Center, it was, appropriately enough, magic hour; the late-afternoon sun bathed the façade of the building in golden light. I'd reached my medical mecca, and it was firmly located on American soil, in a strip mall, in a mythic-sounding place called Rancho Mirage. It was not, however, a medical mirage. It was real—as real as the clinic in Ciudad de Panama. Dr. Lander had left for the evening, but his assistant Marlina gave us a quick tour. On one wall was a framed American flag; it had been presented to Dr. Lander in 1972, on the occasion of his

Outside my medical mecca on the morning of the big day KARINA SALAZAR

twelfth birthday, with a letter from Senator Barry Goldwater. In one of those beautiful coincidences that I've come to see as perhaps not entirely coincidental, Dr. Lander's birthday is July 5—the adoption-birthday of my dog Desiree. The text of Senator Goldwater's letter to twelve-year-old Elliot Lander read, in part: "From the beginnings of America, this flag has represented all that is good in this great country of ours and has been a symbol of our continuing greatness. Please fly this flag in the spirit of patriotism that is the United States', and give it the commanding respect that it so richly deserves." Amen! Here was a perfect, positive omen for the penultimate chapter of my stem cell saga. I'd wanted my first-of-its-kind procedure to take place in the United States, and at the last possible minute I found an all-American doctor with the all-American, can-do spirit needed to perform it. My faith in my homeland's potential as a leader in medical technology was officially restored.

The morning of the big day, January 9, I awoke extra-early and extra-terrified. So much was riding on this! I dabbed my wrists with calming storax essential oil (the Taurean signature scent) and my feet with antibacterial Thieves Oil and ate a light breakfast of fresh, organic fruit and lemon water; the last thing I wanted to do was upset my stomach right before my big procedure. I needed my gut's complete compliance, which was already a challenge, as I was riding a tidal wave of adrenaline. The night before, I'd booked an appointment to get my makeup done at the nearby Aveda salon. While I wanted to keep our footage reporter real, I also didn't want to look like a ghastly ghoul—so I opted for the lightest possible touch of natural-looking makeup (an Aveda specialty) to conceal my dark under-eye circles. I came to the right place: Chatting with Rebecca, the artist doing my makeup, I learned that she, too, had a rescued pit bull. The finishing touch was a smear of pink lip gloss. You can take the girl out of fashion, but there's no need to take fashion out of the girl. A little bit of grooming goes a long way, baby. Always a believer that fashion and beauty have healing powers, I'd once written an article for *Harper's Bazaar* on that very topic almost twenty years earlier. In her book *Why I Wore Lipstick to My Mastectomy*, Geralyn Lucas explains how lip rouge can be a kind of war paint when one is battling a disease. The late cancer surgeon William Cahan, MD, chief of surgery at Memorial

Sloan-Kettering Cancer Center, famously coined the term "lipstick theory," explaining how he was able to tell his patients were improving: "When a woman who is battling cancer starts to put on lipstick, she is on the road to recovery," he said.

If you look good, you feel good: It's a motto I've always taken seriously—seriously enough to style my surgery outfit down to the last detail. For the big day, I craved comfort and courage, and my threads were part of the prep protocol. My instructions from the clinic had included a note about wearing comfortable, loose-fitting clothing so as not to constrict my swollen post-lipo belly. However, I didn't want to sacrifice a stylish silhouette by showing up in sweats, so I'd bought a pair of Lululemon black pants, one size too big, and paired them with a fitted, soft-belted, woolen jacket by H&M that vaguely resembled a ruffled black bathrobe. Black flats completed my stem cell style statement. Arriving at the clinic, I was as ready as I'd ever be, and nervous as hell. Dr. Lander came out to greet me and immediately put me at ease. Not only is he even better-looking in person than in his photographs but also he has a beautiful bedside manner to match.

"Julia," he said, shaking my hand, "I was hoping you'd be fatter!"

Laughing, I told him I'd tried to gain some extra weight, really I had—I'd even mainlined my mom's cheddar-cheese cookies. He put on a sad look. "And you didn't bring us any?"

My rock-star doc proceeded to reassure me that he'd successfully extracted enough fatty tissue from an 87-pound MS patient, so I didn't need to worry—we'd get enough material to work with. We then had a brief consultation in his office. Then it was time to prep for surgery. I was given a sterile blue cap to wear and asked to lie down on an exam table with stirrups at the far end. Shots of numbing lidocaine effectively ensured that I would feel no pain from the foot-long needle used to extract adipose tissue from my belly. Later, Stan told me the size of that needle obliged his squeamish assistant to avert his eyes while holding his camera steady—he feared he might pass out! The tiny OR was packed, for in addition to the doctor, his nurses, Stan, and his assistant, there was also a local photographer I'd hired to take still shots. Without intending to, I managed to approximate the crowded conditions of the

Sun King's operating theater centuries earlier. My job had enabled me to interview a wide range of people from different walks of life in a variety of settings, many of them time-pressed celebrities who were multitasking while in between takes at a photo or film shoot: Sarah Jessica Parker, Chris Isaak, Madeleine Stowe, Iman . . . but I'd never before interviewed a doctor *while* he was performing a procedure on me, and we were both being simultaneously photographed. Dr. Lander spoke to me the entire time, and we had a lively conversation, with Stan interjecting additional interview questions so as to elicit mediagenic answers. The three-way surgical pillow talk turned surreal. When the topic of *Star Trek* came up, Stan asked Dr. Lander what was his favorite episode; naturally, it was the one in which the *Enterprise* officers travel back in time, because Dr. McCoy—Dr. Lander's favorite character—plays a prominent role. Things grew even more surreal when I observed that I felt like I was watching a Food Network show, observing a master chef from the POV of the recipe he was making—I had the bread's-eye view. At which point Dr. Lander held up the tissue he'd collected and agreed with my assessment that the admixture of fat and blood in the syringe looked exactly like pureed sockeye salmon.

Phase one of my procedure was now complete. The doctor helped me sit up, and the nurse outfitted me with a bandage and a wide elastic-and-velcro belt called a binder to hold the bandage in place. With that obi-like contraption encircling my waist, I walked out of the OR with the slow, straight-spined gait of a geisha. Led to a recovery room, I was seated in a comfy chair to wait the estimated ninety minutes for my stem cells to be extracted from my fat sample in a centrifuge machine. The nurse drew my blood for the custom biological "glue" Dr. Lander would be making from my own PRP. An hour and a half later, my cells were ready. Dr. Lander invited me to come and watch the suspenseful moment when a machine called The Countess would reveal the total number of viable stem cells we'd harvested from my fat sample. A dog gets about three million cells per injection; a horse typically gets four million. We needed at least twenty million or we wouldn't have the minimum amount deployed in the Madrid trial—and, since this was America, not Spain, if we didn't obtain enough cells for this treatment, I'd have to return for

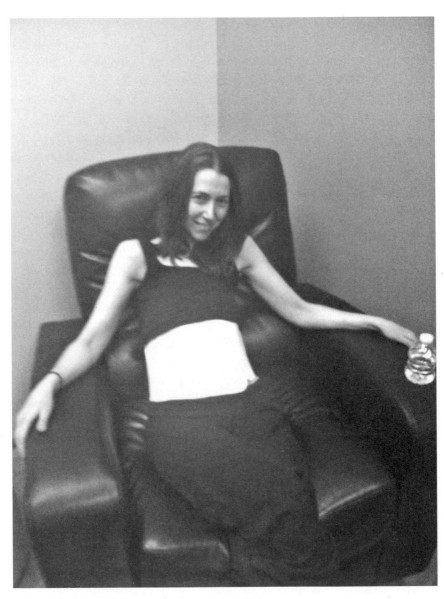

Taking a break, post-liposuction KARINA SALAZAR

another liposuction to receive a booster shot. I watched The Countess like a gambling junkie mentally willing a high-stakes slot machine to make the life-changing payout. The result was in, and the number was . . . forty-two million! Operation Stem Cell had a good chance of being a success.

Twenty million of those cells were then injected intravenously via the catheter installed in my left arm. I silently encouraged the microscopic forces to go find their target—the fistula—and get to work closing it. Once the custom "glue" made from my own PRP was prepared and ready, it was time for the second injection. The remaining twenty-two million cells, combined with the PRP, would be shot into the fistula adjacent to my crack—the fistula created in the emergency room in New York City almost exactly fourteen years earlier and subsequently reopened to permit drainage of pus. For this phase of Operation Stem Cell, I was asked to put my feet in the stirrups—something I've always dreaded doing. Immediately, I tensed up. The area down there had to be injected with numbing painkiller, only this time all those notoriously super-sensitive nerve endings made the painkilling process a killer itself. Trying hard not to scream as I had back in 1999 during the gauze-unpacking ordeal, I squeezed the poor nurse's hand so tightly I feared crushing it; later, I kissed it by way of apology. Once everything was numb down here, the actual infusion of my cells was quick and painless. Dr. Lander installed a tiny funnel into the pinhole opening in the indented scar on my butt and swiftly injected the remaining twenty million cells. It was all over very fast; within minutes, I was sitting up.

The rest is medical history. If I told you that, upon receiving the second injection, I announced that I felt better already, would you believe me? I hardly believed it myself—I'm still a skeptical reporter—but that's precisely what happened. I did feel better already: completely relaxed, as if I'd just had a particularly un-blocking chiropractic adjustment on a sunny beach somewhere. Was it possible to feel a difference that fast? Well, hadn't that been Sam and Sheba's experience with Vet-Stem? Floating back to the recovery room, I was too amped to sit still, so Stan and I shot interviews with Dr. Lander and his colleague Dr. See, with me asking the docs questions off-camera. (Dr. Lander's partner in the practice, clinic cofounder Dr. Berman, was traveling.) At one point, Dr. Lander looked

Proud to be a stem cell junkie! KARINA SALAZAR

at me and remarked, "You don't look like someone who just had surgery, Julia." And indeed, I didn't feel like someone who'd just had surgery. My now hugely swollen belly made me look about three months pregnant, but otherwise, I felt better and more relaxed than I had in a long time. I'd arrived in California armed with several vials of 200c arnica, the highest strength available, confident those potent pellets would let me laugh at the eventual bruising and pain. I casually mentioned my stash to Dr. Lander, who promptly asked me not to take any of it. "We don't know what it will do to your cells," he explained. What, no arnica? I felt like Peanuts' Linus without his security blanket. But I promised to comply with the doctor's request.

After Stan felt satisfied that we had enough footage of the doctors discussing their groundbreaking work, we geared up to return to Los Angeles. That's when I happened to notice a photograph in Dr. Lander's office, of him with Gerald Ford; he'd been Ford's trusted physician for the final ten years of the president's life. So the politician who facilitated a new beginning for my parents was a patient of the doctor who enabled a new beginning for me! It was one of those amazing, stranger-than-fiction coincidences that once again validated my decision to be a writer of nonfiction.

During the drive back to LA, I received a call from Dr. Smith. It was late in the evening in Florida, but he took the time to check in, advising me to do all I could to keep my immune system strong for optimal recovery, including supplementing my diet with zinc, bromelain, and vitamin C. How lucky am I to have him for a medical guardian angel? As the lidocaine wore off, I began to feel the sting of that lipo needle in no small way. Poor Stan witnessed a lot of squirming and groaning as he drove us toward LA, plus the mighty attractive moment when my belly outgrew my underpants by several sizes and I had to shimmy out of those tighties right there in the passenger seat or be strangled down below. But as tempted as I was to override Dr. Lander's no-arnica order, I resisted and resolutely rode out the pain. Installed in my hotel room, I called my parents and a few friends, got up to put the cell phone four feet away from the bed per Dr. Mercola's orders, snuffed my nontoxic aromatherapy candle, shuffled back to bed, and fell fast asleep.

My rock-star doc, Elliot Lander KARINA SALAZAR

The first thing I did upon waking the next morning was—drum roll please—produce a perfect, pain-free poop. Stan stopped by to join me for a farewell breakfast. Walking into my hotel room, he said, "You look like a different person!" Coming from someone whose very living depends on quick, accurate assessments of visual cues, that was tremendously encouraging. I felt like a different person: a much calmer one. It seemed to me as if I'd just experienced less of a medical first than a second birth. Thanks to the California Stem Cell Treatment Center, I *was* reborn—"not in a creepy religious sense," as my friend Eve, a medical doctor, would later say (the girl can't help it; she too is a Vassar-bred "ferocious illiterate"), but in the sense of getting a fresh start, a new leash on life. I even had a temporary new hole in my belly to prove it—at the point where the lipo needle went in. Next, it was off to lunch with my friend the talented actor and photographer Daniel Reichert, yet another proud product of Vassar College. Then I took a cab to Long Beach airport and flew back home to my dogs. The next leg of my healing journey was about to begin: waiting to see whether and how well the procedure had worked. The Madrid trial had had an 83 percent success rate—a solid B. Dr. Lander had made an A+ effort, and I had absolute faith that, whatever the outcome of this procedure, I'd be much the better for having had it done.

CHAPTER 16

Medicine Dog

The recipient of the world's first tissue-engineered organ transplant, Claudia Castillo, reported just five months after her surgery that she could walk up two flights of stairs without becoming breathless. In her own words, "I was a sick woman, now I will be able to live a normal life." Today, at thirty-five, she has no problem keeping up with her daughter and son. She's not a high-profile transplant patient like Dick Cheney or Steve Jobs or Natalie Cole, but Claudia is, in my eyes, every inch the VIP and role model. She's a stem cell pioneer just as much as her heroic doctors are. Her achievement—overcoming illness to enjoy time with her kids—reminds us that the ultimate goal of medicine, even the extraordinary sci-fi kind, is to help ordinary people lead everyday lives, free of discomfort and disease. An ordinary life is the greatest gift, for it permits one to do all the things the human body was meant to do, from taking stairs to walking the dog to, yes, finding relief on the toilet.

I'm not technically a transplant patient, yet the transfer of my own stem cells from my belly fat to my bloodstream was a kind of transplant in which I was both donor and recipient. I was sick, but today, thanks to stem cell technology, I couldn't be more grateful for my healthy, ordinary life. Like my dogs, I finally get to experience what it's like to start the day with a normal bowel movement. If it sounds anticlimactic that my round-the-world journey in search of healing ended with something so mundane, remember the astonishment of Sam's spectacular stem cell success. Think back to that amazing moment, just hours after injection with his own cells—which had twice made their own cross-country trip between New York and San Diego—when my dog lifted his leg to pee for the first time in two years. The hydrant that got hosed that day was a fitting symbol of stem cell success; for me, its counterpart is the porcelain throne. Conquering a fire hydrant, a toilet—these are the little victories that make us feel alive and whole, adding up to improved quality of life. They're not insignificant, even if they are completely ordinary. Besides, so many "ordinary" things are out of this world, starting with shelter dogs.

Certain people and circumstances may have disappointed me, but dogs—my best friends and medical sentinels—have always come through. As long as I can afford to, I promise to feed them the very best food I can get—grain-free, non-GMO, devoid of by-products and chemical preservatives—and to hydrate them with fluoride-free water. I will soup up their food with celery, broccoli, kale, sardines, coconut oil, cinnamon, turmeric, probiotics, Nordic Naturals Omega-3 Pet, and—when their tummies are upset—sweet potato, pureed pumpkin, raw honey, and Coconut Manna. To keep their teeth in top condition, I'll let them chomp on frozen beef bones, preferably from locally raised, grass-fed cows. I'll make sure the toys they tear apart and cuddle up with contain no toxic components to damage their cells. I intend to continue following dogs' wellness lead and advocating on their behalf, to encourage as many people as possible to adopt and discover the ordinary joys, the extraordinary gifts, of life with canine companions. "Dog Is My Co-Pilot" reads *The Bark* magazine's motto, a creative twist on *God Is My Co-Pilot,* the 1943 book authored by the late Brigadier General Robert L. Scott, World War II fighter ace. Apologies to both Brigadier General Scott and to the publishers of *The Bark,* but my motto is, "Dog Is My Doctor."

As I wrote this, I cleared a major hurdle: my forty-eighth birthday. I'm very grateful to have survived age forty-seven. A schoolmate of mine and fellow animal lover was not so lucky. Dr. Katherine Rogers had elected to become a holistic veterinarian in mid-career and earned a devoted following among her patients and clients. After undergoing fertility treatments and giving birth to beautiful twin boys—whom I had the pleasure of seeing as they sweetly slept in their stroller—Dr. Rogers died of ovarian cancer in April 2013 at age forty-seven. In one of life's cruel ironies, it was likely the fertility treatments that killed her; yet they also enabled her to realize her dream of becoming a mother. Knowing how deeply private and how very different from me Dr. Rogers always was, I debated over writing this, but I hope her loved ones understand that I do so because I feel it's important to know how people of one's own age die, so that we may find teaching lessons and become inspired to be proactive about matters of health. The untimely passing of a gifted healer like Dr. Rogers is a terrible loss, not only to her immediate family, friends, and clients, but also to veterinary medicine as a whole, and to the people who depend on its practitioners to maximize time with beloved animals.

Sometimes, giving a "miracle cure" a shot requires a suspension of disbelief. I might not have believed in the healing potential of adult stem cells had I not witnessed their astonishing effects on my dogs. Giving my journalistic skepticism a longer, looser lead enabled me to find healing and share what I learned with others. As with anything, a little skepticism is healthy—but too much is counterproductive. And what we've seen in the media with regard to adult stem cells is a toxic overdose of journalistic skepticism, which has slowed progress by preventing the most widely read media outlets from carrying stories that could really help their audience. I believe helping others is, or should be, the goal of journalism. But writers can't achieve this goal without readers, so I thank you for staying with me and hearing my story to the end. One of the comments on my very first stem cell article for PJMedia mentioned "the leap of faith through God." For me, the leap came through God-spelled-backward. To be effectively healed, whether the illness is critical or chronic, one has to believe in something. If you're agnostic or atheist, then put your faith in science, and the incredible, documented power of the human body to self-heal. Do whatever it takes to combat unhealthy skepticism and make that leap.

Here's something we all can believe in: Veterinarians are leading the way to a bright future of "one medicine" that freely shares human and animal health breakthroughs for the benefit of all. Instead of subjecting laboratory animals to cruel, outdated tests that don't advance scientific progress, we will soon see a more humane model: the Vet-Stem model, in which animal patients are healed and their cases studied with an eye toward improving human health. As of now, the dream of one medicine is just that—a dream—but I'm convinced it will become reality soon. The spirit of James Herriot is alive and well as, inspired by everyone's favorite country vet, new generations of country docs are going forth to treat animals and keep the pet-human bond healthy and strong. Except these days, you can't keep the country doc down on the farm! At the end of the day, Vet-Stem's Bob Harman—internationally recognized stem cell pioneer—is a country vet. Remember Dr. Jo, the country vet I went far out of my way to see? If I wanted to see her today, I'd have to travel all the way to Fiji—yes, Fiji, where she's permanently relocated to work with the Suva SPCA. Dr. Jo is part of a nascent trend of vets-without-borders, traveling to parts of the world where their help is most needed. Long after returning from my Panamanian adventure, I'm glad to receive e-mail alerts from SPAYes, which has spayed, wormed, and vaccinated close to five thousand animals. Remember Tod, my dog Sheba's boyfriend? In 2010 he founded Darwin Animal Doctors, which has a unique mission of care and conservation; by providing free veterinary care to the domestic pets and wildlife of the Galapagos, DAD is helping preserve and protect the biodiversity of these islands whose indigenous animals are found nowhere else on our planet. And, I'm pleased to report, dynamic vets and vet students are signing up in impressive numbers to help realize DAD's goals.

Doug Kramer was a country vet in a big city—Los Angeles—who was so inspired by the author of *All Creatures Great and Small* that he studied at Herriot's alma mater, the University of Glasgow in Scotland, home to the James Herriot Library. Dr. Kramer took the veterinarian's oath so seriously that he repeatedly publicly expressed a willingness to risk going to jail for doing what he perceived as his duty: administering expertly measured doses of medical marijuana to terminally ill animal patients in terrible pain. Meanwhile, in my home town of New York City, a vet named Andrew Kaplan started a 501(c)3 called The Toby Project, which operates mobile surgical vans and stationary "in-neighborhood" clinics, providing targeted, free and low-cost spay and neuter services to those communities that supply or surrender the most animals to municipal shelters. Incidentally, Dr. Kaplan was one of the revered "Dirty Dozen" students at Tufts University School of Veterinary Medicine. In the late 1980s, this brave group of twelve hadn't even taken the veterinarian's oath yet, but already they rejected the old-school "terminal surgery" MO of performing numerous surgeries on healthy animals as a training exercise, then putting them to sleep. These students simply refused to learn how to heal animals by harming them. Standing their ground, they risked expulsion—and, thanks to their efforts, ultimately Tufts changed its vet curriculum. First, the university established a three-year pilot program involving the use of cadavers, client-owned animals who had died of natural causes and whose bodies were donated for this purpose. Finally, Tufts eliminated the traditional lab and externed students to local animal shelters to learn surgery by performing spays and neuters, then doing clinical surgical rotations at the veterinary teaching hospital. Kaplan's advice to today's veterinary students facing a similar challenge? "If you believe in something, dig in your heels in a nonoffensive manner until you either get what you want, or walk the other way by not accepting what they have to offer. Luckily we got the former."

I hope this book has two takeaways. The first is: Take good care of your dogs, and they will take great care of you. My positive outcome was the happy culmination of years of caring for Medicine Dogs—and letting them return the favor. The woof pack enabled me to harness my own health; your canine companions will do the same for you. Between us, my dogs and I have a wealth of experience with three medical conditions that are among the most common worldwide: septicemia, IBD, and osteoarthritis. Sadly, there are so many more disorders plaguing the world's human population—but the good news is that dogs can help us fight any illness. The second takeaway is: Take good care of your cells, so they can take care of you. With proper nutrition, hydration, exercise, and stress management, your cells will rise to the challenge of healing you when stem cell therapy—including the legal culturing of cells—becomes a standard of care in the United States, which I have no doubt it must in the near future. People like you and me will make it happen—all it takes is for us to talk about it and demand it as a basic human right. In the immortal words of Margaret Mead, "Never doubt that a small group of thoughtful, committed citizens can change the world. Indeed, it is the only thing that ever has." If we all work together, we can effect positive change and see a revolution in American health care in our lifetime. I hope you'll join me in bringing pressure on the FDA to approve of adult stem cell culturing, so that procedures like the one that saved Claudia Castillo—which simply wouldn't have been possible without culturing her cells—can be routinely performed on US soil without the ridiculous restriction that currently shackles our medical progress.

Are you less than satisfied with something a doctor has told you, even if you genuinely like your doc? Then become your own patient advocate. Do your homework on the Internet, and respectfully beg to differ. Don't expect others to do the work for you. They won't; they can't. If you get sick, please don't be silent about it. Talk about the problem with as many people as possible, folks you'd never suspect might be able to help. Tweet about it; seek out relevant forums on the web. Not only will you learn more than the average doctor will tell you but also you'll find an understanding ear, or dozens of them. Your fears will diminish exponentially just knowing there are other people who can relate—and by reaching out, you might just help someone else who may be feeling more confused and overwhelmed than you are. Please don't go into denial; own your illness. Remember, you have it, but it doesn't have you.

On my way home from California after treatment, I rededicated myself to extending my dogs' lives. I realize that my commitment to canine life extension constitutes extreme dog ownership and that many of the things I've done make me seem like a weirdo. OK, I'll take it: I'm a weirdo. But wanting to extend a dog's life to the fullest is about more than odd emotional attachment; it's a practical matter of affirming life and health in a toxic world, for the longer a dog stays happy and in optimal health, the longer and better his or her human's life will be. Think about all the time, effort, love, and, yes, money invested in training service dogs to assist blind, deaf, and diabetic people, or therapy dogs that raise the spirits of hospitalized children, like the canine angels of Angels on a Leash. For the thousands of people whose quality of life depends on a service dog, canine life extension is critical. Organizations that train service dogs—groups such as Guide Dogs for the Blind, Southeastern Guide Dogs, Canine Companions for Independence, or Dogs 4 Diabetics—have a special responsibility to provide the best possible health care for their canine alumni. I believe these organizations should StemInsure the puppies they train for a lifetime of service. Labs are especially prone to osteoarthritis, but with their youthful stem cells safely in storage, they won't have to retire early from active duty. They'll be ready and able to assist their human partners longer, and their people can enjoy to the fullest an indescribable bond of trust they worked hard to develop with that one dog.

If you need motivation to take care of your own cells, think of them as your own personal pack of healing hounds, numbering in the tens of millions. Earlier, I compared stem cells to military special forces. Now, considering how bravely tactical canines have conducted themselves in the global theater of war, why not think of the microscopic militia as soldier dogs? If you don't live with a dog, I sincerely hope you'll adopt one soon. I have lots of incentive to preserve my health and protect my longevity: My dogs depend on me. Please don't let life pass you by without letting at least one dog depend on you. Having a pet canine used to be considered a luxury, but I would argue that dogs are an absolute necessity to maintain health and sanity in these manic, maniacal modern times. When you lose a dog, please adopt another as soon as humanly possible. Consider adopting two! This honors the dog you lost, saves a canine life or a couple, and protects your heart—literally, by promoting and prolonging cardiac health. Besides, it's what your dog would want. Take it from Silverdene Emblem O'Neill, also known as Blemie, beloved dalmatian of Nobel Prize winner Eugene O'Neill. The playwright's uplifting "Last Will and Testament of an Extremely Distinguished Dog" is written from Blemie's point of view, and it inspired the composer Steven Mercurio to write a symphony called *A Grateful Tail:*

> *One last request I earnestly make. I have heard my Mistress say, "When Blemie dies we must never have another dog. I love him so much I could never love another one." Now I would ask her, for love of me, to have another. It would be a poor tribute to my memory never to have a dog again. What I would like to feel is that, having once had me in the family, now she cannot live without a dog!*

Every ten seconds in America we kill a perfectly healthy, loving, lovable dog. Think about that: Every ten seconds of every hour, every single day of the year. It's an appalling waste. We humans created this disease state; only we can cure it. Please adopt. There are shelter dogs dying for homes, and there are people dying to have stem cell therapy. I rank them

Going gloveless no longer cramped my style, or my hands.
STEVE YENSEL

as equal in priority. Shelter dogs all have the healing touch—just like the ones I couldn't wait to come home to on the morning of January 11, two days after my historic procedure. I took two days of rest to prepare for resuming my dog-walking routine. Neighbors remarked that I looked "radiant." That's not a word you hear too often from jaded New Yorkers— the same tough, observant species that noticed Sam's newfound agility post-Vet-Stem. *Wow—can they do this for people, too?* Yes, I'm pleased to report, they can. They certainly could for me. I feel fully cured, but if dog forbid I ever experience a setback, I know where to go: back to Rancho.

First, I was reunited with my darling Desiree, who was obliged to wear a cumbersome E-collar to prevent her from worrying her spay sutures. Then, with the help of a friend who'd graciously rented a vehicle for this adventure, I recovered my other dogs from their stay at Unleash. All members of my furry family were now by my side, where they belonged. As the pups were brought out to me one by one, I gave each a short relief walk before putting them in the vehicle. It was biting cold outside, a dramatic contrast to the balmy California weather I'd just enjoyed for the past few days—yet I noticed my hands and feet weren't freezing up the way they had for many years, and I wasn't losing circulation in my fingertips, despite forgetting to wear gloves. Dr. Smith had predicted that the IV injection of my cells would likely help my Raynaud's, too—was that prognosis already coming true? I had three long months of winter ahead of me to find out. Dr. Smith had also encouraged me not to catch the flu, but it so happened that a particularly virulent strain of it began raging around New York after I returned home. By mid-March I fell spectacularly ill. I couldn't write; my brain was cloudy. It was all I could do to walk the hounds, make soup, and collapse in bed with a generous application of Medicine Dogs. On one especially chilly outing, a neighbor cheerfully remarked, "Miss, you're like a soldier with those dogs!" He's a US Army veteran, so that made my day.

Finally, after three weeks of this punishing routine, I broke free of influenza's grip. I started craving oatmeal and sparkling water and was amazed to find both formerly off-menu items agreeing with me. Enjoying that first bowl of Scottish oats in more than a decade, with a sprinkling of cinnamon and a splash of maple syrup, was like partaking of some

For the first time in years, my fingers functioned in the freezing cold!
STEVE YENSEL

long-forbidden fruit; the water might as well have been Champagne. Like the mares and does of the nursery tune, some dogs eat oats without experiencing digestive distress; I was delighted to discover that one of them is Desiree, who gets her own portion, and can hardly wait for the oatmeal pot to cool before she thoroughly pre-washes it for me. Now that I was no longer dead dog-lady walking, exercising the dogs was once again a meditation I couldn't wait to undertake every morning, followed by long sessions in front of my computer. I had a book to write, without delay; it was now more than four years overdue! I knew I wanted our story—my dogs' and mine—to help other people and animals. If it doesn't, I haven't done my job. I aimed to raise awareness of stem cells by chronicling how my dogs had just saved my life. People needed stem cells, now; many didn't have the luxury of waiting. The book had to be finished as soon as possible; there was no more time to waste. But how was I going to get all this down on paper? How to reconcile our story's personal aspects with the science of stem cells? I didn't even have an outline in place, yet I had no doubt my dogs would guide me, just as they had when I undertook the task of churning out five Dogster posts per week. This is really their story;

Desiree, best friend and medical sentinel DANIEL REICHERT

to tell it, all I had to do was observe them for cues. If you're a writer and you're blocked, here's another incentive to adopt from your local animal shelter: Just walk the dog and watch the ideas flow.

Stepping outside with Cupcake to start our daily dog-walk routine (this is done in shifts, so each dog gets an individual outing), we paused— she to observe a squirrel in her crosshairs, me to admire the grove of trees along the Pelham Parkway, where, if you squint, you can pretend you're not in New York City. The scent of honeysuckle was intoxicating. As I looked up to see the blossoms doing their springtime thing, my mind wandered back to X's broken promise. We never did go for that motorcycle ride along the tree-lined path, causing the blossoms to shower down. I'd spent years regretting this, to the point of searching online for men with motorbikes who might take me for that fantasy ride. Argh! I'd had my head in my butt for so long that my judgment was flawed on this and a few other things. What does fighting prolonged illness do to one's mental faculties? In my case, it gave me a microscopically narrow focus, a fancy form of tunnel vision: fistula vision. I was like one of the animals my heart broke for at the neighborhood pet store: the betta fish in a glass bowl no bigger than a Christmas ornament; the sociable parrot confined to a solitary cage. Of all the healing gifts I received from my stem cells, perhaps the mesenchymal Medicine Dogs' greatest legacy was restoring my ability to see past the limited sphere of my fistula and appreciate the bigger picture—and what a nice picture it was shaping up to be. I was forty-eight years young, with the second half of my life to look forward to. As soon as my book was done, I would get my motorcycle operator's license and find that flower-lined path myself.

I was brought up short by the more immediate task at hand: Cupcake was preparing to make number two. She scoped out a tree-box to her liking, then circled, squatted, and extruded a picture-perfect poop. Cupcake completed this peristalsis performance by digging her hind feet deep in the tree-box, scratching at the earth behind her, feeling light, energized, and ready for the day's adventures. Ah, sweet relief! Stooping to clean up after her, then sweeping stray soil back in to the box with my boot, I smiled to realize that, for the first time in fourteen years—maybe the first time ever—I now knew exactly how that felt.

ACKNOWLEDGMENTS

Depending on your perspective, this book was five years in the making, or fifteen, or forty-eight. A big thank you from the bottom of my heart to everyone who conspired to make writing it possible:

My parents, Martha and George Szabo, for a lifetime of spot-on health care and literary criticism . . .

Lara Asher and the team at Lyons Press, for giving *Medicine Dog* a wonderful home (special kudos to Lauren Brancato and Mary Ballachino) . . .

The dynamic Dr. Damián García-Olmo, for historic contributions to colorectal medicine that made so many people feel better . . .

The brilliant Dr. Bob Harman, for enabling disabled animals to walk again . . .

Dr. Elizabeth Higgins, my pups' peerless personal physician . . .

The rest of the best vets: Dr. Jennifer Chaitman, Dr. Dennis "Tim" Crowe, Dr. Jill Elliot, Dr. Dennis Geiser, Dr. Andrew Kaplan, Dr. Patty Khuly, Dr. Diane Levitan, Dr. Jo Olver, Dr. Heather Peikes, Dr. Michael Rubinstein, Dr. Julie Ryan Johnson, Dr. Shingo Soeda, Dr. Andrew Turkell, Dr. Michele Yasson . . .

Dr. Doug Kramer, whose important work with medical marijuana for animals was tragically interrupted when he died at age thirty-six, as this book was going to press (for a completely legal, over-the-counter alternative, contact the Seattle company Canna-Pet.com). . . .

The Olympian Healers: Neil Riordan, Dr. Leonard Smith, Dr. Mark Berman, Dr. Elliot Lander . . .

Everybody at the Humane Society of New York, especially Sandra DeFeo, Virginia Chipurnoi, William Berloni, Sarah DeVries, Joe Fischer, Denise Meachum, Anne Marie Karash, Rebecca Meyers, Elizabeth Dewer, Mary Ann Zanella, and Desiree's favorite, Richie Zanella . . .

Wendy Gallart, Barbara Ross, and Dr. Anthony Fischetti of the Animal Medical Center . . .

Melissa Barton and the Yale Committee on Literary Property . . .

Heather Green, for joining me on many exciting journeys of discovery, including our first trip to Spain . . .

Mary Shomon, beloved friend, charismatic leader, passionate and compassionate patient advocate, for illuminating so many on the path to wellness; Scott Rose, for introducing me to Mary, and for fabulous fluency with so many languages; and Julia Schopick, for "Googling it Up" . . .

Daniel Reichert, brilliant polymath, for the post-treatment photo session that resulted in this book's cover and the other valiant, virtuous Virgos: Jim Thiel, Chris Hulbert, Jefferson Spady, Matt Metzgar, Anne Bredon . . .

Aaron Hanscom, for the opportunity to connect with PJMedia's readers . . .

Janine Kahn, for letting this non-vet share get-well tricks with Dogster readers . . .

The people who kept me from falling apart: Susan Ainsworth, Alain Amouyal, John Bartlett, Chantal Desmoulins, Arsen Gurgov, Thomas Lee Hudson, Dr. Jennifer Jablow, Emily Lansbury, Louis Licari, Louisa McCune-Elmore, Jenn Mohr, Helen Murray, Dr. Joyce Nawy, Enid O, Gail O'Connell-Babcock, Susan Raimond, Leigh Rossini, Natasha Salman . . .

For random acts of kindness: Dawn Bauer-Wood, Michelle Gonzales Bleza, Steve Carrington, Lisa Cook, Hilary Couture, Jim Crosby, Marie-Dominique Pecorini, Diana and Isabel Downing, Tod Emko, Ferrell Hancock, Sue Harman, Ruth Hernandez, Amelia Kinkade, Jana Kohl, Celia Kutcher, Susan Matheson, Lisa and Steven Mercurio, Monique Muhlenkamp, Dr. Laurie Nadel, Sandra Quilico, Amanda and Martin St. John, Violeta Valentino, Jasmine White . . .

For gracious permission to reproduce photographs: Anneli Adolfsson, Janise Bogard, Marie Fetzer, Circe Hamilton, Jonathon Kambouris, Dana Rose Lee, Wyatt Marshall, Catherine Nance, Karina Salazar, Daniela Stallinger, Steve Yensel . . .

Edgar Otto, tireless champion of Hyperbaric Veterinary Medicine . . .

My beautiful Medicine Dogs: I will try to be less overprotective, but please bear with me—this is hard because I cannot stand to lose you!

Finally, to the one who always got the last word, the one without whom none of this would have ever happened: my former spouse. As you used to say, "I love you anyway." *Vaya con perros.*

Resources

Chapter 1

To learn about dogs at high risk of being euthanized at NYCACC, follow and "like" Urgent Part 2 Urgent Death Row Dogs on Facebook, and please go adopt (for shelter info, visit www.nycacc.org).

To make an appointment at the Animal Medical Center, or walk in on an emergency basis, visit www.amcny.org.

To commission a portrait by sculptor Jennifer Weinik, visit www.jennweinik.com.

To learn more about Vet-Stem, visit www.vet-stem.com.

To adopt a dog (or cat), visit the Vladimir and Wanda Toscanini Horowitz Adoption Center at the Humane Society of New York, home to the clinic where Sam, Sheba, and Desiree underwent Vet-Stem treatment (www.humanesocietyny.org).

Chapter 3

To learn more about IBD, visit the Crohn's & Colitis Foundation of America (www.ccfa.org).

To learn more about obstetric fistula, visit the Worldwide Fistula Fund (www.fistulafund.org).

To learn more about the Christopher & Dana Reeve Foundation (whose focus is embryonic stem cells, versus the non-embryonic stem cells that this book champions), visit www.christopherreeve.org.

For IBD sufferers, the Washlet is a dogsend: This modern spin on the bidet helps you feel clean and reduces your carbon paw-print by reducing toilet paper consumption (totousa.com).

To acquire a platform that will permit you to squat on your toilet for efficient elimination, visit www.naturesplatform.com.

CHAPTER 5

To learn more about hyperbaric oxygen therapy for animals, and how your veterinarian may lease a hyperbaric chamber, visit www.hvmed.com.

To purchase CDs by Harp Healer Susan Raimond, visit www.petpause2000.com.

My favorite products containing neem oil are by Organix-South (www.organix-south.com).

To make an appointment with Dr. Jill Elliot, visit www.nyholisticvet.com.

CHAPTER 7

For couples who live in close quarters and must share one toilet, try PooPourri (www.poopourri.com).

To make an appointment with animal communicator Dawn Allen, visit www.dawnallen.org.

CHAPTER 8

For updates from Dr. Marty Becker, "America's Vet," and his team, visit www.drmartybecker.com and www.vetstreet.com.

To book a phototherapy session with Circe, visit www.circephoto.com.

To learn more about dog-friendly Crypton Super Fabrics, including items sporting patterns designed by artist William Wegman, visit www.cryptonathome.com.

To learn more about products by Buck Mountain Botanicals, available to veterinarians, visit www.buckmountainbotanicals.com.

To learn about the best dog boarding facility in New York City, visit www.unleashbrooklyn.com.

CHAPTER 9

To learn more about comedian Ben Morrison, visit http://ben
morrison.org.

To learn more about the Stem Cell Institute, visit www.cellmedicine
.com.

To make an appointment with Dr. Michele Yasson (who conducts
telephone consultations), visit www.holvet.net.

To learn more about my favorite probiotic supplements, visit www
.renewlife.com.

CHAPTER 10

To learn more about the work of Dr. Stanley Jones, visit www.spine
careusa.com.

CHAPTER 11

To learn more about North Shore Animal League America and its
events, visit www.animalleague.org.

To learn more about the Stem Cell Center of Excellence in Tijuana,
visit www.stemcellmx.com.

CHAPTER 12

To learn more about the Mayor's Alliance for NYC's Animals, visit
www.animalalliancenyc.org.

To delve deeper into the principles of food combining, visit www
.bodyecology.com.

To learn more about the work of author and wellness advocate
Suzanne Somers, visit www.suzannesomers.com.

Chapter 13

To learn more about stylist Louis Licari, including his upcoming "Ambush Makeover" appearances on NBC's *Today*, visit www.louis licari.com.

Damián García-Olmo, Jose Manuel García-Verdugo, Jorge Alemany, José A. Gutiérrez-Fuentes, eds. 2008. *Cell Therapy*. McGraw-Hill/Interamericana de España S.A.U.

My success in the pool was due in no small part to wearing performance swim gear by Tyr; learn more at www.tyr.com.

To make an appointment with Dr. Diane Levitan, whose practice is called Peace Love Pets Veterinary Care, visit www.peacelovepets.org.

Chapter 14

When in Madrid, by all means visit the Mercado de San Miguel (www.mercadodesanmiguel.es).

To follow a few excellent doctors, visit the following websites: www .cleanprogram.com, www.drwhitaker.com, www.drsinatra.com, www .drlark.com, www.mercola.com, and www.drkarenbecker.com (no relation to Dr. Marty Becker).

Chapter 15

To find out whether you are eligible for treatment at the California Stem Cell Treatment Center or one of the affiliates of the Cell Surgical Network, visit www.stemcellrevolution.com.

To make an appointment with Food Healer and radio host Celia Kutcher, visit www.foodhealer.com; to find out when she's appearing on air, visit www.heritageradionetwork.com.

To make an appointment with medical intuitive Jennifer Kaye Dickinson, visit www.jenniferkaye.com.

If you are planning to be treated at the California Stem Cell Treatment Center, an excellent place to stay is the Omni Rancho Las Palmas (www.rancholaspalmas.com). I also highly recommend its farm-to-table restaurant, Bluember (www.rancholaspalmas.com/bluember).

Storax essential oil is available from Gritman Essential Oils (www.gritman.com).

Thieves Oil is a proprietary blend made by Young Living Essential Oils (www.living-essential-oils.com).

The aromatherapy candles my dogs and I swear by are made by Sniff (www.sniffpetproducts.com).

CHAPTER 16

To read Dog Is My Doctor, visit www.pet-reporter.com/blog/.

To purchase CDs and find out about upcoming performances of "A Grateful Tail," visit the composer's website, www.stevenmercurio.com.

If you're considering making a donation to a worthy animal charity, please consider these: Suva SPCA in Fiji (www.spayfiji.org/fiji-spca); SPAYes (www.spaypanamasanimals.com); Darwin Animal Doctors (www.darwinanimaldoctors.org); and The Toby Project (www.tobyproject.org).

To locate stores that carry Yaff Bar, Desiree's favorite energy snack, visit www.muddandwyeth.com.

About the Author

Julia Szabo, nationally recognized Pet Reporter and animal health advocate, produced the popular "Pets" column in the *New York Post* for eleven years. The author of six previous books, she is the Health Editor of Dogster.com, a frequent contributor to PJMedia.com, and pens the blog *Dog Is My Doctor.* Her writings on dogs have also appeared in the *New York Times, Reader's Digest, The New Yorker, Travel + Leisure, Cesar's Way, The Bark,* and *FIDOFriendly.* She lives in New York City with her family of rescued dogs and cats. Follow her on Twitter @PetReporter1, and visit her website, pet-reporter.com.